Spreadsheets for Accounting

Tutorial

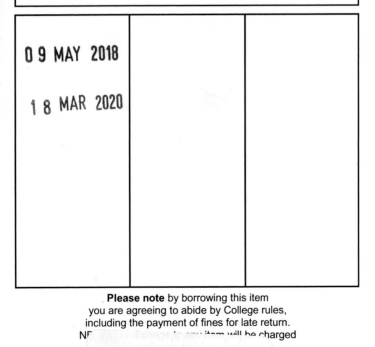

Wend

Published by Osborne Books Limited
Tel 01905 748071
Email books@osbornebooks.co.uk
Website www.osbornebooks.co.uk

Design by Laura Ingham

Printed by CPI Group (UK) Limited, Croydon, CR0 4YY, on environmentally friendly, acid-free paper from managed forests.

British Library Cataloguing in Publication Data
A catalogue record for this book is available from the British Library

ISBN 978 1909 173 842

Contents of this book

Quick guide to the contents of this book

List of practice exercises

Also available from Osborne Books...

Workbooks

Practice questions and assessments
with answers

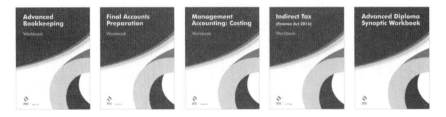

Wise Guides

Handy pocket-sized study and revision guides

Student Zone

Login to access your free ebooks and
interactive revision crosswords

Download **Osborne Books App** free from the App Store or Google Play Store
to view your ebooks online or offline on your mobile or tablet.

www.osbornebooks.co.uk

Introduction

Qualifications covered

This book has been written specifically to cover the Unit 'Spreadsheets for Accounting' which is mandatory for the following qualifications:

■ AAT Advanced Diploma in Accounting – Level 3

■ AAT Advanced Diploma in Accounting at SCQF – Level 6

The book contains a clear text with worked examples and case studies, chapter summaries and key terms to help with revision. Each chapter concludes with a wide range of activities, many in the style of AAT computer based assessments.

To speed up the learning process in the later exercises, Osborne Books has provided a number of spreadsheet files for free download from its website www.osbornebooks.co.uk. Access to these can be gained through the 'Products and Resources' button on the menu bar and then via the *Spreadsheets for Accounting Tutorial* book page.

Which spreadsheet software?

The illustrations in this text are based on Excel 2013, part of the Microsoft Office suite, but it is appreciated that a variety of software will be in use at any one time. The text therefore aims to be generic wherever possible so that all users can be catered for.

Note that the downloads referred to above are also provided as CSV files, which can be used to import the required raw data into most spreadsheet programs.

Osborne Study and Revision Materials

Our materials are tailored to the needs of students studying this unit and revising for the assessment. They include:

■ **Student Zone:** access to Osborne Books online resources

■ **Osborne Books App:** Osborne Books ebooks for mobiles and tablets

Visit www.osbornebooks.co.uk for details of study and revision resources and access to online material.

Contents – a quick guide

This section explains at a glance the main contents of each of the eight chapters in this book.

1 Spreadsheet basics

This chapter covers the following basic principles and techniques:
- Some preliminaries
- Basic spreadsheet structure
- Dealing with worksheets
- Dealing with workbooks
- Enter data into cells
- Copy the data in cells
- Rows and columns
- Change the height of a row or width of a column
- Using basic formulas

2 Formatting the spreadsheet data

This chapter covers the formatting of a spreadsheet:
- Formatting - style
- Formatting - fonts and size
- Number formats
- Cell alignment
- Date format
- Printing and page setup

3 Advanced formatting

This chapter covers more advanced formatting and improving spreadsheet presentation:
- Cell display – borders, fill colours
- Moving rows and columns
- Hiding rows and columns
- Specifying row height and column width
- Cell and sheet protection
- Conditional formatting
- Data validation

4 Spreadsheet functions

This chapter explains the use of built-in functions which are found in most common spreadsheet software packages:
- Formulas
- Mathematical operators

- Functions
- Ranges
- Mathematical functions
- Cell addressing
- Date functions
- Logical functions and operators
- Lookup functions
- Circular references in formulas

5 Sorting, checking and importing data

This chapter explains some of the built-in tools found in normal spreadsheet packages:
- Formula validation
- Spell check
- Find and replace
- Sorting and filtering data
- Introducing subtotals
- Embedding, linking and screenshots
- Import/Export

6 Statistical functions and charts

This chapter explains and illustrates some of the statistical functions and data analysis tools which you can use. It covers:
- Simple statistical functions
- Analysis tools
- Remove duplicates
- Comments

7 Charts

This chapter provides guidance on working with charts
- Types of charts
- Chart creation
- Modification of charts
- Chart printing

8 Pivot tables and workbook management

This chapter deals with Pivot Tables and other techniques for manipulating data:
- Managing windows – freeze panes
- Working with multiple worksheets and workbooks
- Using Paste Special
- Creating and formatting pivot tables
- Using subsets of data
- What-if scenarios

- Goal seeking
- Data tables
- Hyperlinks

List of practice exercises

Practice exercises

Learning about spreadsheet software is an essentially practical process and this book contains a wide range of practical exercises which will enable students to gain the spreadsheet skills needed to tackle the AAT assessment. These exercises and details of their contents are set out on the next page.

Some exercises require the download of spreadsheet files from www.osbornebooks.co.uk ('Products and Resources'). These files are in Excel (2013) format and are also provided as csv files.

1 Spreadsheet basics

this chapter covers...

This chapter is an introduction for those new to spreadsheets. It explains and takes you through some of the basic concepts and techniques for working with spreadsheets.

By the time you have finished this chapter and carried out the exercises which follow, you should be competent in setting up and manipulating a basic spreadsheet. The concepts and techniques covered are:

- *some preliminaries*

- *basic spreadsheet structure*

- *dealing with worksheets*

- *dealing with workbooks*

- *entering data into cells*

- *copying the data in cells*

- *dealing with rows and columns*

- *changing the height of a row or the width of a column*

- *using basic formulas*

Note that the step by step instructions given in this chapter are based on the Microsoft® Excel model, but the concepts and techniques described relate to all spreadsheet packages.

SOME PRELIMINARIES

numbers

Within a spreadsheet, a series of digits (0 - 9) will be treated as a NUMBER provided there are no spaces. A number can also have a decimal point (.) eg 12.99 would be twelve point nine-nine.

To ease interpretation of a number it can include commas(,) to represent thousands eg 34,567 would represent thirty four thousand, five hundred and sixty seven.

dates

Dates are normally entered in the form 31/10/16, day, month, year separated by / (slash).

text

Any series of characters which cannot be recognised as a number or a date is known as TEXT.

mouseclick

Whenever a CLICK of the mouse is mentioned, this is referring to a click of the LEFT mouse button. Any RIGHT mouse clicks will be specifically preceded by RIGHT. DOUBLE click refers to two clicks in quick succession of the LEFT mouse key.

undo

If at any stage you wish to Undo the changes which you have just made, click on the Undo icon (left pointing curved arrow) to remove the last edit to a cell. To remove the edit before that, click the Undo icon again and so on.

redo

Following an Undo of some changes which you have just made, if you change your mind and want to reinstate those edits, click on the Redo icon (right pointing curved arrow) to put the last changes back. To redo the edit before that, click the Redo icon again and so on.

keyboard

Keys on the keyboard which you will need to be familiar with are:

RETURN (or ENTER)	ESC
TAB	CTRL (CONTROL)

So it is worth spending a minute or two identifying where these keys are located.

menus

As with all computer programs, there is a main menu bar, with tabs identifying different options available. These are usually grouped by relevance; the common tabs which we will make use of are:

■ FILE, HOME, INSERT, PAGE LAYOUT, FORMULAS, DATA, REVIEW and VIEW

It is possible your menu may differ, depending on your software installation.

Often, some of the more common options can be accessed by RIGHT mouse click.

help

If you require additional information or clarification on any action, formula or general query, Help is available within your spreadsheet program by clicking the Help icon (usually a ? in a blue circle situated to the far right of the main menu bar). Alternatively, press the F1 function key.

SPREADSHEET STRUCTURE

definition

A spreadsheet is a grid or table of rows and columns which is used to manipulate numbers and perform calculations.

rows, columns and cells

Rows are in a horizontal direction, and are identified by numbers: 1, 2, 3, and so on.

Columns are vertical, and are identified by letters: A, B, C, and so on through the alphabet.

Columns beyond Z (26) continue in the format AA, AB, AC and so on, changing to BA, BB etc. for columns 53 and onwards.

The maximum number of rows and columns allowed in a spreadsheet is determined by the software package you are using and the memory within your computer. For Excel® you can have more than one million rows and more than 16 thousand columns if your computer has the capacity.

Where a row and column cross or intersect, it is called a **cell**.

The cell is referred to by a combination of a letter (the column identifier) and a number (the row reference) to identify its location. This is known as a **cell reference**.

Cell reference D7 would refer to the cell at the intersection of column D (the fourth column) and row 7. See the cell highlighted on the screen image on the previous page.

The lines marking the edges of the rows and columns are called **gridlines**. **Scroll bars** are provided to cater for larger spreadsheets and allow scrolling both vertically and horizontally, changing the rows and columns displayed as you move up, down and across the spreadsheet.

WORKBOOKS AND WORKSHEETS

A **workbook** is the computer file created when you start a new spreadsheet.

A **workbook** contains a set of **worksheets**.

Each **worksheet** is an individual **spreadsheet**.

For example, a workbook could have two worksheets, one worksheet with data, and a second worksheet containing a chart representing the data.

files and folders

Each workbook is held as one file. A file is the computer equivalent of a paper document containing the information which you have entered. Each file has a name which you specify when it is created. This should be chosen to be meaningful and help identify what the file contains, for example Timesheet March 2016.

To organise our files in a logical way we store related files in a **folder**, which we again name when we create it to clarify the sort of files/documents the folder will contain. For example: Timesheets 2016-2017.

Within Excel the File and Folder tools mentioned below are available whenever you select one of the menu options such as OPEN, SAVE AS or SHARE, all of which are located under the FILE menu.

create a folder

Creating a folder can be achieved by using the **New Folder** option, and naming the folder appropriately.

finding a file

If you are unable to locate a file, you can use the **Search tool** provided when you select OPEN within the FILE menu.

renaming a file

To rename a file, click the filename, once then once more and type in the new name. Press **RETURN** or click somewhere else to complete the edit. **ESC** will cancel the edit.

sharing a file

This can be done in two ways, either using the SHARE option within Excel, or by allowing direct access to the file either on the network, or your computer.

The **SHARE** option, found under the **FILE** menu, allows you to save the file online, and Invite people to share it, or you can email the file to one or more people directly, in a variety of formats, such as PDF.

To allow the sharing of a file on the network, or on your computer, the file needs to be in a folder which is accessible to other people. By right mouse clicking on the folder name, and setting the **share with** options as required, you can specify who can access the file.

worksheets

Each **worksheet** has a name, which is usually displayed as a tab at the bottom of the spreadsheet work area.

When you create a new workbook it will contain at least one worksheet – named Sheet1, more may be included, depending on how your Excel is set up.

Worksheet **names** can be changed, by double clicking on the name tab, and entering the required text of the new name.

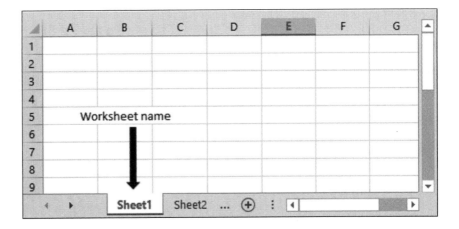

It is possible to add one or more additional worksheets should you require them.

New worksheets are added one at a time, either by clicking on the the plus (+) symbol in the circle next to the sheet name tabs, or by using **Insert**, and selecting **Worksheet**.

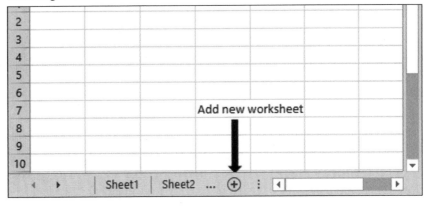

Worksheets which are not required can be deleted, by using **Delete** from the **Home** menu by selecting the worksheet, or right mouse clicking on the sheet to be deleted, and selecting **Delete**.

You can easily change the relative order of the worksheets within the workbook, just by selecting the name tab, holding the mouse down, and dragging the worksheet to its new position in the order.

Each worksheet can represent one spreadsheet, or data from different worksheets may be linked together to form one more complex spreadsheet.

Switching between worksheets is achieved by clicking on the name tab of the worksheet which you want to see on the screen.

workbooks

As noted earlier, a **workbook** is a collection of worksheets ranging from one worksheet upwards to a maximum number which will be dependent on the software package and available computer memory.

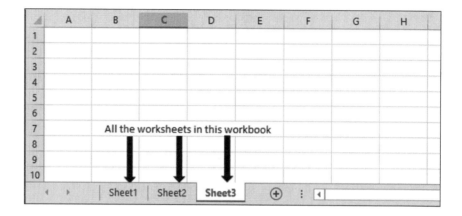

For example, a workbook could have two worksheets, one worksheet with data, and a second worksheet containing a chart representing the data.

When you want to start your first spreadsheet, you will select **New** from the File menu, select **Blank Workbook** from the available templates, and a new workbook will open, usually containing 1 or more blank worksheets ready for you to enter data.

The information which you have entered should be regularly saved using the standard disk icon, or **Save** under the File menu.

To open a previously saved workbook, you would either select **Open** from the File menu, navigate to the required folder and select the required workbook from the appropriate folder or, if it is listed, select the workbook from the list of recently used documents.

To save a copy of the workbook with a different name either as a backup or as a fresh starting point, you would use **Save as** usually found under the File menu and supply a new name for the copy of the workbook. You would also use **Save as** if you wanted to save the workbook as different type of file, e.g. PDF to send to other people. For security purposes a copy of an important workbook should be saved to removable media such as a memory stick and stored off-site.

It is also good practice to add a version number or part of a date to the filename so that different versions can be saved as the spreadsheet evolves. This also allows a previous version to be identified and opened, if required, or just kept as an archive copy of the original workbook.

ENTER DATA INTO CELLS

Within the grid of cells on your worksheet, you can move around from cell to cell using various methods:

■ the mouse

■ the arrow keys

■ the **TAB** key

■ or the **RETURN** key (also known as the **ENTER** key)

The current cell, known as the active cell is highlighted.

The active cell reference is shown in the **Name Box** above column A; this is B5 in the example below.

To enter data into a cell:

■ click on the cell where you want the data to go

■ type your data into the cell

■ either press the **RETURN** key, or click on another cell with the mouse

Other useful keys when entering data are the **TAB** key which moves the active cell to the next cell in the current row, and the **ESC** key which cancels the current data entry.

If you just wish to edit the current data, you will see the data held in the current cell displayed in the **Formula Bar**, (in this example Income forecast).

To modify the contents of a cell:

■ click on the required cell

■ either enter the new data directly

■ *or* click into the Formula Bar

■ make any changes

■ press **RETURN**

If at any time you wish to cancel the changes, press the **ESC** key before pressing **RETURN**, or if you have pressed RETURN, click on the Undo icon as described in the preliminaries.

To remove data:

■ select the cell to be changed

■ press the **Delete** key

■ *or* select **Clear Contents** from the drop down menu displayed when you right mouse click on the cell

selecting multiple cells

If at any time you wish to select more than one cell:

■ select the first cell by clicking on the cell

■ keep the left mouse button pressed and drag the mouse over the other cells you wish to select

A series of selected cells is shown below.

◢	A	B	C	D	E	F	G
1	.						
2		February	March	April	May	June	
3							

If the cells you wish to select are not consecutive (ie not next to each other):

■ select the first cell by clicking on the cell

■ hold down the **CONTROL** key while clicking on the other cells you want to select (as shown below)

◢	A	B	C	D	E	F	G
1							
2							
3		February	March	April	May	June	
4							

It is often useful to be able to select multiple cells as you will see in the following sections.

COPYING CELLS

The simplest method of copying data in a cell is to:

■ move to the cell you wish to copy

■ from the Home menu, select **Copy**

■ move to the cell where you wish to place the copy

■ from the Home menu select **Paste**

If you wish to paste the data into more than one cell, select all the cells where the data is to go, then select **Paste**.

Alternatively, to copy the selected cell, you could click on the **Copy** icon on the tool bar if there is one, or press **CTRL** and **C** together; then to paste, click on the **Paste** icon, or press **CTRL** and **V** together.

It is also possible to move the contents of one cell to a new cell reference:

■ click on the data cell to move

■ move the cursor over the edge of the cell until you see a four headed arrow, press down on the left mouse key

■ drag to the cell where the data is to go

■ release the mouse

You will see the data move to the new location.

If at any time you wish to copy more than one cell at a time:

■ select the cells to copy by clicking on the first cell

■ keeping the left mouse key pressed drag the mouse in the appropriate direction until all the required cells are selected

■ select **Copy** and **Paste** as described above

Alternatively, click on the first cell, move to the last of the cells to be selected, hold down the **SHIFT** key and click the mouse.

If the cells which you wish to copy are not consecutive, for each of the cells to be copied, hold down the **CTRL** key and click the cell, as described in the section on selecting multiple cells.

DEALING WITH ROWS AND COLUMNS

On a worksheet, each column is identified by a letter or combination of letters; this is called the **Column header**.

Similarly each row is identified by a number called the **Row header**.

One click on a column header will select the entire column. Similarly with a row header, one click on the row header will select the whole row.

If you realise that you have missed out a row or a column once you have entered data, it is straightforward to insert extra rows or columns.

inserting a column

■ select the column to the right of where you want to insert another column, by right clicking on the column header

■ select **Insert** from the menu displayed

The new column will be inserted at the position of the selected column, and all existing columns will move right, as shown in the example below. You can then enter data in the new column.

Note that for some spreadsheet packages you may need to select **Insert**, then **Column** from the menus.

	A	B	C	D	E	F	G
1	Expenditure forecast						
2							
3		January		March	April	May	June
4							
5							
6							

inserting a row

If we take an example expenditure worksheet as shown in the image below.

	A	B	C	D	E	F	G
1	Expenditure forecast						
2							
3		January	February	March	April	May	June
4							
5	Salaries						
6	Rent						
7	Accountancy						
8	Advertising						
9	Postage						
10	Stationery						

To insert a row:

- ▪ select the row below where you want to insert another row, by right clicking on the row header

- ▪ select **Insert** from the dropdown menu displayed; for some spreadsheet packages you may need to select Insert, then Row from the menu

In the screen below a new row has been inserted between the rows for Salaries and Rent (rows 5 and 6), and the text 'Insurance' has been entered in cell A6. Note that the new row will be inserted at the selected row (row 6), and all the existing rows will then move down. You can then enter data in the new row.

	A	B	C	D	E	F	G
1	Expenditure forecast						
2							
3		January	February	March	April	May	June
4							
5	Salaries						
6	Insurance						
7	Rent						
8	Accountancy						
9	Advertising						
10	Postage						
11	Stationery						

For some spreadsheet packages you may need to select **Insert**, then **Row** from the menus.

deleting a column

To delete a column:

- select the column to be deleted, by right clicking on the column header
- select **Delete** from the menu displayed.

For some spreadsheet packages you may need to select **Delete**, then **Column** from the menus.

deleting a row

To delete a row:

- select the row to be deleted, by right clicking on the row header
- select **Delete** from the menu displayed

For some spreadsheet packages you may need to select **Delete**, then **Row** from the menus.

changing the width of a column

	A	B	C	D	E	F	G
1	Expenditure forecast						
2							
3		January	February	March	April	May	June
4							
5	Salaries						
6	Insurance						
7	Rent						
8	Accountancy						
9	Advertising						
10	Postage						
11	Stationery						

If you look at the example above, you will see that some of the text in the selected cell in column A overflows into column B. Once we put data into column B, the full text in column A will no longer be visible, so we need to make column A wider.

To make a column wider:

■ click on the column header

■ move the cursor to the line at the right edge of the column header box, the cursor changes shape to a black cross with arrow heads

■ press the mouse down

■ drag to the right as far as is required to display all information correctly

■ release the mouse

Column A is then made wider, as shown below:

	A	B	C	D	E	F	G
1	Expenditure forecast						
2							
3		January	February	March	April	May	June
4							
5	Salaries						
6	Insurance						
7	Rent						
8	Accountancy						
9	Advertising						
10	Postage						
11	Stationery						

There are several alternative ways to make a column wider. If you double click on the right edge of the column header box, the column will automatically widen to contain the longest data within the column.

Also if you right click on the column header, you can select **Column Width** from the drop down menu and specify a width as a number from 0 to 255 which represents the number of characters that can be displayed in a cell that is formatted with the standard font.

If a cell contains a date, number or result of a formula, and the column is not wide enough to display the whole of the value, you will see ###### displayed in the cell instead. To resolve this, just make the column wider until all is displayed.

changing the height of a row

The method used to modify the height of a row is very similar:

- click on the row header

- move the cursor to the bottom edge of the row header box, the cursor changes shape to a black cross with arrow heads

- press the mouse down

- drag down or up until you are satisfied with the row height

- release the mouse

You can see in the image below how we have made the height of row 1 containing 'Expenditure forecast' larger to make it stand out as a heading.

	A	B	C	D	E	F	G
1	Expenditure forecast						
2							
3		January	February	March	April	May	June
4							
5	Salaries						
6	Insurance						
7	Rent						
8	Accountancy						
9	Advertising						
10	Postage						
11	Stationery						

Also, if you right click on the row header, you can select Row Height and specify the height as a number from 0 to 409, which represents the height measurement in points (1 point equals approximately 1/72 inch or 0.35mm). If the row height is set to zero, the row is hidden.

turning off gridlines

If you do not wish to see gridlines when you are working on your spreadsheet, they can be turned off.

To turn off gridlines:

■ select the **File** menu

■ select **Options**

■ select **Advanced**

■ scroll down to **Display options for this worksheet**, and uncheck **Show gridlines**

To turn gridlines back on again, repeat the above, and check Show gridlines.

Note: Gridlines do not appear on your printed output unless you request them to appear in your printing selections.

USING BASIC FORMULAS

The most powerful feature of a spreadsheet is its ability to perform calculations. To **create a formula**, click on the cell where you wish to place the formula. Enter the "=" sign to indicate that this cell is going to contain a formula. The formula can contain numbers, cell references and arithmetic symbols, eg '+' as shown below:

A simple formula for **addition** might be something like

=B4+B5+B6+42

This would add up the values in the cells B4, B5, B6 and the number 42.

A simple formula for **subtraction** is: =B4–B5

For **multiplication**: =B4*B5

And **division**: =B4/B5

To make one cell always hold the same value as another, eg B2 having the same value as A1, enter the formula =A1 in cell B2.

In the example on the next page, we want to enter formulas to calculate the totals for each month.

B11	▾	⋮	✕ ✓ *fx*	=			

◢	A	B	C	D	E	F	G
1	Expenditure Forecast						
2							
3		January	February	March	April	May	June
4	Salaries	£80,000	£80,000	£80,000	£90,000	£90,000	£90,000
5	Insurance	£1,000	£500	£0	£0	£0	£500
6	Rent	£3,500	£3,500	£3,500	£3,500	£3,500	£3,500
7	Accountancy	£270	£0	£270	£0	£270	£0
8	Advertising	£0	£1,500	£0	£0	£0	£1,800
9	Postage	£95	£190	£95	£80	£95	£150
10	Stationery	£57	£90	£0	£90	£0	£90
11	Totals	=					

The formula we could enter in cell B11 to add up column B, would be
=B4+B5+B6+B7+B8+B9+B10

There is an alternative way of adding these numbers, using the built-in function **SUM( )**.

The equivalent formula would be =SUM(B4:B10) which will add up all the cells from B4 to B10 inclusive.

This formula could then be copied to each of the cells in the Totals row in each column to produce a monthly total for the expenditure forecast, using **Copy** and **Paste** as described previously.

Note that as the formula is copied to the new cells it will **automatically change** to reflect the new row/column references.

B11	▾	⋮	✕ ✓ *fx*	=SUM(B4:B10)			

◢	A	B	C	D	E	F	G
1	Expenditure Forecast						
2							
3		January	February	March	April	May	June
4	Salaries	£80,000	£80,000	£80,000	£90,000	£90,000	£90,000
5	Insurance	£1,000	£500	£0	£0	£0	£500
6	Rent	£3,500	£3,500	£3,500	£3,500	£3,500	£3,500
7	Accountancy	£270	£0	£270	£0	£270	£0
8	Advertising	£0	£1,500	£0	£0	£0	£1,800
9	Postage	£95	£190	£95	£80	£95	£150
10	Stationery	£57	£90	£0	£90	£0	£90
11	Totals	£84,922	£85,780	£83,865	£93,670	£93,865	£96,040

calculating averages

The next requirement is to calculate the **average expenditure** for each expense type over the six months, into column H. To do this we can use the function **AVERAGE**.

The formula in this case would be =AVERAGE(B4:G4). This calculates the average value of all cells from B4 to G4 inclusively.

Again, this formula can be copied to all the other cells in the Average column, producing the results shown below in Column H.

H4			f_x	=AVERAGE(B4:G4)			
	A	B	C	D	E	F	G	H
1	Expenditure Forecast							
2								
3		January	February	March	April	May	June	Average
4	Salaries	£80,000	£80,000	£80,000	£90,000	£90,000	£90,000	£85,000
5	Insurance	£1,000	£500	£0	£0	£0	£500	£333
6	Rent	£3,500	£3,500	£3,500	£3,500	£3,500	£3,500	£3,500
7	Accountancy	£270	£0	£270	£0	£270	£0	£135
8	Advertising	£0	£1,500	£0	£0	£0	£1,800	£550
9	Postage	£95	£190	£95	£80	£95	£150	£118
10	Stationery	£57	£90	£0	£90	£0	£90	£55
11	Totals	£84,922	£85,780	£83,865	£93,670	£93,865	£96,040	

There are many built-in functions which are available to use within your spreadsheet. A number of these will be covered in subsequent chapters.

Chapter Summary

In this chapter we have covered the following spreadsheet concepts and techniques:

■ some preliminaries

■ basic spreadsheet structure

■ worksheets

■ workbooks

■ entering data into cells

■ copying the data in cells

■ rows and columns

■ changing the height of a row or the width of a column

■ using basic formulas

You should now carry out some or all of the exercises on the next few pages in order to practise and reinforce your learning.

Activities

Exercise 1 – setting up a new worksheet

In this first exercise we will create a simple spreadsheet to record time worked on various activities.

Stage 1

This stage is all about entering some text to form the basic layout of our spreadsheet.

1.   Open a new workbook.

2.   Move to Sheet1.

3.   Change the name of the sheet to **Time data**.

4.   Move to cell A1, enter **Work bookings**.

5.   Move to cell A2, enter **Client**.

6.   Enter **Week1**, **Week2**, **Week3** in cells B2, C2, D2 respectively.

7.   Enter **Smiths Ltd**, **Jones and Partner**, **Redwoods**, **Underhills** in cells A3, A4, A5, A6 respectively.

8.   Save the workbook with the name **Exercise1**.

Your spreadsheet should appear as shown in the screen below:

A1	▼	:	✕	✓	*fx*	Work bookings		✓
	A	**B**	**C**	**D**	**E**	**F**	**G**	
1	Work bookings							
2	Client	Week1	Week2	Week3				
3	Smiths Ltd							
4	Jones and Partner							
5	Redwoods							
6	Underhills							
7								

Time data | Sheet ... ⊕

Stage 2

We are going to improve the layout and enter some values.

1.   Widen column A to allow for the longest entry in column A.

2.   Insert a row below Work bookings to improve the presentation.

3.   For Smiths Ltd, enter the value **15** for Week1 (cell B4), copy this value into Week2 (cell C4), and Week3 (cell D4).

4.   Similarly for Jones and Partner, enter the following values **12**, **8**, **10**.

5.   For Redwoods enter **13**, **20**, **11**.

6.   The values for Underhills are the same as those for Redwoods. Use Copy and Paste to put these values in cells B7, C7, D7.

7.   Save your spreadsheet (keeping the same name: **Exercise1**).

Your spreadsheet should appear as shown in the screen below:

A1		X	✓	*fx*	Work bookings			
	A	**B**	**C**	**D**	**E**	**F**	**G**	
1	Work bookings							
2								
3	Client	Week1	Week2	Week3				
4	Smiths Ltd	15	15	15				
5	Jones and Partner	12	8	10				
6	Redwoods	13	20	11				
7	Underhills	13	20	11				
8								

Time data   Sheet2   ...   ⊕

Stage 3

We are now going to use some formulas to get the spreadsheet to do some calculations for us.

1. In cell A9 enter **Totals**.

2. Cell B9 is the first cell where we want to enter the formula to total cells B4 through to B7 (using the SUM function).

3. Copy the formula from cell B9 into C9 and D9 to calculate the other totals.

4. Save your spreadsheet.

Your spreadsheet should appear as shown in the screen below.

B9		fx	=SUM(B4:B7)				
	A	B	C	D	E	F	G
1	Work bookings						
2							
3	Client	Week1	Week2	Week3			
4	Smiths Ltd	15	15	15			
5	Jones and Partner	12	8	10			
6	Redwoods	13	20	11			
7	Underhills	13	20	11			
8							
9	Totals	53	63	47			
10							

Time data   Sheet2   ...

Stage 4

One more calculation is needed.

1. In cell E3 enter **Average**.

2. Cell E4 is the first cell where we want to enter the formula to calculate the average of cells B4 through to D4.

3. Copy the formula from cell E4 into E5 through to E7 to calculate the other averages.

4. Save your spreadsheet.

The final spreadsheet is shown below.

E4			X ✓ *fx*	=AVERAGE(B4:D4)			
	A	B	C	D	E	F	G
1	Work bookings						
2							
3	Client	Week1	Week2	Week3	Average		
4	Smiths Ltd	15	15	15	15		
5	Jones and Partner	12	8	10	10		
6	Redwoods	13	20	11	14.66667		
7	Underhills	13	20	11	14.66667		
8							
9	Totals	53	63	47			

Time data   Sheet2

Exercise 2 – correcting and extending data, adding formulas

In this next exercise we will modify the previous time recording spreadsheet to make some corrections and extend the data recorded.

You will notice that changes to the data automatically change the values in those cells where we have a formula.

Stage 1

This stage involves making changes within an existing spreadsheet.

1.   Open the workbook created in the previous exercise **Exercise1**.

2.   Save the workbook with a new name **Exercise2**.

3.   Week2 for Smiths Ltd should read **5** not 15, change the value in cell C4.

4.   Week2 for Underhills should read **12** not 20, change the value in cell C7.

5.   Underhills should be **Underhills Ltd**, change the entry in cell A7.

6.   Change all the text in row 3 to capital letters (these are our headings within the spreadsheet).

7.   Save the workbook still with the name **Exercise2**.

Your spreadsheet should appear as shown in the screen below.

A1	▼ :	✕ ✓ *fx*	Work bookings				✔
	A	B	C	D	E	F	G
1	Work bookings						
2							
3	CLIENT	WEEK1	WEEK2	WEEK3	AVERAGE		
4	Smiths Ltd	15	5	15	11.66667		
5	Jones and Partner	12	8	10	10		
6	Redwoods	13	20	11	14.66667		
7	Underhills Ltd	13	12	11	12		
8							
9	Totals	53	45	47			
10							

Time data   Sheet2   ...   ⊕

Stage 2

We are going to enter some additional values because we now have data for Week4, and a new client.

1. Insert a column after Week3 and before Average (between columns D and E).

2. Enter text **WEEK4** in cell E3.

3. Time booking for each client for Week4 is 6 hours. Use Copy and Paste to enter 6 in cells E4, E5, E6 and E7.

4. Enter the formula for the total for Week4 in cell E9 (**Note**: You can either use Copy and Paste to copy the formula from one of the other Total cells, or enter the formula using Sum, and include all cells from E4 through to E7.

5. A new client was taken on in Week4. Insert a row below Underhills Ltd, still leaving a blank row above Totals.

6. The new client name is Abbey Builders. Enter **Abbey Builders** in cell A8.

7. For Abbey Builders, enter the value **0** for Week1 (cell B8), copy this value into Week2 (cell C8), and Week3 (cell D8) and then enter the value **13** into Week4 (cell E8).

8. Check the formulas for Totals for each week, making sure they include the new row (Abbey Builders in Row 8). Modify and copy across to each week if necessary.

9. Save your spreadsheet.

Your spreadsheet should now look as shown below:

B10	▾	⋮	✕ ✓ ƒx	=SUM(B4:B8)			▾
◢	A	B	C	D	E	F	G
1	Work bookings						
2							
3	CLIENT	WEEK1	WEEK2	WEEK3	WEEK4	AVERAGE	
4	Smiths Ltd	15	5	15	6	10.25	
5	Jones and Partner	12	8	10	6	9	
6	Redwoods	13	20	11	6	12.5	
7	Underhills Ltd	13	12	11	6	10.5	
8	Abbey Builders	0	0	0	13		
9							
10	Totals	53	45	47	37		

Time data   Sheet2   ...   ⊕   ⋮

Stage 3

We are now going to introduce some more formulas to get the spreadsheet to do some additional calculations for us.

1.   We no longer need the Average column. Delete column F.

2.   We want to calculate the total number of hours for each client. Enter **CLIENT TOTAL** in cell F3.

3.   Widen column F so that the **CLIENT TOTAL** text fits within the column.

4.   Enter the formula in cell F4 to total cells B4 through to E4.

5.   Copy the formula from cell F4 into cells F5, F6, F7, and F8 to calculate the other totals.

6.   Enter **EXTENDED** in cell G3.

7.   Widen column G so that the text fits within the column.

8.   Each client total is to be multiplied by 1.5. Enter the formula in G4 to give Smiths Ltd total (F4) multiplied by 1.5.

9.   Copy the formula from F4 into cells F5,F6,F7,F8.

10.   Save your spreadsheet.

Your spreadsheet should look as shown below:

G4		fx	=F4*1.5				
	A	B	C	D	E	F	G
1	Work bookings						
2							
3	CLIENT	WEEK1	WEEK2	WEEK3	WEEK4	CLIENT TOTAL	EXTENDED
4	Smiths Ltd	15	5	15	6	41	61.5
5	Jones and Partner	12	8	10	6	36	54
6	Redwoods	13	20	11	6	50	75
7	Underhills Ltd	13	12	11	6	42	63
8	Abbey Builders	0	0	0	13	13	19.5
9							
10	Totals	53	45	47	37		

Time data   Sheet2   She ...

Exercise 3 – creating another workbook, using formulas to check data

In this exercise we will create a simple spreadsheet for bank transactions.

Stage 1

This stage involves entering some text to form the basic layout of our spreadsheet.

1.   Open a new workbook.

2.   Move to Sheet1.

3.   Change the name of the sheet to **July**.

4.   Move to cell A1, enter **Bank transactions**.

5.   Move to cell A3, enter **Opening balance**.

6.   Widen column A so that all text is contained within the column.

7.   Enter **1500** in cell B3.

8.   Enter **Date** in cell A5, **Debit** in B5, **Credit** in C5, **Balance** in D5.

9.   Save the workbook with the name **Exercise3**.

Your spreadsheet should look as shown below:

	A	B	C	D	E	F	G
1	Bank transactions						
2							
3	Opening balance	1500					
4							
5	Date	Debit	Credit	Balance			
6							
7							
8							
9							
10							

July

Stage 2

We are going to enter details of some transactions.

1.   Starting in row 6 enter **02/04/16** in column A, **95.34** in column B, **0** in column C.

2.   In row 7, enter **11/04/16**, **0**, **25.5** in columns A, B, C respectively.

3.   In row 8, enter **15/04/16**, **0**, **34.78** in columns A, B, C respectively.

4.   In row 9, enter **22/04/16**, **67.9**, **0** in columns A, B, C respectively.

5.   In row 10, enter **28/04/16**, **17.99**, **0** in columns A, B, C respectively.

6.   Save your spreadsheet.

Your spreadsheet should now look as shown below:

	A	B	C	D	E	F	G
1	Bank transactions						
2							
3	Opening balance	1500					
4							
5	Date	Debit	Credit	Balance			
6	02/04/2016	95.34	0				
7	11/04/2016	0	25.5				
8	15/04/2016	0	34.78				
9	22/04/2016	67.9	0				
10	28/04/2016	17.99	0				

July

Stage 3

We are now going to enter some formulas to calculate the balance after each transaction.

1. On the first row of data (row 6) the value in the Balance column is going to be calculated using the opening balance. Enter a formula in cell D6, which takes the opening balance (B3), subtracts the debit (B6), and adds the credit (C6).

2. Enter the formula in D7, which uses the previous balance from D6, subtracts the debit (B7), and adds the credit (C7).

3. Enter a formula for the remaining rows of data.

4. Save your spreadsheet.

Your spreadsheet should now look as shown below:

D6	▾	⋮	✕	✓	*fx*	=B3-B6+C6		
◢	A	B	C	D	E	F	G
1	Bank transactions						
2							
3	Opening balance	1500					
4							
5	Date	Debit	Credit	Balance			
6	02/04/2016	95.34	0	1404.66			
7	11/04/2016	0	25.5	1430.16			
8	15/04/2016	0	34.78	1464.94			
9	22/04/2016	67.9	0	1397.04			
10	28/04/2016	17.99	0	1379.05			
◂ ▸	July	⊕			⋮	◂	▸

Stage 4

We are now going to finalise the spreadsheet and enter some formulas to carry out some cross checks.

1.   Enter **Closing balance** in cell A4.

2.   Insert a row between row 4 and row 5.

3.   The value of the closing balance will be the balance after the last transaction (D11 in this instance).

      Enter a formula in B4 so that this cell always holds the value of D11.

4.   The transaction of 28/04/16 is incorrect, the Debit figure should be 107.99. Change the value in cell B11; see how the value in B4 changes to the new closing balance figure.

5.   Enter **Totals** in cell A12.

6.   Enter a formula in cell B12 to total the debits. (Adding up B7 through to B11.)

7.   Enter a formula in cell C12 to total the credits.

8.   In cell E12, enter a formula which takes the opening balance, subtracts the total debits, and adds in the total credits. (This should give the same value as the closing balance – a useful reconciliation.)

9.   Save your spreadsheet.

Your spreadsheet should now appear as shown below:

E12	▼ :	X ✓	f_x	=B3-B12+C12		
	A	B	C	D	E	F	G
1	Bank transactions						
2							
3	Opening balance	1500					
4	Closing balance	1289.05					
5							
6	Date	Debit	Credit	Balance			
7	02/04/2016	95.34	0	1404.66			
8	11/04/2016	0	25.5	1430.16			
9	15/04/2016	0	34.78	1464.94			
10	22/04/2016	67.9	0	1397.04			
11	28/04/2016	107.99	0	1289.05			
12	Totals	271.23	60.28		1289.05		
	◄ ► July	⊕		:	◄		►

2 Formatting the spreadsheet data

this chapter covers...

In this chapter we describe ways of formatting data within a spreadsheet using different text fonts and styles. We also explain different ways of representing numeric data, including currencies and dates. Page layouts will also be explained.

When you have finished this chapter and carried out the exercises which follow, you should be competent in formatting and also printing a spreadsheet.

The concepts and techniques covered are:

■ *formatting – style*

■ *formatting – fonts and size*

■ *number formats*

■ *cell alignments*

■ *date formats*

■ *printing and page setup*

Note that the step-by-step instructions given in this chapter are based on the Microsoft® Excel model, but the concepts and techniques described relate to all spreadsheet packages.

FORMATTING – STYLE

Text formatting within a spreadsheet, as with other types of document, is often used to make an item stand out or to emphasise specific data.

We will use the expenditure worksheet shown below as an example.

A1	▼	⋮	✕ ✓ *fx*	Expenditure forecast			⌄

	A	B	C	D	E	F	G
1	Expenditure forecast						
2							
3		January	February	March	April	May	June
4							
5	Salaries						
6	Insurance						
7	Rent						
8	Accountancy						
9	Advertising						
10	Postage						
11	Stationery						

Sheet1   ⊕

making data bold

To make data bold:

■ click on the required cell

then

■ click on the **Bold** icon on the menu bar if visible

or

■ right click on the selected cell

■ select **Format cells**

■ select **Font**

■ make the font style **Bold**

or

■ press **CTRL** and **B** together (hold down the **CONTROL** key and tap the **B** key and release)

Now look at the next page to see the result.

◢	A	B	C	D	E	F	G
1	**Expenditure forecast**		◄━━━━━━━		**Now bold**		
2							
3		January	February	March	April	May	June
4							
5	Salaries						

To make **more than one cell bold**:

■ select all the required cells

■ and follow the steps set out on on the previous page

using italics

To use **italics in one cell**:

■ click on the required cell

then

■ click on the **Italics** icon on the menu bar if visible

or

■ right click on the selected cell

■ select **Format cells**

■ select **Font**

■ make the font style **Italics**

or

■ press **CTRL** and **I** together (hold down the **CONTROL** key and tap the **I** key and release)

See the spreadsheet screen below.

To make **more than one cell italicised:**

■ select all the required cells

■ and follow one of the formatting choices explained above

4							
5	*Salaries*						
6	*Insurance*						
7	*Rent*						
8	*Accountancy*	◄━━━━━		*Now Italics*			
9	*Advertising*						
10	*Postage*						
11	*Stationery*						

underlining data

To **underline data**:

■ click on the required cell

then

■ click on the **Underline** icon on the menu bar if visible

or

■ right click on the selected cell, select **Format cells**, select **Font** and make the underline style **Single**

or

■ press **CTRL** and **U** together (hold down the **CONTROL** key and tap the **U** key and release)

◢	A	B	C	D	E	F	G
1	Expenditure forecast		◄━━━━━━━━		Now Underlined		
2							
3		January	February	March	April	May	June
4							
5	Salaries						

To underline data in more than one cell, select all the required cells and follow the steps set out above.

To **double underline** data:

■ click on the required cell

Then

■ click on the drop down arrow by the **U**nderline icon

■ select **D**ouble underline

Or

■ Right click on the selected cell, select **Format cells**, select **Font** and make the underline style **double**

◢	A	B	C	D	E	F	G
1	Expenditure forecast		◄━━━━━━━━		Now Double Underlined		
2							
3		January	February	March	April	May	June
4							
5	Salaries						

note – changing back to normal text

To turn off the style, such as bold, underline, italics, you follow exactly the same steps described above and the style will change back to normal.

FORMATTING TEXT – FONT AND SIZE

font face

The **font face** (often known as the '**font**') of text is the style of the lettering:

This is Times   This is Helvetica

To change the font face:

■ click on the required cell

then

■ click on the **Font** list dropdown on the menu bar if visible

■ select the required font

or

■ right click on the selected cell

■ select **Format cells**

■ select **Font**

■ choose the required **Font** from the list

To change the font in more than one cell, select all the required cells and follow the steps above.

	A	B	C	D	E	F	G
1	Expenditure forecast						
2							
3		January	February	March	April	May	June
4							
5	Salaries						
6	Insurance						
7	Rent						
8	Accountancy			Font changed to Arial			
9	Advertising						
10	Postage						
11	Stationery						

font size

To change the font size:

■ click on the required cell

then

■ click on the **Font size** dropdown on the menu bar if visible

■ select the required font face size

or

■ right click on the selected cell, select **Format cells**, select **Font** and choose the required font size from the list

	A	B	C	D	E	F	G
1	**Expenditure forecast**					Now larger font	
2							
3		January	February	March	April	May	June
4							
5	*Salaries*						
6	*Insurance*						

To change the font size in more than one cell, select all the required cells and follow the steps above.

font colour

To change the font colour:

■ click on the required cell

then

■ click on the **Font color** drop-down on the menu bar if visible (usually displayed as a capital A, with the current colour displayed as a bar underneath)

■ select the required font colour

or

■ right click on the selected cell, select Format cells, select Font and choose the required colour from the list

To change the font colour in more than one cell, select all the required cells and follow the steps above.

mini toolbar

Depending on the set up of your spreadsheet program, when you select text to modify, you may see the mini toolbar appear, as shown below.

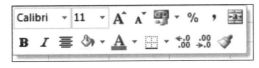

This toolbar provides a quick way of getting to formatting options which you might require when working on your spreadsheet. If you are using Excel, and it does not appear, you can change this as described on the next page.

■ select the File menu

■ select Options

■ select General

■ scroll down to **User Interface Options**, and **check Show Mini Toolbar** on selection

To turn off the Mini Toolbar, repeat the above, and **uncheck Show Mini Toolbar** on selection

FORMATTING – NUMBERS

The word '**format**' is used in this context to describe the way in which a number will be displayed.

dealing with decimal places

When you enter a number into a cell it is displayed exactly as you type it, except that any **trailing zeros** (zeros after the last non-zero digit on the right of the decimal point), and **leading zeros** (zeros before the first non-zero digit at the front of the number) will be ignored.

For example, if you type **0000125.76000** into a cell and press **RETURN** (Enter) you will see **125.76** displayed.

If you want to see trailing zeros after a decimal point, you will need to change the number of decimal places which are displayed.

For example, if you are dealing with money amounts, you will want to see £34.10 rather than £34.1, which looks very odd. Therefore it is quite common that you would want all values in a particular column or row to display to a certain number of decimal places, to give a consistent view to the spreadsheet.

You can see in the example at the top of the next page that several of the data entries are displayed with only one digit after the decimal point.

(Note that throughout this example a 'credit' means a payment into the bank and a 'debit' means a payment out – just as you would see on a bank statement, but not in double-entry.)

	A	B	C	D	E	F	
1	Bank transactions						
2							
3	Opening balance	1500					
4	Closing balance	1289.05					
5							
6	Date	Debit	Credit	Balance			
7	02/04/2016	95.34	0	1404.66			
8	11/04/2016	0	25.5	~~1100.10~~	One decimal place		
9	15/04/2016	0	34.78	1464.94			
10	22/04/2016	67.9	0	1397.04			

To change the number of decimal places:

■ select the required cells, row or column

■ right click on the selection

■ select **Format cells**

■ select the **Number** tab

■ select category **Number**

■ adjust the number of decimal places as required

You can see the effect below where the number formats for columns B and C have been changed to display 2 decimal places.

	A	B	C	D	E	F	
1	Bank transactions						
2							
3	Opening balance	1500.00					
4	Closing balance	1289.05					
5							
6	Date	Debit	Credit	Balance			
7	02/04/2016	95.34	0.00	1404.66			
8	11/04/2016	0.00	25.50	1430.16			
9	15/04/2016	0.00	34.78	1464.94			
10	22/04/2016	67.90	0.00	1397.04			
11	28/04/2016	107.99	0.00	1289.05		.	
12	Totals	271.23	60.28		1289.05		

displaying commas in figures

In order to make numbers more readable, we often insert a comma to identify when the number is over a thousand, and a further comma for over a million and so on.

To display a , (comma) to represent thousands:

■ select the required cells, row or column

■ right click on the selection

■ select **Format** cells

■ select the **Number** tab

■ select **category Number**

■ tick the **Use 1000 Separator** box

As you can see in the image below the comma can make a big difference to the readability of the spreadsheet. Compare Column D below with Column D on the the screen shown on the previous page.

	A	B	C	D	E	F
1	Bank transactions					
2						
3	Opening balance	1500.00				
4	Closing balance	1289.05				
5						
6	Date	Debit	Credit	Balance		
7	02/04/2016	95.34	0.00	1,404.66		
8	11/04/2016	0.00	25.50	1,430.16		
9	15/04/2016	0.00	34.78	1,464.94		
10	22/04/2016	67.90	0.00	1,397.04		
11	28/04/2016	107.99	0.00	1,289.05		
12	Totals	271.23	60.28		1,289.05	

dealing with currencies

Often when we are dealing with money it is simpler to use the built in format of currency for our data. A format of currency does not affect the values but merely the way the data is displayed.

One of the most commonly used currencies is the UK pound sterling.

To display data as **Currency sterling** with a £ symbol:

■ select the required cells, row or column

■ right click on the selection

■ select **Format** cells

■ select the **Number** tab

- select category **Currency**

- adjust the decimal places as required

- for **Symbol** select the £ (pound sterling) from the list displayed

The effect of formatting columns B, C and D as currency sterling is shown below.

	A	B	C	D	E	F
1	Bank transactions					
2						
3	Opening balance	£1,500.00				
4	Closing balance	£1,289.05				
5						
6	Date	Debit	Credit	Balance		
7	02/04/2016	£95.34	£0.00	£1,404.66		
8	11/04/2016	£0.00	£25.50	£1,430.16		
9	15/04/2016	£0.00	£34.78	£1,464.94		
10	22/04/2016	£67.90	£0.00	£1,397.04		
11	28/04/2016	£107.99	£0.00	£1,289.05		
12	Totals	£271.23	£60.28		£1,289.05	

If the values we had entered were euros, we could use the same procedure as for the pound sterling (see above) and select the euro as the symbol from the list displayed. The spreadsheet would then appear as follows:

	A	B	C	D	E	F
1	Bank transactions					
2						
3	Opening balance	€1,500.00				
4	Closing balance	€1,289.05				
5						
6	Date	Debit	Credit	Balance		
7	02/04/2016	€95.34	€0.00	€1,404.66		
8	11/04/2016	€0.00	€25.50	€1,430.16		
9	15/04/2016	€0.00	€34.78	€1,464.94		
10	22/04/2016	€67.90	€0.00	€1,397.04		
11	28/04/2016	€107.99	€0.00	€1,289.05		
12	Totals	€271.23	€60.28		€1,289.05	

dealing with percentages

It is also possible to display a number as a **percentage** (%).

If you enter numbers followed by a % sign, the data will be recognised as a percentage and the % sign will be displayed.

If you have a calculation, and you want the result to **display as a percentage**, rather than decimals, you would use the format options to change the way the result is displayed. For example, you may want to show the closing balance in the spreadsheet on the opposite page as a percentage of the opening balance.

To do this, you would first insert an appropriate text description in cell D4 and then the formula =B4/B3 in cell E4 (see pages 17-18 for formulas) to calculate the closing balance divided by the opening balance.

E4	▾ ⋮	✕ ✓ *fx*	=B4/B3			
	A	B	C	D	E	F
1	Bank transactions					
2						
3	Opening balance	€ 1,500.00				
4	Closing balance	€ 1,289.05		C.Bal/O.Bal	0.86	
5						
6	Date	Debit	Credit	Balance		
7	02/04/2016	€ 95.34	€ 0.00	€ 1,404.66		
8	11/04/2016	€ 0.00	€ 25.50	€ 1,430.16		
9	15/04/2016	€ 0.00	€ 34.78	€ 1,464.94		
10	22/04/2016	€ 67.90	€ 0.00	€ 1,397.04		
11	28/04/2016	€ 107.99	€ 0.00	€ 1,289.05		
12	Totals	€ 271.23	€ 60.28		€ 1,289.05	

The spreadsheet would then look like this (note top bar and cells D4 and E4):

To make cell E4 display as a **percentage**:

■ select the required cell

■ right click on the selection

■ select **Format** cells

■ select the **Number** tab

■ select category **Percentage**

■ adjust the decimal places as required

The spreadsheet will then appear as shown at the top of the next page.

E4	▼	:	✕ ✓ *fx*	=B4/B3		

▲	A	B	C	D	E	F
1	Bank transactions					
2						
3	Opening balance	€ 1,500.00				
4	Closing balance	€ 1,289.05		C.Bal/O.Bal	85.94%	
5						
6	Date	Debit	Credit	Balance		
7	02/04/2016	€ 95.34	€ 0.00	€ 1,404.66		
8	11/04/2016	€ 0.00	€ 25.50	€ 1,430.16		
9	15/04/2016	€ 0.00	€ 34.78	€ 1,464.94		
10	22/04/2016	€ 67.90	€ 0.00	€ 1,397.04		
11	28/04/2016	€ 107.99	€ 0.00	€ 1,289.05		
12	Totals	€ 271.23	€ 60.28		€ 1,289.05	

Note: applying a format of percentage will automatically multiply the selected cell (or cells) by 100 to create a percentage.

CELL ALIGNMENT

Alignment is used to describe the relative position of data within a cell.

With **left alignment** the data is shown up against the left edge of the cell.

Right alignment means that the data is shown up against the right edge of the cell.

For **centre alignment** the data is positioned in the centre of the cell.

Examples of all of these are shown in the screen below. By default any text entered is aligned to the left. Data which is recognised as a number will be automatically aligned to the right.

▲	A	B	C	D	E	F
1	Bank transactions					
2						
3	Opening balance	£1,500.00				
4	Closing balance	£1,289.05				
5						
6	Date	Debit	Credit	Balance		
7	02/04/2016	£95.34	£0.00	£1,404.66	◄──────	Left
8	11/04/2016	£0.00	£25.50	£1,430.16		
9	15/04/2016	£0.00	£34.78	£1,464.94	◄──────	Right
10	22/04/2016	£67.90	£0.00	£1,397.04		
11	28/04/2016	£107.99	£0.00	£1,289.05	◄──────	Centre
12	Totals	£271.23	£60.28		£1,289.05	

To change the way data is aligned in a cell or cells:

- select the required cells, row or column
- right click on the selection
- select **Format** cells
- select the **Alignment** tab
- on the Horizontal dropdown select **Left**, **Right** or **Centre** as required

or with the cells selected

- click on the appropriate **Alignment** icon on the menu bar if visible

merged cells

Sometimes we have some text which we specifically want to spread across several cells, perhaps as a heading, and we may wish it to be centred across these cells.

To achieve this we effectively **merge** the cells together to make one big cell and then apply standard alignment options within this **merged cell**.

	A	B	C	D	E	F	G
1	Bank transactions						
2							
3	Opening balance	£1,500.00					
4	Closing balance	£1,289.05					
5							
6			Transactions		◄ Merged and centred		
7	Date		Debit	Credit	Balance		
8		02/04/2016	£95.34	£0.00	£1,404.66		
9		11/04/2016	£0.00	£25.50	£1,430.16		
10		15/04/2016	£0.00	£34.78	£1,464.94		
11		22/04/2016	£67.90	£0.00	£1,397.04		
12		28/04/2016	£107.99	£0.00	£1,289.05		
13	Totals		£271.23	£60.28		£1,289.05	

You can see in the example above that the merged cells (B6, C6, D6) are now treated as just one cell, when selected, and this allows us to centre the text over the three columns B, C and D.

To merge cells:

- select the required cells
- right click on the selection
- select **Format** cells
- select the **Alignment** tab
- on the text control section click the **Merge cells** checkbox

or with the cells selected

■ click on the **Merge cells** option from the Merge & Center dropdown menu available on the Home menu ribbon

To unmerge cells:

■ select the required cells

■ right click on the selection

■ select **Format** cells

■ select the **Alignment** tab

■ on the text control section click the **Merge cells** checkbox so that it is unchecked

or with the cells selected

■ click on the **Unmerge cells** option from the Merge & Center dropdown menu available on the Home menu ribbon

DATE FORMATS

There are a variety of different ways in which dates can be displayed.

The common way of describing dates is to use 'd' for day, 'm' for month and 'y' for year.

If we take the date of 10th February 2016, it can be displayed in the following formats (for UK dates):

■ dd/mm/yyyy would display as 10/02/2016

■ dd/mm/yy would display as 10/02/16

To change the way a date is displayed:

■ select the required cells
■ right click on the selection
■ select **Format** cells
■ select the **Number** tab
■ select category **Date**
■ choose the format you require from the dropdown list

The spreadsheet at the top of the next page shows the year date amended from 2016 to 16.

	A	B	C	D	E	F
1	Bank transactions					
2						
3	Opening balance	£1,500.00				
4	Closing balance	£1,289.05				
5						
6			Transactions			
7	Date	Debit	Credit	Balance		
8	02/04/16	£95.34	£0.00	£1,404.66		
9	11/04/16	£0.00	£25.50	£1,430.16		
10	15/04/16	£0.00	£34.78	£1,464.94		
11	22/04/16	£67.90	£0.00	£1,397.04		
12	28/04/16	£107.99	£0.00	£1,289.05		
13	Totals	£271.23	£60.28		£1,289.05	

You can also use other date formats which are available under category **Custom**.

dates and time

Occasionally it is useful to include the time within a date, or even just to show the time on its own. There are specific formats to allow for this, within the format options. The common way of describing times is to use 'h' for hour, 'm' for minutes and 's' for seconds. The default time format is hh:mm:ss

For example, 40 seconds after half past one in the afternoon could be displayed as:

13:30:40

Or

01:30:40 PM

Additional date and time formats are available under the category **Custom**.

PAGE SETUP AND PRINTING

Once we have created and formatted our spreadsheet it is quite possible that we will want to print it.

Spreadsheets are not like word-processed documents – they do not automatically fit within one horizontal page width and flow on downwards.

The first step is to see what the spreadsheet would look like when printed, without actually printing. From the **File** menu, select **Print**. You will then see all the print settings which you can change, together with a **Print Preview** of the worksheet on the right hand side of the screen. Alternatively, you can select **Page Setup** from the **Page Layout** menu, then **Print Preview**.

If you need to make adjustments to the layout for printing, this can be done through **Settings** within the **Print** option, or **Page Setup** within the **Page Layout** menu.

Page Setup allows you to:

- change the **orientation**, so if the spreadsheet is slightly too wide to fit on one page width, you might change the orientation to **Landscape**

- adjust the **Margins** – you might want to reduce these to a minimum to give as much space as possible

- select **Fit to page** – you can specify how many pages wide, by how many pages tall you want to fit the spreadsheet into; it is important to make sure that the text of the spreadsheet remains legible

- check or uncheck the **gridlines** box if you want to see gridlines for the rows and columns included on your printout

The two images that follow show print previews where the page orientations are:

- portrait – one is taller than it is wider – like a portrait picture

- landscape – the other is wider than it is taller – like a landscape painting

The image below shows a print preview where the page orientation is **Portrait**.

The image below shows a print preview where the page orientation is **Landscape**.

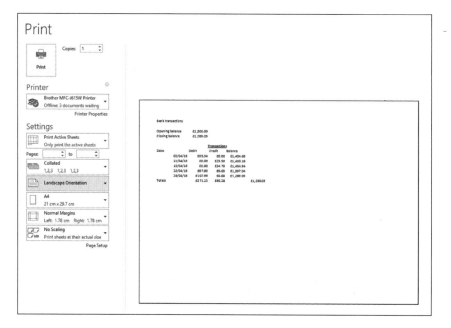

print area

If you want to print just a particular group of cells on your spreadsheet, you can set a print area, this could be different for each worksheet and the details of any print areas are saved when the workbook is saved.

To set a print area:

- select a range or group of cells

- select the **Page Layout** menu

- select **Print Area**

- select **Set Print Area**

To clear a print area:

- select the **Page Layout** menu

- select **Print Area**

- select **Clear Print Area**

headers and footers

It is sometimes useful to add a **header** or a **footer** to your spreadsheet.

As you would expect a **header** is something which will usually appear at the top of each page when printed. This could be something like "Company Confidential" and the date.

A **footer** will appear at the bottom and is often used to include the author and a page number if the printing covers more than one page.

To create a header or a footer:

■ select **Page setup** (within **Page Layout**)

■ select **Header/Footer**

■ either select one of the built in choices from the drop down list for the header or footer such as page number or date

■ or create your own custom piece of text

An example Header, selected from the list is shown in the screen below:

An example Footer, selected from the list is shown in the screen below:

There are a number of additional items which can be inserted into either a header or a footer. These are available if you select Custom for your header or footer, and then pick the items you want and where you want to position them, for example:

■ text

■ time

■ filename

■ picture

This can be seen in the image on the next page:

Header

To format text: select the text, then choose the Format Text button.
To insert a page number, date, time, file path, filename, or tab name: position the
   insertion point in the edit box, then choose the appropriate button.
To insert picture: press the Insert Picture button. To format your picture, place the
   cursor in the edit box and press the Format Picture button.

| A | | | | | | | | | |

Left section:	Center section:	Right section:
Confidential	&[Date]	Page &[Page]

pagebreak

If we wish to format our printed output so that part of the information is on one page and the remainder on another page, we can insert what is known as a page break.

To insert a page break:

▪ select the **Page Layout** menu

▪ click on the cell to be the start of the new page

▪ select **Breaks**

▪ select **Insert Page Break**

Other packages will usually provide the same facilities presented in a different way. We recommend that you experiment and gain an understanding of the page setup options.

| **Chapter Summary** | This chapter has covered in detail the following topics: |

▪ formatting – style

▪ formatting – fonts and size

▪ number formats

▪ cell alignments

▪ date formats

▪ page setup

You should now carry out some or all of the exercises on the next few pages in order to practise and reinforce your learning.

Activities

Exercise 1 – setting up a costing worksheet

In this exercise, we will create a spreadsheet, insert rows and columns, create some simple formulas, and do some formatting. The spreadsheet will be an example of production costing.

Stage 1

This stage is about creating our basic layout.

1.   Create a **New** workbook.

2.   Move to Sheet1.

3.   Enter the spreadsheet title **Production costs**.

4.   In cell B2, C2, D2, enter **No of Units**, **Unit Cost**, **Total Cost** respectively, widening columns as necessary to fit the text.

5.   In A3, A4 enter **Materials**, **Labour** respectively.

6.   Insert a row between the Production costs title (row1) and the column headings (row 2).

7.   Increase the height of row 1 to 25, to make it stand out more.

8.   In cell B4 and cell B5 enter **12000** for the No of units.

9.   Enter the unit cost for materials (C4) **£5**.

10.   Enter the unit cost for labour (C5) **£2**.

11.   In cell D4, enter the formula to calculate the total materials cost for these 12000 units (=B4*C4).

12.   Similarly in cell D5, enter the formula for total labour costs.

13.   Format cells C4 to C7 and D4 to D7 as **currency, no decimal places** with **currency symbol £**.

14.   Save the workbook as **T2Exercise1**.

Your workbook should look as shown below:

D4	▾	⋮	✕ ✓ *fx*	=B4*C4		
◢	A	B	C	D	E	F
1	Production costs					
2						
3		No of Units	Unit Cost	Total Cost		
4	Materials	12000	£5	£60,000		
5	Labour	12000	£2	£24,000		
6						

Stage 2

We are going to introduce some further values and do some more calculations.

1. Continuing with the **T2Exercise1** workbook.

2. In cell A6, enter **Fixed Costs** widening column A as necessary.

3. In cell D6, enter **£36000**.

4. In cell A7, enter **Total**.

5. In cell D7, enter the formula to calculate the sum of the Total Cost values.

We will now work out the unit cost for the Fixed Costs.

6. In cell B6, enter **12000** for the no of units.

7. Enter a formula in cell C6, to calculate the unit cost for Fixed Costs (=D6/B6).

Now we have the overall total cost for the manufacture of 12000 units we can calculate the overall unit cost based on materials, labour, and Fixed Costs.

8. Enter a formula in C7 to sum the unit costs.

9. Save the workbook.

Your workbook should look as shown below:

C6		✕ ✓ *fx*	=D6/B6		
	A	B	C	D	E	F
1	Production costs					
2						
3		No of Units	Unit Cost	Total Cost		
4	Materials	12000	£5	£60,000		
5	Labour	12000	£2	£24,000		
6	Fixed Costs	12000	£3	£36,000		
7	Total		£10	£120,000		

Stage 3

Changing our layout and improving the structure of our costing worksheet.

1.   Continuing with the **T2Exercise1** workbook.

2.   Insert 2 rows between the current row 2, and row 3. (This should move the current row 3 down to below 5.)

3.   Copy cell B5 (No of Units) into cell A3.

4.   In Cell C3 enter 12000 (or copy B6).

What we need to do now is modify our formulas so that they all refer to the one cell which defines the number of units we want to produce (which is going to be cell C3), rather than having that value multiple times within our spreadsheet.

5.   Modify the formula for Total Cost for Materials (D6) to use Materials Unit Cost (C6) and No of Units (C3).

6.   Similarly modify the formula for Total Cost for Labour (D7).

7.   For Fixed Costs, modify the formula which calculates the Unit Cost (C8) to use Total Fixed Costs (D8) and No of Units (C3).

The values shown in the cells should look exactly as before, as shown in the image below:

D6		f_x	=C3*C6		
	A	B	C	D	E	F
1	Production costs					
2						
3	No of Units		12000			
4						
5		No of Units	Unit Cost	Total Cost		
6	Materials	12000	£5	£60,000		
7	Labour	12000	£2	£24,000		
8	Fixed Costs	12000	£3	£36,000		
9	Total		£10	£120,000		

It is only the formulas which are different, as shown in the image on the next page:

A1	▾ : ✕ ✓ 𝑓𝑥	Production costs		
	A	**B**	**C**	**D**
1	Production costs			
2				
3	No of Units		12000	
4				
5		No of Units	Unit Cost	Total Cost
6	Materials	12000	5	=C3*C6
7	Labour	12000	2	=C3*C7
8	Fixed Costs	12000	=D8/C3	36000
9	Total		=SUM(C6:C8)	=SUM(D6:D8)

We no longer need column B, holding the repeated No of Units.

8. Delete column B.

If, when you do this you get #REF appearing in any of the cells, it means you have not changed all the formulas correctly, and they are still using the values in Column B. (Use Undo to put the column back, and check each of the formulas.)

9. Change the No of Units to 18000.

See how making one change now reflects through all of our calculations.

If we wanted to compare the effect of two different quantities at once, we could do this by copying all the relevant cells to a new area, and the formulas will be copied.

10. Select cells B3 to C9.

11. Select **COPY**.

12. Move to cell E3, select **PASTE**.

13. Change cell B3 back to 12000.

14. **Merge and centre** the heading Production Costs in row 1 across columns A to F.

15. Save the workbook.

You can now compare the different costings for two different levels of production, as shown in the image below.

	A	**B**	**C**	**D**	**E**	**F**
1			Production costs			
2						
3	No of Units	12000			18000	
4						
5		Unit Cost	Total Cost		Unit Cost	Total Cost
6	Materials	£5	£60,000		£5	£90,000
7	Labour	£2	£24,000		£2	£36,000
8	Fixed Costs	£3	£36,000		£2	£36,000
9	Total	£10	£120,000		£9	£162,000

Exercise 2 – using percentages and decimal places

In this exercise we will create a simple spreadsheet to create the line-by-line detail for an invoice.

Stage 1

This stage is about creating the basic layout of our spreadsheet.

All text should be entered in the default typeface, font size 11, normal style.

1.   Open a new workbook.

2.   Move to **Sheet1**.

3.   Rename the worksheet **Invoice 201**.

4.   Starting in cell A1, enter the text as shown below to create the layout of the invoice.

Invoice Date:							
Customer No.:							
Product	Description	Qty	Price	Unit	Total	Discount	Net
Code			£		£	%	£

5.   Widen column A so that all the text fits within the column.

6.   Widen column B to 18.

7.   Format the columns for Price, Total and Net as **Currency**, **£**, **two decimal places** (columns D, F and H).

8.   Format discount % to **percentage** with **one decimal place**.

9.   **Underline** Invoice Date and Customer No. (cells A1 and A3).

10.   Enter **1/2/2016** for Invoice Date (cell B1).

11.   Enter **1498** for Customer No.

12.   Make the column headings in rows 5 and 6 **Bold**.

13.   Enter the details of the products sold, as shown in the table below:

Product	Description	Qty	Price	Unit
PAPER-R	Paper -Ream	4	2.15	each
PEN-50	Pens box - 50	2	9.99	each
A4FOLD-3	A4 Ring Folder - 3	3	2.50	each
PAD-1	Lined pads - 1	6	1.70	each
ENVA4-100	Envelopes A4 -100	3	10.99	each

14. Format the Price column (column D) to show **two decimal places** (no currency sign).

15. Save your workbook as **T2Exercise2**.

Your worksheet should look as shown below:

	A	B	C	D	E	F	G	H	I
1	Invoice Date:	01/02/2016							
2									
3	Customer No.:	1498							
4									
5	Product	Description	Qty	Price	Unit	Total	Discount	Discount	Net
6	Code			£		£	%	£	£
7	PAPER-R	Paper -Ream	4	2.15	each				
8	PEN-50	Pens box - 50	2	9.99	each				
9	A4FOLD-3	A4 Ring Folder - 3	3	2.50	each				
10	PAD-1	Lined pads - 1	6	1.70	each				
11	ENVA4-100	Envelopes A4 -100	3	10.99	each				

Invoice 201 | Sheet2 | Sheet3

Stage 2

During this stage we are going to enter the formulas for Totals and Discount values:

1. In the Total column, cell F7, enter the formula to calculate the Total price for the Paper item (Qty * Price).

2. Enter the formulas for the Total for the remaining items.

3. Format the Total column (column F) to show **two decimal places** (no currency sign).

4. Format the Discount column (column G) to **percentage no decimal places**.

5. Enter **Discount values** of **5**, **10**, **5**, **2** and **4** in cells G7 through to G11 respectively.

To help us do our calculations relating to the discount value, we are going to include an extra column on our invoice which would not normally be shown on an invoice. The calculation would usually be done in just one step, rather than two.

6. Insert a column between the Discount and the Net columns (G and H). This column is going to hold the calculated value of the discount.

7. In cell H5, enter **Discount**, and in cell H6, enter £.

8. Format the Discount £ column (column H) to show **two decimal places** (no currency sign).

9. In cell H7, enter the formula to calculate the Discount £ for the Paper item (Total * Discount %), copy this formula into cells H8 to H11.

10. Save your workbook.

Your worksheet should look as shown below:

	A	B	C	D	E	F	G	H	I
1	Invoice Date:	01/02/2016							
2									
3	Customer No.:	1498							
4									
5	Product	Description	Qty	Price	Unit	Total	Discount	Discount	Net
6	Code			£		£	%	£	£
7	PAPER-R	Paper -Ream	4	2.15	each	8.60	5%	0.43	
8	PEN-50	Pens box - 50	2	9.99	each	19.98	10%	2.00	
9	A4FOLD-3	A4 Ring Folder - 3	3	2.50	each	7.50	5%	0.38	
10	PAD-1	Lined pads - 1	6	1.70	each	10.20	2%	0.20	
11	ENVA4-100	Envelopes A4 -100	3	10.99	each	32.97	4%	1.32	

Stage 3

We are going to complete the invoice in this stage:

1. In the Net column, cell I7, enter the formula to calculate the Net price for the Paper item (Total £ – Discount £).

2. Enter the formulas for the Net £ for the remaining items.

We are now going to total the invoice and add the VAT:

3. In cell H12, enter **Subtotal**, and in I12, enter the formula to total the Net Values (I7 to I11).

4. In cell H13, enter **VAT (20%)**, and in I13, enter the formula to calculate the VAT at 20% (=I12*20/100) or (=I12*0.2).

5. In cell H14, enter **TOTAL** and in cell I14, enter the formula to calculate the invoice TOTAL by adding the Subtotal and the VAT.

6. **Double underline** your TOTAL value (cell I14).

7. Having completed the invoice you see an error. Change the Qty of Envelopes to 6 (cell C11).

8. Also, change the Price for pens to **10.99** (cell D8).

9. Save your workbook.

Your worksheet should look as shown below:

	A	B	C	D	E	F	G	H	I
1	Invoice Date:	01/02/2016							
2									
3	Customer No.:	1498							
4									
5	Product	Description	Qty	Price	Unit	Total	Discount	Discount	Net
6	Code			£		£	%	£	£
7	PAPER-R	Paper -Ream	4	2.15	each	8.60	5%	0.43	8.17
8	PEN-50	Pens box - 50	2	10.99	each	21.98	10%	2.20	19.78
9	A4FOLD-3	A4 Ring Folder - 3	3	2.50	each	7.50	5%	0.38	7.13
10	PAD-1	Lined pads - 1	6	1.70	each	10.20	2%	0.20	10.00
11	ENVA4-100	Envelopes A4 -100	6	10.99	each	65.94	4%	2.64	63.30
12								Subtotal	108.38
13								VAT (20%)	21.68
14								TOTAL	130.05

Exercise 3 – using formatting and printing

In this exercise we will use the invoice spreadsheet created in the previous exercise to practise using different formats.

Stage 1

1.   Open the workbook **T2Exercise2** created in the previous exercise.

2.   Save the workbook with name **T2Exercise3**.

3.   Edit cell A5 to be **Product Code**.

4.   Edit cell G5 to be Discount %.

5.   Edit cell H5 to be Discount Value.

6.   Widen all columns as necessary so that column text is fully visible.

7.   Delete row 6.

8.   Format the values for Price, Total, Discount Value and Net to **currency, 2 decimal places, symbol £**.

9.   Set the **alignment** of the column headings for Qty, Price, Total, Discount Value and Net to be **right aligned**.

10.   Save your workbook.

Your worksheet should look as shown below:

	A	B	C	D	E	F	G	H	I
1	Invoice Date:	01/02/2016							
2									
3	Customer No.:	1498							
4									
5	Product Code	Description	Qty	Price	Unit	Total	Discount %	Discount Value	Net
6	PAPER-R	Paper -Ream	4	£2.15	each	£8.60	5%	£0.43	£8.17
7	PEN-50	Pens box - 50	2	£10.99	each	£21.98	10%	£2.20	£19.78
8	A4FOLD-3	A4 Ring Folder - 3	3	£2.50	each	£7.50	5%	£0.38	£7.13
9	PAD-1	Lined pads - 1	6	£1.70	each	£10.20	2%	£0.20	£10.00
10	ENVA4-100	Envelopes A4 -100	6	£10.99	each	£65.94	4%	£2.64	£63.30
11								Subtotal	£108.38
12								VAT (20%)	£21.68
13								TOTAL	£130.05

Stage 2

1. Change the font size of cells A1, A2, A3, B3 to 12, change column widths to fit text if necessary.

2. Change the font style of the column headings to Italics.

3. Change the format of the Invoice Date to show just two digits for the year.

4. Align the column heading Description (column B) in the centre.

5. Keep the **Discount%** values as percentage, change to also display one decimal place.

6. In cell A12, enter the text Euro Rate.

7. In cell B12, enter the value 1.3 to represent the euro exchange rate, i.e. number of euros to the pound.

8. Enter **Euro Value** in cell J5 as a column heading.

9. Enter formulas in cells J6 to J10 to calculate the Net value in euros from the £ value in the Net column. (Net Value * Euro Rate.)

10. Set the format of cells J6 to J9 to currency, 2 decimal places, symbol euro.

You will notice that cell J9 has the value 12.99, not 13 as expected.

11. To understand why, select cell I9, change the format to show 4 decimal places.

You can see that the value in this cell is slightly less than 10 when you show more decimal places. When only two decimal places are shown, it is rounded up. So 9.9960 is shown as 10.00 when you are only showing 2 decimal places.

12. **Undo** this format change to cell I9 so that only 2 decimal places are shown.

13. Save your workbook.

Your worksheet should look as shown below:

	A	B	C	D	E	F	G	H	I	J
	J6			X ✓ *fx*	=I6*B12					
1	Invoice Date:	01/02/16								
2										
3	Customer No.:	1498								
4										
5	*Product Code*	*Description*	*Qty*	*Price*	*Unit*	*Total*	*Discount %*	*Discount Value*	*Net*	*Euro Value*
6	PAPER-R	Paper - Ream	4	£2.15	each	£8.60	5.0%	£0.43	£8.17	€ 10.62
7	PEN-50	Pens box - 50	2	£10.99	each	£21.98	10.0%	£2.20	£19.78	€ 25.72
8	A4FOLD-3	A4 Ring Folder - 3	3	£2.50	each	£7.50	5.0%	£0.38	£7.13	€ 9.26
9	PAD-1	Lined pads - 1	6	£1.70	each	£10.20	2.0%	£0.20	£10.00	€ 12.99
10	ENVA4-100	Envelopes A4 -100	6	£10.99	each	£65.94	4.0%	£2.64	£63.30	€ 82.29
11							Subtotal		£108.38	
12	Euro Rate	1.3					VAT (20%)		£21.68	
13							TOTAL		£130.05	

Stage 3

In this stage we are going to look at headers and footers, and how to print the spreadsheet.

1. Using **Page Setup** options, create a **custom header** which is to appear on our printed documents. The header should have the **date** in the left section, and the **sheet name** (which in this case is the invoice number) in the right section. Within the custom header section as you move the mouse over each of the options you will see what they represent.

2. Now create a footer which displays **page number of total number** of pages use page 1 of ?.

3. Select **Print** from your menu.

Within the preview, you will see that not all of our columns can be seen. Several columns get pushed on to a second page. To confirm this, the footer displays Page 1of 2, as shown below.

11/02/2016							Invoice 201

Invoice Date:	01/02/16	
Customer No.:	1498	

Product Code	Description	Qty	Price	Unit	Total	Discount %
PAPER-R	Paper -Ream	4	£2.15	each	£8.60	5.0%
PEN-50	Pens box - 50	2	£10.99	each	£21.98	10.0%
A4FOLD-3	A4 Ring Folder - 3	3	£2.50	each	£7.50	5.0%
PAD-1	Lined pads - 1	6	£1.70	each	£10.20	2.0%
ENVA4-100	Envelopes A4 -100	6	£10.99	each	£65.94	4.0%

Euro Rate	1.3

Page 1 of 2

4.   Within **Settings**, change the orientation so that the page will print Landscape.

This now fits on one page, but we want to try some other alternatives.

5.   Change the orientation to Portrait.

6.   Change the scaling to Fit All Columns on One Page.

7. From **Page Setup** in the Print menu, remove the footer (set to none).

8. Modify the custom header, in the centre section put the text **Page** followed by a space, then select **page number** from the available options.

9. Save your workbook.

The preview should appear as shown below:

11/02/2016				Page 1						Invoice 201
Invoice Date:		01/02/16								
Customer No.:		1498								
Product Code	Description	Qty	Price	Unit	Total	Discount %	Discount Value		Net	Euro Value
PAPER-R	Paper-Ream	4	£2.15	each	£8.60	5.0%	£0.43		£8.17	€10.62
PEN-50	Pens box-50	2	£10.99	each	£21.98	10.0%	£2.20		£19.78	€25.72
A4FOLD-3	A4 Ring Folder-3	3	£2.50	each	£7.50	5.0%	£0.38		£7.13	€9.26
PAD-1	Lined pads-1	6	£1.70	each	£10.20	2.0%	£0.20		£10.00	€12.99
ENVA4-100	Envelopes A4-100	6	£10.99	each	£65.94	4.0%	£2.64		£63.30	€82.29
						Subtotal			£108.38	
Euro Rate		1.3				VAT (20%)			£21.68	
						TOTAL			£130.05	

Note:

It is useful to practise further with **Print Settings**, to see the effects of the many different options, also setting up your own headers and footers.

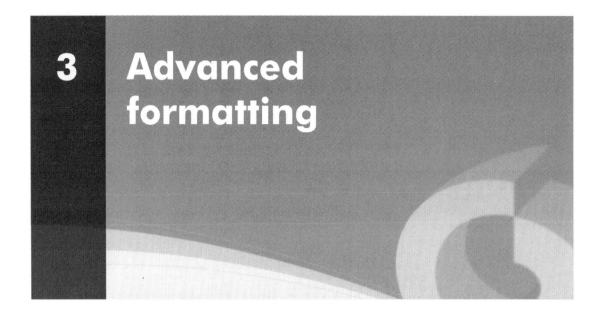

3 Advanced formatting

this chapter covers...

This chapter provides an introduction to advanced formatting for those new to spreadsheets. It explains and takes you through the basic concepts and techniques listed below. By the time you have finished this chapter and carried out the exercises which follow, you should be able to produce clearly formatted, easy-to-read spreadsheets. The concepts covered are:

■ *cell display – borders, fill colours*

■ *moving rows and columns*

■ *hiding rows and columns*

■ *specifying row height and column width*

■ *cell and sheet protection*

■ *conditional formatting*

■ *data validation*

Note that the step-by-step instructions given in this chapter are based on the Microsoft® Excel model, but the concepts and techniques described relate to all spreadsheet packages.

CELL DISPLAY

using borders

We sometimes want to make a cell or group of cells stand out within the spreadsheet.

One of the ways we can do this is to use **Borders**, which are just lines which we add around the edges of a cell or group of cells.

Borders can vary in colour and thickness; they can also be dotted or broken.

They can also be used to split groups of numbers to improve legibility by applying the border to just one edge of a cell.

	A	B	C	D	E	F	G
1	Bank transactions						
2							
3	Opening balance	£1,500.00			border around one cell		
4	Closing balance	£1,289.05					
5							
6	Date	Debit	Credit	Balance			
7	02/04/2016	£95.34	£6.00	£1,404.66			
8	11/04/2016	£0.00	£25.50	£1,430.16			
9	15/04/2016	£0.00	£34.78	£1,464.94		borders splitting groups	
10	22/04/2016	£67.90	£0.00	£1,397.04		of numbers	
11	28/04/2016	£107.99	£0.00	£1,289.05			
12	Totals	£271.23	£60.28		£1,289.05		

To apply borders:

■ select all the required cells

■ right click on the selected cell or cells

■ select **Format cells**

■ select **Border**

■ choose the **Line style** and **Color**

■ apply to the required edges using either preset borders

■ *or* clicking within the Border box to select edges (as shown in the screen illustration on the next page)

Number	Alignment	Font	Border	Fill	Protection

Line

Style:

None

Color:

Automatic

Presets

None Outline Inside

Border

Text

using font and fill colour

It is possible to change both the colour of the **Font** and the colour of the background within a cell, known as the **Fill color**.

	A	B	C	D	E	F
1	Bank transactions					
2						
3	Opening balance	£1,500.00		Cell fill color grey		
4	Closing balance	£1,289.05		with a thin border		
5						
6	Date	Debit	Credit	Balance		
7	02/04/2016	£95.34	£0.00	£1,404.66		
8	11/04/2016	£0.00	£25.50	£1,430.16		
9	15/04/2016	£0.00	£34.78	£1,464.94		
10	22/04/2016	£67.90	£0.00	£1,397.04		
11	28/04/2016	£107.99	£0.00	£1,289.05		
12	Totals	£271.23	£60.28		£1,289.05	

To change the Font colour:

- select all the required cells
- right click on the selected cell or cells
- select **Format cells**
- select **Font**
- choose the **Color** you require

To set the cell Fill color:

- select all the required cells
- right click on the selected cell or cells

- select **Format cells**
- select **Fill**
- choose the Background **Color** you require

In addition to the Fill colour, you can also apply shading to make a particular row, column, or group of cells stand out. A variety of different patterns are available.

In the example below we have applied shading to the Totals row.

	A	B	C	D	E	F
1	Bank transactions					
2						
3	Opening balance	£1,500.00				
4	Closing balance	£1,289.05				
5						
6	Date	Debit	Credit	Balance		
7	02/04/2016	£95.34	£0.00	£1,404.66		
8	11/04/2016	£0.00	£25.50	£1,430.16		
9	15/04/2016	£0.00	£34.78	£1,464.94		
10	22/04/2016	£67.90	£0.00	£1,397.04		
11	28/04/2016	£107.99	£0.00	£1,289.05		
12	Totals	£271.23	£60.28		£1,289.05	

To set the shading:

- select all the required cells
- right click on the selected cell or cells
- select **Format cells**
- select **Fill**
- choose the **Pattern Color,** and **Pattern Style** you require

ADVANCED CELL ALIGNMENT

wordwrap

If the text which you enter into a cell is longer than the width of the cell, the text entered will appear as a single line of text across adjacent cells, as shown in the example on the next page:

If we want to force the text to fit in just column C, we can use word wrap, and the row height will automatically adjust to fit the text, without changing the column width, wrapping it into one cell. This can be seen in the image below:

To apply word wrap to a cell:

■ select the required cells

either

■ select **Wrap Text** from the Home menu ribbon

or

■ right click on the selection

■ select **Format cells**

■ select the **Alignment** tab

■ on the text control section click the **Wrap text** checkbox

justify

If we have some text which has been word wrapped and occupies multiple lines within a cell, it is possible to justify the text, either horizontally or vertically. The example at the top of the next page shows some text in a cell:

If we now format the cell to justify horizontally, the text reformats as shown:

The text has been spread horizontally, to fill the cell to the edges as much as possible.

To justify the contents of a cell:

■ select the required cells

■ right click on the selection

■ select **Format cells**

■ select the **Alignment** tab

■ on the text alignment section for **Horizontal**, select **Justify** from the **Horizontal** drop-down list, or for **Vertical**, select **Justify** from the **Vertical** drop-down list. **Note**: Justification can be applied as a format to any cell, not just those containing text.

orientation

Orientation is the direction in which the text reads when it is displayed in a cell, the default which we use most of the time is horizontal and left to right, this can be changed using the **Format Cells** options. In the example below we have merged cells A2 through to A13, and entered the text 2015-2016 into the merged cells:

	A	B	C	D	E	F	G
1	Year	Month					
2		Jan					
3		Feb					
4		Mar					
5		Apr					
6		May					
7		Jun					
8		Jul					
9		Aug					
10		Sep					
11		Oct					
12		Nov					
13	2015-2016	Dec					

If we now change the orientation of the text in the merged cells, we can make it easier to read and clarify which cells it applies to, as shown below:

	A	B	C	D	E	F	G
1	Year	Month					
2		Jan					
3	2	Feb					
4	0	Mar					
5	1	Apr					
6	5	May					
7	-	Jun					
8	2	Jul					
9	0	Aug					
10	1	Sep					
11	6	Oct					
12		Nov					
13		Dec					

Here we have changed the orientation to 90 degrees, still with the text centered vertically.

To change the orientation of the contents of a cell:

■   select the required cells

and

- right click on the selection

- select **Format cells**

- select the **Alignment** tab

| Number | Alignment | Font | Border | Fill | Protection |

Text alignment

Horizontal:
Center ⌄ Indent:

Vertical:
Center ⌄ 0 ⬍

☐ Justify distributed

Text control

☐ Wrap text
☐ Shrink to fit
☑ Merge cells

Right-to-left

Text direction:
Context ⌄

Orientation

90 ⬍ Degrees

- on the orientation section for **Vertical**, click on **Text** in the vertical box or for greater flexibility click on the **red diamond**, and drag up or down to specify the orientation of the text or enter a specific value (between 90 and –90) in the **degrees** box. You will also normally make the Vertical text alignment **center** to centre the text in the merged cells.

  There are many different settings for orientation so it is worth trying a variety to see their effect.

or

- click on the **Orientation** option available on the Home menu ribbon

- select the appropriate option

shrink to fit

When text is too large to fit in a cell, rather than resize the cell, if you don't want to change the column width, due to retaining a specific layout format, it is possible to shrink the text to fit within the cell.

To shrink text:

- select the required cells

and

- right click on the selection

■ select **Format cells**

■ select the **Alignment** tab

■ click on **Shrink to fit**

MOVING A COLUMN OR A ROW

Sometimes we may wish to change our basic layout and **move either a column or a row** within the layout. If we look at our Expenditure forecast worksheet as shown below.

	A	B	C	D	E	F	G	H
1	Expenditure Forecast							
2								
3		January	February	March	April	May	June	Totals
4	Salaries	£80,000	£80,000	£80,000	£90,000	£90,000	£90,000	£510,000
5	Insurance	£1,000	£500	£0	£0	£0	£500	£2,000
6	Rent	£3,500	£3,500	£3,500	£3,500	£3,500	£3,500	£21,000
7	Accountancy	£270	£0	£270	£0	£270	£0	£810
8	Advertising	£0	£1,500	£0	£0	£0	£1,800	£3,300
9	Postage	£95	£190	£95	£80	£95	£150	£705
10	Stationery	£57	£90	£0	£90	£0	£90	£327
11	Totals	£84,922	£85,780	£83,865	£93,670	£93,865	£96,040	£538,142

We might wish to move the Totals column to display before the months, as you can see in the image below:

B4	▼	⋮	✕	✓	*fx*	=SUM(C4:H4)		

	A	B	C	D	E	F	G	H
1	Expenditure Forecast							
2								
3		Totals	January	February	March	April	May	June
4	Salaries	£510,000	£80,000	£80,000	£80,000	£90,000	£90,000	£90,000
5	Insurance	£2,000	£1,000	£500	£0	£0	£0	£500
6	Rent	£21,000	£3,500	£3,500	£3,500	£3,500	£3,500	£3,500
7	Accountancy	£810	£270	£0	£270	£0	£270	£0
8	Advertising	£3,300	£0	£1,500	£0	£0	£0	£1,800
9	Postage	£705	£95	£190	£95	£80	£95	£150
10	Stationery	£327	£57	£90	£0	£90	£0	£90
11	Totals	£538,142	£84,922	£85,780	£83,865	£93,670	£93,865	£96,040

Notice how the formulas in the Totals column have automatically changed so that they are still adding each of the monthly columns.

Alternatively, we might want to move the rows around so that the Salaries row comes before the Stationery row, as shown below.

C11			✕ ✓ $f\!x$	=SUM(C4:C10)			

◢	A	B	C	D	E	F	G	H
1	Expenditure Forecast							
2								
3		Totals	January	February	March	April	May	June
4	Insurance	£2,000	£1,000	£500	£0	£0	£0	£500
5	Rent	£21,000	£3,500	£3,500	£3,500	£3,500	£3,500	£3,500
6	Accountancy	£810	£270	£0	£270	£0	£270	£0
7	Advertising	£3,300	£0	£1,500	£0	£0	£0	£1,800
8	Postage	£705	£95	£190	£95	£80	£95	£150
9	Salaries	£510,000	£80,000	£80,000	£80,000	£90,000	£90,000	£90,000
10	Stationery	£327	£57	£90	£0	£90	£0	£90
11	Totals	£538,142	£84,922	£85,780	£83,865	£93,670	£93,865	£96,040

To move a row:

■ right click on the row header of the row to move

■ select **Cut**

■ right click on the row header to where you want to move the row

■ select **Insert cut cells**

or

■ insert a row in the position that you want to move the row to

■ click on the row header of the row to move and move the cursor over the lower edge of the row selected until the four headed arrow appears

■ press the left mouse key down and drag the row to the blank row and release

To move a column:

■ right click on the column header of the column to move

■ select **Cut**

■ right click on the column header where you to move the column to

■ select **Insert cut cells**

or

■ insert a column in the position that you want to move the column to

■ click on the column header of the column to move and move the cursor over the lower edge of the column header until the four headed arrow appears

■ press the left mouse key down and drag the column to the blank column and release

HIDE A ROW OR A COLUMN

Sometimes we may wish to hide certain data or calculations used in a spreadsheet from public view, for example salary data. The Hide row or column option allows us to do this and still make use of the data within our spreadsheet. In the spreadsheet below, Column B the Totals column has been hidden.

	A	C	D	E	F	G	H
1	Expenditure Forecast						
2							
3		January	February	March	April	May	June
4	Insurance	£1,000	£500	£0	£0	£0	£500
5	Rent	£3,500	£3,500	£3,500	£3,500	£3,500	£3,500
6	Accountancy	£270	£0	£270	£0	£270	£0
7	Advertising	£0	£1,500	£0	£0	£0	£1,800
8	Postage	£95	£190	£95	£80	£95	£150
9	Salaries	£80,000	£80,000	£80,000	£90,000	£90,000	£90,000
10	Stationery	£57	£90	£0	£90	£0	£90
11	Totals	£84,922	£85,780	£83,865	£93,670	£93,865	£96,040

To hide a row:

■ right click on the row header

■ select **Hide**

To hide a column:

■ right click on the column header

■ select **Hide**

It is also possible to unhide a row or column to make modifications.

To unhide a row:

■ select the row headers of the rows either side of the hidden row

■ select **Format**

■ select **Unhide Rows**

To unhide a column:

■ select the column headers of the columns either side of the hidden column

■ select **Format**

■ select **Unhide Columns**

SPECIFYING ROW HEIGHT AND COLUMN WIDTH

There are several ways of setting the height of a row, or width of a column.

So far in this book we have looked at dragging the boundaries of the row or column to set the size.

For columns, it is also possible to specify the size as a number from 0 to 255 which represents the number of characters that can be displayed in a cell that is formatted with the standard font.

With a column width of zero, the column will be hidden.

For rows, it is possible to specify the size as a number from 0 to 409, which represents the height measurement in points (1 point equals approximately 1/72 inch or 0.35mm).

If the row height is set to zero, the row is hidden.

To set a column to a specific width:

■   select the column or columns that you want to change

■   select **Format, Column Width**

or

■   RIGHT CLICK on the column header, select Column Width

then

■   enter the required value

◢	A	B	C	D	E	F	G	H
1	Expenditure	Forecast						
2								
3		Totals	January	February	March	April	May	June
4	Insurance	£2,000	£1,000	£500	£0	£0	£0	£500
5	Rent	£21,000	£3,500	£3,500	£3,500	£3,500	£3,500	£3,500
6	Accountancy	£810	Column Width	?	✕	£0	£270	£0
7	Advertising	£3,300	Column width: 11			£0	£0	£1,800
8	Postage	£705				£80	£95	£150
9	Salaries	£510,000	£8	OK	Cancel	£90,000	£90,000	£90,000
10	Stationery	£327	£57	£90	£0	£90	£0	£90
11	Totals	£538,142	£84,922	£85,780	£83,865	£93,670	£93,865	£96,040

To set a row to a specific height:

■   select the row or rows that you want to change

■   select **Format, Row Height**

or

■ RIGHT CLICK on the row header, select Row Height then

■ enter the required value as shown below

◢	A	B	C	D	E	F	G	H
1	Expenditure Forecast							
2								
3		Totals	January	February	March	April	May	June
4	Insurance	£2,000	£1,000	£500	£0	£0	£0	£500
5	Rent	£21,000	£3,5 Row Height ? ×		£3,500	£3,500	£3,500	
6	Accountancy	£810	£2			£0	£270	£0
7	Advertising	£3,300	Row height: 22.5			£0	£0	£1,800
8	Postage	£705	OK Cancel			£80	£95	£150
9	Salaries	£510,000	£80,0			0,000	£90,000	£90,000
10	Stationery	£327	£57	£90	£0	£90	£0	£90
11	Totals	£538,142	£84,922	£85,780	£83,865	£93,670	£93,865	£96,040

CELL AND WORKSHEET PROTECTION

It can be important that the values within certain cells do not get changed by a user, for example a formula.

To prevent a cell being changed we can lock it. The default setting for a cell is usually locked. Locking a cell has no effect until the worksheet (also know as a 'sheet') containing the cell is protected. If a user tries to change a locked cell on a protected worksheet he/she will get a message to the effect that the cell is protected and therefore read-only.

To lock a cell or cells:

■ select all the required cells

■ right click on the selected cell or cells

■ select **Format cells**

■ click the **Protection** tab

■ check the **Locked** box (see the screen below)

Format Cells	? ×
Number Alignment Font Border Fill **Protection**	
☑ Locked	
☐ Hidden	
Locking cells or hiding formulas has no effect until you protect the worksheet (Review tab, Changes group, Protect Sheet button).	

Alternatively,

- select **Format** from the menu ribbon, then **Lock Cell**

The Lock Cell menu option acts as an on /off switch.

If the cell(s) are already locked, you will see the square around the padlock, next to the Lock Cell menu item, as shown ⟶ in the image on the right.

If the cell(s) are NOT already locked, you will just see the the the padlock, as shown in this image.

⟶

To unlock a cell or cells:

- select all the required cells

Either

- right click on the selected cell or cells
- select **Format cells**
- click the **Protection** tab
- uncheck the **Locked** box

or

- select **Format** from the menu ribbon, Lock Cell

If locking a cell is to have any effect the worksheet containing the locked cells **must be protected**.

To protect a worksheet:

- select the sheetname tab of the required worksheet
- select **Protect sheet** from the **REVIEW** menu bar
- enter a memorable password as requested

It is very important to keep a note of the password, because if you lose a password, **you cannot recover it**. Without the necessary password all changes to protected cells would not be permitted, even by the creator of the worksheet.

If you do have the password and wish to change cells you first need to **unprotect the sheet**:

- select the sheetname tab of the required worksheet
- select **Unprotect sheet** from the **REVIEW** menu bar
- enter the password as requested

CONDITIONAL FORMATTING

We have covered the concepts of displaying cells with different fill colours and text colours, by selecting and changing.

Sometimes we may want a cell to change colour or display a different font face automatically depending on the value it may hold; this is known as **conditional formatting**. This is especially useful if we have a large amount of data, where it would be easy to miss seeing certain values.

Conditional formatting allows you to define a rule or rules, and if the data meets the rules (conditions), it will display in the format that you have specified, in a different font or fill colour. For example we may want all values less than £1,000 on a financial worksheet to be displayed in red text, so that they stand out. Another example would be to display all negative (less than zero) values within a row or column in red.

logical operators

We can apply comparison 'operators' to create rules where **conditional formatting** can be used. These include:

- equal to
- greater than
- between
- less than
- text that contains
- a date occurring

Alternatively, we can create a **top/bottom** rule, these include:

- top 10 items
- top 10%
- bottom 10 items
- bottom 10%
- above average
- below average

You can define more than one rule, and each rule can have several conditions within it. Once you have created a conditional formatting rule, you can edit the rule, to change the criteria, change cells you want to apply it to, or change the way the cells meeting the criteria are displayed.

In the example below we have created a conditional formatting rule to apply to the Postage costs in Cells C8 through to H8. If the value is greater than 100, we want to fill the cell with a grey background.

The rule is displayed below:

Conditional Formatting Rules Manager			? ✕

Show formatting rules for: This Worksheet ⌄

| New Rule... | Edit Rule... | ✕ Delete Rule | ▲ ▼ |

Rule (applied in order shown)	Format	Applies to	Stop If True
Cell Value > 100	AaBbCcYyZz	=$C$8:$H$8	☐

Note: $ symbols are automatically inserted within the cell range; the meaning of these $ symbols is described later in the book. As you can see in the image below, all cells where Postage costs are greater than £100 are shown filled with a grey background.

◢	A	B	C	D	E	F	G	H
1	Expenditure Forecast							
2								
3		Totals	January	February	March	April	May	June
4	Insurance	£2,000	£1,000	£500	£0	£0	£0	£500
5	Rent	£21,000	£3,500	£3,500	£3,500	£3,500	£3,500	£3,500
6	Accountancy	£810	£270	£0	£270	£0	£270	£0
7	Advertising	£3,300	£0	£1,500	£0	£0	£0	£1,800
8	Postage	£705	£95	£190	£95	£80	£95	£150
9	Salaries	£510,000	£80,000	£80,000	£80,000	£90,000	£90,000	£90,000
10	Stationery	£327	£57	£90	£0	£90	£0	£90
11	Totals	£538,142	£84,922	£85,780	£83,865	£93,670	£93,865	£96,440
12								
13					Values exceed £100			

To set conditional formatting for a group of cells:

- select the required cells

- select **Conditional formatting** from the menu bar

- enter the rule which you want to apply using the drop down list of 'greater than, less than, equal to' etc, and the required value

- select the **Font style** and **Colour**, together with the fill colour and any other effects

  either from choices in the drop-down list,

  or by selecting **Custom format** from the bottom of the list, and choosing from the standard format cells options.

To clear conditional formatting for a group of cells:

■   select the required cells

■   select **Conditional formatting**

■   select **Clear Rules**, then **Clear rules from selected cells**

To clear all conditional formatting for a worksheet:

■   select **Conditional formatting**

■   select **Clear Rules**, then **Clear rules from entire sheet**

DATA VALIDATION

When a spreadsheet is being used, it is possible we may only want to allow certain values in a particular cell; this might be to prevent data entry errors such as misspelling or to ensure consistency across the data.

It is possible to restrict the type of data which may be entered, such as a date, a whole number, or to provide a list of acceptable values, which will then be displayed as a drop down list when the user moves to the cell. This restriction of values is called **data validation**.

In the image below we have restricted the values allowed in cells in the month column (column A) to three character month names. When you move to one of these cells, a drop down list appears showing the acceptable choices. You are only allowed to select from this list.

In the image below you can see that the choice of Product has also been restricted to allow only four specific values. When you select any of the cells in the product column the drop down list of products is displayed and you can choose from this list.

B6			✕ ✓ f_x			
	A	B	C	D	E	F
1	Sales					
2						
3	Month	Product	Value			
4	Feb	Clothing	£1,500.00			
5	Feb	Jewellery	£220.00			
6	Mar		▾			
7		Accessories				
8		Clothing				
		Footwear				
9		Jewellery				
10		Other				

To define the data validation for a group of cells:

■ select the required cells

■ select **Data validation** from the menu bar

■ select the validation criteria from the drop down list (as seen in the screen below)

■ if you select **List**, enter the values you want to allow, separated by commas

The data validation for our restricted months in column A looks like:

Data Validation	? ✕

Settings | Input Message | Error Alert

Validation criteria

Allow:

| List | ☑ Ignore blank |

Data:

| between | ☑ In-cell dropdown |

Source:

| Jan,Feb,Mar,Apr,May,Jun,Jul,Aug,Sep,Oct,Nov,[🔢 |

And for the Product column:

Data Validation	?	✕

Settings | Input Message | Error Alert

Validation criteria

Allow:

List	⌄	☑ Ignore blank

Data:

| between | ⌄ | ☑ In-cell dropdown |

Source:

| Accessories, Clothing, Footwear, Jewellery, Other | 🔣 |

If we wanted to restrict a cell or group of cells to contain just dates between April and September, example settings are shown below:

Data Validation	?	✕

Settings | Input Message | Error Alert

Validation criteria

Allow:

Date	⌄	☑ Ignore blank

Data:

| between | ⌄ |

Start date:

| 01/04/16 | 🔣 |

End date:

| 01/09/16 | 🔣 |

☐ Apply these changes to all other cells with the same settings

| Clear All | | OK | Cancel |

It is also possible to apply **data validation** to cells that already contain data. For example, suppose we had values in column A as shown below.

	A	B	C	D	E
1	ID				
2	1				
3	2				
4	3				
5	4				
6	5				
7	6				
8	7				
9	8				
10	-9				
11	10				

We want to restrict the values in cells A2 to A11 to numbers between 1 and 10.

To do this,

- Select cells A2 to A11,

- Select **Data Validation, Settings**

- And set as follows:

  Allow: **whole number**

  Data: **Between**

  Minimum: **0**

  Maximum: **10**

As shown in the image below.

Note: although we now have data validation on these cells, invalid values are not automatically highlighted.

To identify any invalid values:

Select **Data Validation, Circle Invalid Values**

And as shown below, the -9 value is highlighted.

	A	B	C	D	E
1	ID				
2	1				
3	2				
4	3				
5	4				
6	5				
7	6				
8	7				
9	8				
10	-9				
11	10				

To remove the red validation circles:

Select **Data Validation, Clear Validation Circles**

a note on copying data validation

Once you have formatted a cell with data validation, if you want to apply that same validation to another cell or cells, you can use normal **Copy** and **Paste** facilities and the data validation will apply to the cells where you paste.

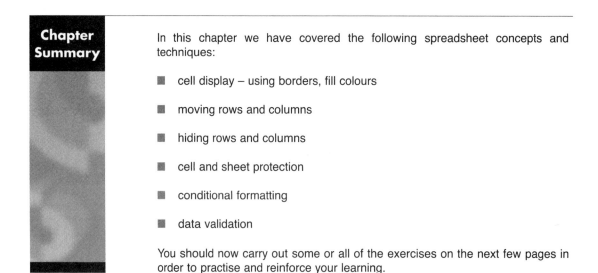

Chapter Summary

In this chapter we have covered the following spreadsheet concepts and techniques:

▩ cell display – using borders, fill colours

▩ moving rows and columns

▩ hiding rows and columns

▩ cell and sheet protection

▩ conditional formatting

▩ data validation

You should now carry out some or all of the exercises on the next few pages in order to practise and reinforce your learning.

Activities

Exercise 1 – formatting, including data validation and presentation

In this first exercise we will create a simple time recording spreadsheet to record details of time spent on client work by a firm of accountants.

Stage 1

In this stage we create the basic layout of our spreadsheet. All text should be entered in the default typeface, font size 10, normal style.

1.   Open a new workbook.

2.   Move to Sheet1.

3.   Change the name of the sheet to **Time record**.

4.   Move to cell A1, enter **Client work log**.

5.   Move to cell A3, enter **Name**.

6.   Format cell B3 so that it has a thin solid black border all the way round, and is filled with a light grey.

7.   In cell A4 enter **Department**.

8.   Format cell B4 so that it has a thin solid black border all the way round, and is filled with a light grey.

9.   In cell A5 enter **Month**.

10.   Move to cell B5, apply data validation to the cell, to allow the user to pick the name of the month from a list of three character month names, ie Jan, Feb, Mar, and so on for the whole year, displayed in calendar order.

11.   Format cell B5 so that it has a thin solid black border all the way round, and is filled with a light grey.

12.   Widen column A to ensure all text is enclosed within it.

13.   Widen column B to allow enough space for a full name.

14.   Save the workbook with the name **T3Exercise1**.

Your spreadsheet should appear as shown in the screen at the top of the next page:

Stage 2

We will continue creating the basic template for entry of client time recording information.

1.　In cell A7, enter **Date**.

2.　In cell B7, enter **Client**.

3.　In cell C7, enter **Hours**.

4.　Column A from row 8 onwards is where we are going to enter date information, so format this column to display dates in the form dd/mm/yy (eg 14/03/16).

5.　For the hours column we will restrict the entry to only allow whole or half hours. Apply data validation to cell C8, giving a list of values from 0.5 through to 4.0, ie 0.5,1.0,1.5, etc.

6.　To apply the same data validation to C9 through to C30, copy cell C8 to cells C9 through to C30.

7.　Merge cells A1, B1, C1 and centre the text "Client work log" across the three cells.

8.　Save your spreadsheet (keeping the same name – **T3Exercise1**).

Your spreadsheet should appear as shown in the screen below:

Stage 3

We will now use borders to improve the spreadsheet presentation. All borders should be a thin solid black border unless otherwise specified.

1.   Apply a border to the top and bottom edges of A7 through to C7.

2.   Apply a border to the left and right edges of C7 through to C30.

3.   Apply a border to the lower edge of A30 through to C30.

4.   Apply a border to the left and right edges of A7 through to A30.

5.   Insert a column before column A.

6.   Set the width of column A to 4.

7.   Save your spreadsheet (keeping the same name – **T3Exercise1**).

Your spreadsheet should appear as shown in the screen below.

Stage 4

We are now going to complete the formatting and leave the sheet ready to be used for data entry.

1.   Insert 2 rows above row 7.

2.   In cell C7 enter **Total**.

3.   In cell D7 enter the formula to add cells D10 through to D32.

4.   Format D7 to display with one decimal place and with a bold font.

5.   Put a double line border on the bottom edge of cells C7 and D7.

6.   Make rows 2, 6, and 8 height 6.

7.   Lock all cells with text or values already in.

8.   Unlock cells C3, C4, C5, B10 through B32, C10 through C32, D10 through D32.

9.   Protect the sheet with password **ex3**.

10.   Save your spreadsheet.

Your spreadsheet should appear as shown in the screen below.

	A	B	C	D	E	F	G·	H
1			Client work log					
2								
3		Name						
4		Department						
5		Month						
6								
7			Total	0.0				
8								
9		Date	Client	Hours				
10								
11								
12								
13								
14								
15								

Time record ⊕

Exercise 2 – conditional formatting

In this second exercise we are going to make use of conditional formatting in an inventory situation, to help us identify when inventory of a product is low.

Stage 1

In this stage we are going to work with an inventory list which has already been created.

1.   Download the file **T3InventoryList**.

2.   Save this workbook with the name **T3Exercise2**.

The workbook should look as shown below:

	A	B	C	D	E	F
1	Inventory report					
2						
3	Product code	Inventory	Price	Value	Re-order Level	
4	ab1	967	£2.50	£2,416	174	
5	ab2	946	£3.25	£3,074	286	
6	ab3	458	£0.99	£453	677	
7	ab4	149	£0.45	£67	32	
8	ab8	73	£3.29	£241	454	
9	ab10	663	£2.25	£1,492	177	
10	ab11	890	£1.35	£1,201	790	
11	bb4	7	£0.45	£3	961	
12	bb8	825	£3.29	£2,715	650	

The **Re-order Level** column tells us the inventory of each item we like to hold. If the **Inventory** figure has fallen below this number, then we need to re-order.

In column F we are going to compare the Inventory figure, with the Re-order Level.

3.   Set column F width to 11.

4.   In cell F3, enter the text **Inventory v Re-order**, set the cell format to word wrap.

5.   In cell F4, enter the formula for **Inventory** minus **Re-order Level**.

6.   Copy the formula for each of the products.

7.   Apply conditional formatting (**Highlight cell rules**), to column F, so that all cells where the number is negative (less than 0) are displayed with a custom format, black text and a dark grey fill.

8.   Save your workbook.

The image on the next page shows the results.

	A	B	C	D	E	F
1	Inventory report					
2						
3	Product code	Inventory	Price	Value	Re-order Level	Inventory v Re-order
4	ab1	967	£2.50	£2,416	174	793
5	ab2	946	£3.25	£3,074	286	660
6	ab3	458	£0.99	£453	677	-219
7	ab4	149	£0.45	£67	32	117
8	ab8	73	£3.29	£241	454	-381
9	ab10	663	£2.25	£1,492	177	486
10	ab11	890	£1.35	£1,201	790	100
11	bb4	7	£0.45	£3	961	-954
12	bb8	825	£3.29	£2,715	650	176

Stage 2

In this stage we are going to experiment with some other conditional formatting.

We want to look at the values of inventory which we are holding.

1. In the Value column (column D), using conditional formatting, highlight the top 10 inventory values, display with a custom format, black border, fill with background colour light grey and pattern style dots (first row, top right in choices).

The first few rows are shown below:

	A	B	C	D	E	F
1	Inventory report					
2						
3	Product code	Inventory	Price	Value	Re-order Level	Inventory v Re-order
4	ab1	967	£2.50	£2,416	174	793
5	ab2	946	£3.25	£3,074	286	660
6	ab3	458	£0.99	£453	677	-219
7	ab4	149	£0.45	£67	32	117
8	ab8	73	£3.29	£241	454	-381
9	ab10	663	£2.25	£1,492	177	486
10	ab11	890	£1.35	£1,201	790	100
11	bb4	7	£0.45	£3	961	-954
12	bb8	825	£3.29	£2,715	650	176

We now want to identify our 10 lowest priced items.

2.   In the Price column (column C), using conditional formatting, highlight the lowest 10 priced item values, display with a custom format, italic font, and a light grey fill.

3.   Save your workbook.

The first few rows are shown below:

▲	A	B	C	D	E	F
1	Inventory report					
2						
3	Product code	Inventory	Price	Value	Re-order Level	Inventory v Re-order
4	ab1	967	£2.50	£2,416	174	793
5	ab2	946	£3.25	£3,074	286	660
6	ab3	458	£0.99	£453	677	-219
7	ab4	149	£0.45	£67	32	117
8	ab8	73	£3.29	£241	454	-381
9	ab10	663	£2.25	£1,492	177	486
10	ab11	890	£1.35	£1,201	790	100
11	bb4	7	£0.45	£3	961	-954
12	bb8	825	£3.29	£2,715	650	176

Exercise 3 – data validation and worksheet protection

In this exercise we are again going to create a spreadsheet containing summary invoice details. The spreadsheet will utilise data validation and validation circles.

Stage 1

This stage is about creating the basic layout of our spreadsheet.

All text should be entered in the default typeface, font size 10, normal style.

1.   Open a new workbook.

2.   Rename the worksheet Sheet1 to **Invoices**.

3.   Using worksheet Invoices, enter **Invoice summary** in cell A1.

4.   Enter **Invoice Date**, **Customer**, **Gross**, and **Date Paid** in cells A2 through to D2 respectively.

5.   Make the column headings, row 2, bold and underlined.

6.   Details for the first two invoices are as follows:

   01/4/2016, **Farmhouse Foods**, **147.59**.

   09/4/2016, **The Halal Centre**, **286.68**.

   Enter these details on rows 3 and 4.

7.   Insert a row between rows 1 and 2 to create space below the title.

8. Widen column A to fit the column title Invoice Date.

9. Widen column B (the customer column) to 20.

10. Save the workbook with the name **T3Exercise3.**

Your spreadsheet should appear as shown in the screen below.

	A	B	C	D	E	F
1	Invoice summary					
2						
3	Invoice Date	Customer	Gross	Date Paid		
4	01/04/2016	Farmhouse Foods	147.59			
5	09/04/2016	The Halal Centre	286.68			
6						

Invoices ⊕ ⋮ ◄

Stage 2

We are now going to apply some formatting, and enter more invoices:

1. Enter the invoices from the table as shown below:

Invoice date	Customer	Gross
13/04/16	Edwards Farm	114.54
01/05/16	W B Meats	262.74
15/04/16	T F Curries	381.59
20/04/16	Ahmed Foods	81.15

2. Format the Gross column (column C), as **Currency Euro €**, with **no decimal places**.

3. Change the font size of Invoice summary (cell A1) to 14.

4. Change the format of the Date column (A) to show just two digits for the year.

We have missed some invoices.

5. Enter the invoices from the table as shown below between rows 4 and 5 to keep the invoices in date order.

Invoice date	Customer	Gross
04/04/16	Fast Foods	68.34
05/04/16	The Snack Bar	234.54

6. Make each of the column headings in row 3, font style **italics** and **underlined**.

7. In cell B12, enter the text **Gross Totals** in **bold**.

8. Now total the Gross values in cells C12.

9. **Double underline** and make **bold** the totals value.

10. Align the column heading for **Gross** to the **right**.

11. Save your workbook.

Your workbook should look as shown below:

	A	B	C	D	E
1	Invoice summary				
2					
3	*Invoice Date*	*Customer*	*Gross*	*Date Paid*	
4	01/04/16	Farmhouse Foods	€148		
5	04/04/16	Fast Foods	€68		
6	05/04/16	The Snack Bar	€235		
7	09/04/16	The Halal Centre	€287		
8	13/04/16	Edwards Farm	€115		
9	01/05/16	W B Meats	€263		
10	15/04/16	T F Curries	€382		
11	20/04/16	Ahmed Foods	€81		
12		**Gross Totals**	**€1,577**		

Stage 3

All of the invoices have now been paid.

1. Enter paid dates as shown in the table below.

Invoice date	Customer	Gross	Date paid
01/04/16	Farmhouse Foods	€148	01/05/16
04/04/16	Fast Foods	€68	28/05/16
05/04/16	The Snack Bar	€235	08/05/16
09/04/16	The Halal Centre	€287	09/04/16
13/04/16	Edwards Farm	€115	30/04/16
01/05/16	W B Meats	€263	05/06/16
15/04/16	T F Curries	€382	12/05/16
20/04/16	Ahmed Foods	€81	21/05/16

We only want invoices from April to be included in this analysis.

2. Apply **Data Validation** to the Invoice Dates, to allow only Dates between 1st April, and 30th April. As shown in the image below.

Settings	Input Message	Error Alert

Validation criteria

Allow:

Date	☑ Ignore blank

Data:

between

Start date:

01/04/2016

End date:

30/04/2016

Nothing visibly changes.

3. Now select **Circle Invalid Data**.

You should see the invoice dated 01/05/16 circled, since this is a May invoice, as shown below.

	A	B	C	D	E
1	Invoice summary				
2					
3	*Invoice Date*	*Customer*	*Gross*	*Date Paid*	
4	01/04/16	Farmhouse Foods	€148	01/05/2016	
5	04/04/16	Fast Foods	€68	28/05/2016	
6	05/04/16	The Snack Bar	€235	08/05/2016	
7	09/04/16	The Halal Centre	€287	09/04/2016	
8	13/04/16	Edwards Farm	€115	30/04/2016	
9	01/05/16	W B Meats	€263	05/06/2016	
10	15/04/16	T F Curries	€382	12/05/2016	
11	20/04/16	Ahmed Foods	€81	21/05/2016	
12		**Gross Totals**	**€1,577**		

4. Delete the row containing the 01/05/16 invoice.

We now want to look at how long it is taking for the invoices to be paid.

5.   In cell E3, enter text **Days to Pay**.

6.   In cell E3, set the alignment to **shrink the text** to fit the column.

This makes the headings look inconsistent.

	A	B	C	D	E
1	Invoice summary				
2					
3	*Invoice Date*	*Customer*	*Gross*	*Date Paid*	*Days to Pay*
4	01/04/16	Farmhouse Foods	€148	01/05/2016	
5	04/04/16	Fast Foods	€68	28/05/2016	

We will use alignment, Wrap Text instead.

7.   For cell E3, turn off shrink to fit, and select **wrap text**, and set horizontal alignment to **justify**.

8.   Enter a formula in E4 to calculate the number of days taken to pay the invoice (D4 – A4).

The result may look like a date, if so, change the format to number, rather than date.

9.   Format E4 to **Number**, no decimal places.

10.   Copy this formula into cells E5 through to E10.

11.   In cell E11, enter a formula to calculate the **Average** of the Days to Pay.

12.   Save your workbook.

Your workbook should look as shown below.

E11	▼ : ✕ ✓ *fx*	=AVERAGE(E4:E10)		

	A	B	C	D	E
1	Invoice summary				
2					
3	*Invoice Date*	*Customer*	*Gross*	*Date Paid*	*Days to Pay*
4	01/04/16	Farmhouse Foods	€148	01/05/2016	30
5	04/04/16	Fast Foods	€68	28/05/2016	54
6	05/04/16	The Snack Bar	€235	08/05/2016	33
7	09/04/16	The Halal Centre	€287	09/04/2016	0
8	13/04/16	Edwards Farm	€115	30/04/2016	17
9	15/04/16	T F Curries	€382	12/05/2016	27
10	20/04/16	Ahmed Foods	€81	21/05/2016	31
11		**Gross Totals**	**€1,314**		27

Stage 4

We are just going to make a few small changes to the format, to complete the exercise.

1.   Move the Date Paid column to before the Customer column.

2.   Insert 2 rows above row 3 the column titles row.

3.   In cell B3, enter the text **Average days to Pay**.

4.   **Merge** cells B3 and C3 and centre the text, also make it **bold**.

5.   Enter a formula in cell D3, so that it holds the value of cell E13 (the average), make sure it is formatted as Number, no decimal places.

6.   Hide column E (The Days to Pay column).

7.   Save your workbook.

Your workbook should look as shown below.

D3	▼ ⋮	✗ ✓ ƒx	=E13		
	A	B	C	D	F
1	Invoice summary				
2					
3		**Average Days to Pay**		27	
4					
5	*Invoice Date*	*Date Paid*	*Customer*	*Gross*	
6	01/04/16	01/05/2016	Farmhouse Foods	€148	
7	04/04/16	28/05/2016	Fast Foods	€68	
8	05/04/16	08/05/2016	The Snack Bar	€235	
9	09/04/16	09/04/2016	The Halal Centre	€287	
10	13/04/16	30/04/2016	Edwards Farm	€115	
11	15/04/16	12/05/2016	T F Curries	€382	
12	20/04/16	21/05/2016	Ahmed Foods	€81	
13			**Gross Totals**	**€1,314**	

4 Spreadsheet functions

this chapter covers...

This chapter covers the creation of formulas, and shows how you can make use of some of the built-in calculation facilities provided by spreadsheet software. It explains and takes you through the concepts and techniques listed below. By the time you have finished this chapter and carried out the exercises which follow, you should be able to produce spreadsheets which perform a variety of calculations. The concepts and techniques covered are:

■ *formulas*

■ *mathematical operators*

■ *functions*

■ *ranges*

■ *mathematical functions*

■ *cell addressing*

■ *date functions*

■ *logical functions and operators*

■ *lookup functions*

■ *circular references in formulas*

Note that the step-by-step instructions given in this chapter are based on the Microsoft® Excel model, but the concepts and techniques described relate to all spreadsheet packages.

FORMULAS

As we have seen in previous chapters, whenever we wish to carry out a calculation or enter a formula into a cell within our spreadsheet, we move to the cell where we want the formula to appear and start by entering an equal sign =.

The formula can take a very simple form, containing just numbers, or a mixture of numbers and cell references, or as we have seen earlier, a function and cell references.

Examples of formulas include:

=3 + 2

=D6 – 1.15

=D6 * D7

=D32

Note that as we create the formula, any spaces we insert within the formula are automatically ignored.

One of the most significant points about formulas which has already been mentioned, is that when we copy a formula from one cell to another cell or group of cells, the row and column numbers automatically change as appropriate. they will automatically relate to the row or column references of the new cell to which the formula has been copied.

MATHEMATICAL OPERATORS

The common mathematical operators which we will use in our formulas are as follows:-

■ Addition: +

■ Subtraction: –

■ Multiplication: *

■ Division: /

We also make use of brackets: ( )

As with our normal mathematics there is an **order** that will be followed when a formula is interpreted, known as the **operator precedence**.

The order of calculations within any formula is as follows:

■ any calculation contained in brackets is done first

■ division and multiplication are ranked the same

■ addition and subtraction are ranked the same

So, if we want to group parts of our calculation to ensure that certain parts are calculated before a subsequent part, then we would use brackets.

For example:

$$= (B3 + 5)/100$$

Here 5 is added to B3 and the result is divided by 100.

This gives a different result to

$$= B3+5/100$$

Here 5 is divided by 100 and the result is added to B3

As you can see brackets play a very important part in our construction of formulas.

FUNCTIONS – AN EXPLANATION

Spreadsheet packages contain built-in formulas called **Functions** that make it easy to perform common calculations on data. For example, =**SUM( )** is a function which can be used to add up values, as we have seen in the earlier chapters of this book.

Most functions are designed to accept data which is then used in the calculations. This data is entered within the round brackets which follow the function's name.

For example, =**SUM(A1,A2,A3)** is a formula which uses the SUM function to add up the values of the three cells.

These values are also known as '**arguments**'.

As you can see, each argument (or value) is usually separated from the previous argument (value) by a comma.

The **type** of argument will vary from function to function: it could be a number, or a cell reference, or group of cells.

The **number** of arguments may also vary from function to function.

The most common forms of argument are a cell reference, or group of cell references, as we shall see in the examples which follow. Look at cell A1 in the screen at the top of the next page.

As you can see in this screen, the SUM function is prompting the user to enter the first argument or number to be added. This could be a cell reference or an actual number.

If an argument is **optional** (ie you don't have to enter it) you will see the argument in square brackets, for example [number2], as shown above.

The result which a function creates is said to be the value **returned** by the function, and is known as the **return** value.

RANGES

A range is a **group or block of cells in a worksheet**. It is essentially a shorthand way of specifying the first and last cell and automatically including all the cells in-between.

A range is identified by the cell reference of the first cell (upper left cell), followed by a colon, then the cell reference of the last cell (bottom right).

Examples of a range of cells include:

D4:D11   – all the cells are in the same column

C4:F4   – all the cells are in the same row

D4:F10   – a block of cells across several rows and columns

A range of cells as described above can be used as an argument within a function, for example =SUM(D4:D11).

MATHEMATICAL FUNCTIONS

The functions we are going to cover in this section are as follows:

- ABS
- INT
- SUM

We are also going to explain the AUTOSUM facility, which is available to help create formulas within Microsoft Excel.

ABS

The ABS function 'returns' the **absolute value** of a number, which is the value of a number **without its sign**:

> =ABS(number)

The ABS function has just one argument:

- a number is required

    For example:

    > =ABS(-2) . . . means that the number's sign will be removed and will return the value 2

    > =ABS(2) . . . will also return the value 2

INT

The INT function rounds a number down to the integer (ie whole number):

> =INT(number)

The INT function has just one argument:

- the number may contain decimals which you wish to round down to an integer

    For example: =INT(2.45) would return the value 2

    =INT(2.99) would also return the value 2

SUM

We have already used the SUM function in this book. The SUM function adds all the numbers that you specify as arguments. Each argument can be a number, a cell reference, a range of cells, or the result of another function:

> =SUM(number1, [number2], [number3],...)

The SUM function has these arguments:

▓ number1 is required

▓ number2, number3 . . . are optional

You can specify up to a total of 255 arguments (values) to be added together. For example:

=SUM(C2,C16,C20)

This would return the sum of the numbers in the cells C2, C16, and C20.

The screen illustrated below adds the values for the 'odd' numbered weeks for Smiths Ltd, using =SUM(B4, D4, F4), producing a total value of 45.

G4	▾ :	✕ ✓	*fx*	=SUM(B4,D4,F4)		
◢	A	B	C	D	E	F	G
1	Work bookings						
2							
3	Client	Week1	Week2	Week3	Week4	Week5	Odd weeks
4	Smiths Ltd	15	15	15	15	15	45
5	Jones and Partner	12	8	10	9	9	
6	Redwoods	13	20	11	7	8	
7	Underhills	13	20	11	2	9	

When we are positioned on a cell containing a formula, if we click on the formula, in the formula bar, all cells used in that formula are highlighted, as can be seen below.

PPMT	▾ :	✕ ✓	*fx*	=SUM(B4,D4,F4)		
◢	A	B	C	D	E	F	G
1	Work bookings						
2							
3	Client	Week1	Week2	Week3	Week4	Week5	Odd weeks
4	Smiths Ltd	15	15	15	15	15	=SUM(B4,D4,F4)
5	Jones and Partner	12	8	10	9	9	
6	Redwoods	13	20	11	7	8	
7	Underhills	13	20	11	2	9	

SUM is often used for a **range of cells**, for example:

=SUM(C2:C16)

This would return the sum of all the numbers in the range C2 to C16, ie cells C2,C3,C4,C5 etc... all the way to C16.

The screen illustrated overleaf uses the formula =SUM(B4:F4,50) to total all five weeks for Smiths Ltd and add a value of 50. This produces a total of 125.

G4		▼	⋮	✕ ✓ fx		=SUM(B4:F4,50)	

◢	A	B	C	D	E	F	G
1	Work bookings						
2							
3	Client	Week1	Week2	Week3	Week4	Week5	Forecast
4	Smiths Ltd	15	15	15	15	15	125
5	Jones and Partner	12	8	10	9	9	
6	Redwoods	13	20	11	7	8	
7	Underhills	13	20	11	2	9	

AUTOSUM

This is a facility available in Microsoft® Excel, which may not be available in other spreadsheet packages. It provides a quick way of selecting ranges of cells, usually for totalling, without having to manually specify or select the start and end cells for the range.

You select the cell where you want to position a total, and **AUTOSUM** will guess which cells above, or to the left you want to add up.

PPMT		▼	⋮	✕ ✓ fx		=SUM(B4:B7)	

◢	A	B	C	D	E	F	G
1	Work bookings						
2							
3	Client	Week1	Week2	Week3	Week4	Week5	Forecast
4	Smiths Ltd	15	15	15	15	15	125
5	Jones and Partner	12	8	10	9	9	
6	Redwoods	13	20	11	7	8	
7	Underhills	13	20	11	2	9	
8		=SUM(B4:B7)					
9		SUM(**number1**, [number2], ...)					

In the example above, we have selected cell B8, then selected AUTOSUM from the menu bar. You can see that the formula =SUM(B4:B7) is automatically shown in the cell. If you just press **RETURN** this formula will be entered into the cell.

how to use AUTOSUM

- select a cell below the column of numbers or to the right of the row of numbers

- select AUTOSUM from the menu bar; a dotted rectangle will be displayed, highlighting the numbers to be included

- if the appropriate cells are included, press **RETURN**

- if not, use the mouse to drag the boundaries of the rectangle to include the appropriate cells

MORE ON RANGES

It is also possible to assign a name to a cell or range of cells, this can be useful if you are using a particular cell(s) in many formulas, or to give clarity within a formula by using a meaningful name.

For example, if we look at the example Profit & Loss sheet below, we could name the cell holding the total Sales values as **Sales** and the Cost of sales value as **CostofSales**, then we could use these names in the formula for Gross profit, which makes for an easy to understand formula.

Sales ▾ ⋮	✕ ✓ *fx*	=SUM(D8:D10)				
	A	B	C	D	E	F	G
1			ABC Traders				
2							
3			Statement of profit or loss				
4			for the year ended 31 March 2016				
5							
6			£	£			
7	Sales revenue						
8	Software			251,783			
9	Hardware			161,723			
10	Consultancy			55,276			
11				468,782			
12							
13	Cost of Sales			120,156			
14							
15	Gross Profit			348,626			

We have named cell D11 **Sales**, and now whenever we select it, and the name sales is displayed in the name box.

Similarly in the image on the next page, we have named cell D13, as **CostofSales**.

We can now enter a formula in D15 just using these names, as shown below:

CostofSales ▾	:	✕ ✓ *fx*	120156			
	A	B	C	D	E	F	G
1				ABC Traders			
2							
3				Statement of profit or loss			
4				for the year ended 31 March 2016			
5							
6			£	£			
7	Sales revenue						
8	Software			251,783			
9	Hardware			161,723			
10	Consultancy			55,276			
11				468,782			
12							
13	Cost of Sales			120,156			
14							
15	Gross Profit			348,626			

Alternatively, as mentioned we could name a group of cells, as illustrated below, where we have named D8 through to D10 as **Sales Values**.

SalesValues ▾	:	✕ ✓ *fx*	251783			
	A	B	C	D	E	F	G
2							
3				Statement of profit or loss			
4				for the year ended 31 March 2016			
5							
6			£	£			
7	Sales revenue						
8	Software			251,783			
9	Hardware			161,723			
10	Consultancy			55,276			
11				468,782			
12							
13	Cost of Sales			120,156			
14							
15	Gross Profit			348,626			

We could then make use of this name in the formula in cell D11 for the total sales in cell D11, as shown on the next page.

| Sales | ▾ | : | ✕ | ✓ | *fx* | =SUM(SalesValues) |

▲	A	B	C	D	E	F	G
2							
3				**Statement of profit or loss**			
4				for the year ended 31 March 2016			
5							
6			£	£			
7	**Sales revenue**						
8	Software			251,783			
9	Hardware			161,723			
10	Consultancy			55,276			
11				468,782			
12							
13	Cost of Sales			120,156			
14							
15	**Gross Profit**			348,626			

To assign a name to a range of cell(s):

■ select the required cells

■ select the FORMULAS menu

■ select **Define Name**

■ enter the name we want to use to refer to this range of cells

As shown in the image below, we are about to define a name for cell D8. To make any changes to Names which we have defined, use the Name Manager option, found within the FORMULAS menu.

| D8 | ▾ | : | ✕ | ✓ | *fx* | 251783 |

▲	A	B	C	D	E	F	G	H	I
1				**ABC Traders**					
2									
3				**Statement of profit or loss**					
4				for the year ended 31 March 2016					
5									
6			£	£					
7	**Sales revenue**								
8	Software			251,783					
9	Hardware			161,723					
10	Consultancy			55,276					
11				468,782					
12									
13	Cost of Sales			120,156					
14									
15	**Gross Profit**			348,626					
16									

New Name ? ✕

Name: |

Scope: Workbook ▾

Comment:

Refers to: =Sheet1!$D$8

OK   Cancel

FUNCTION WIZARD

Within Excel®, there is a function wizard which helps us use any functions. It is found in the FORMULAS menu, Insert function, and also the fx symbol displayed just above the spreadsheet columns.

	A	B	C	D	E	F	G
1				Monthly Sales Value			
2							
3	Customer Name	Month1	Month2	Month3	Month4	Month5	Month6
4	Farmhouse Foods		£112				£26
5	Engineering Services					£67	
6	Another Food Service				£58	£116	
7	Top Quality Supplies		£56				
8	Halal Foods						
9	Edwards Farm					£40	
10	Allen and co	£45	£68	£231	£0	£331	£37
11	Ahmed and son						
12	Green & Sons Wholesalers	£700		£104			
13	Higginbottom and son						
14	W B Meats		£45				
15	The Halal Centre			£50			£0
16							

If in our spreadsheet, we select a cell, say cell C16, and then select Insert function we get the following:

Insert Function   ?   ✕

Search for a function:

Type a brief description of what you want to do and then click Go   Go

Or select a category: Most Recently Used   ⌄

Select a function:

SUM
COUNTA
PPMT
ISPMT
CUMPRINC
CUMIPMT
POWER

SUM(number1,number2,...)
Adds all the numbers in a range of cells.

Let's assume we want to total some values, we will select the SUM function from the list offered. (If the function we want to use is not listed, we can just type the name or a description in the SEARCH for box.)

We can now enter the function arguments, (it is possible that some cell references are automatically inserted as the tool tries to guess which cells we want to add up), as shown below.

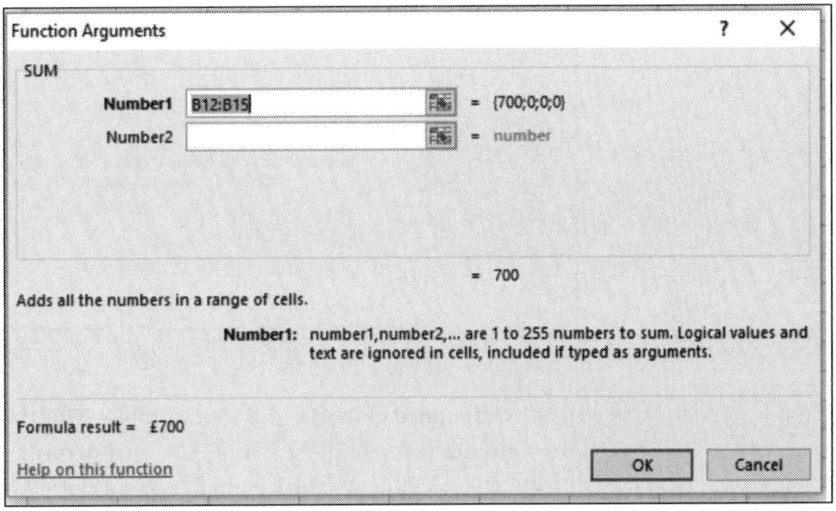

This isn't what we want, so make sure the entry in box Number1 is highlighted and then drag the cursor to select the cells we want to sum, e.g. B4 to B15.

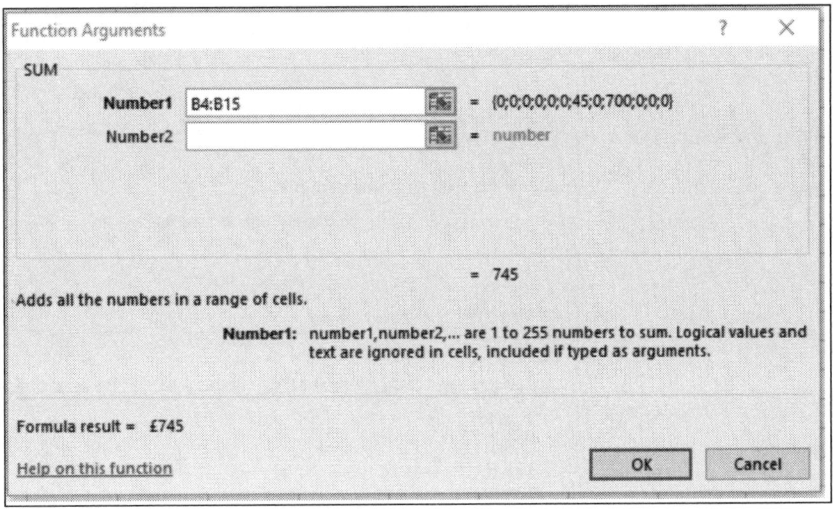

This is what we want, so click OK and the formula will be inserted.

If we already have a formula which we wish to edit, select the cell containing the formula, click on the **Insert Function** and make your changes.

To add the contents of an entire column:

To include all the values in row 4, would be 4:4.

If we had named cells B4 to B15 as a range **Month1**, we could easily insert this into the formula by selecting **Use in Formula** from the **FORMULAS** menu and selecting Month1 from the list of defined ranges.

CELL ADDRESSING

The way in which a cell is referenced is known as its address, for example A12, B49. This becomes important when we are using formulas. We have two ways of referencing cells within formulas:

- relative addressing
- absolute addressing

relative addressing

As we have seen, when we copy a formula from one cell to another, the formula is automatically adjusted to reflect the row or column of the new cell. This is called **relative addressing**: the formula is adjusted relative to the new cell.

We have seen that if you copy the formula **=SUM(B3:E3)** down a row from cell F3 to cell F4, the formula becomes **=SUM(B4:E4)**

Similarly, for columns, if you copy the formula **=SUM(B4:B8)** from cell B9 across a column to cell C9, the formula becomes **= SUM(C4:C8)**

absolute addressing

Sometimes we do not want the cell reference to change as we copy a formula – we want to keep a reference to an original cell or cells. To do this we use the dollar sign: $.

For example, $B$3 would refer to cell B3, and, when placed in a formula and copied, the copies would all also refer to B3.

In the example below we have entered an hourly rate in cell B3, which we wish to apply to all the totals. We have created a formula in cell G6 to give us a monetary value for the work carried out for the client using the formula:

=F6 * B3

PPMT ▾	⋮	✕ ✓ *fx*	=F6*B3			
	A	B	C	D	E	F	G
1	Work bookings						
2							
3	Hourly rate	£20					
4							
5	Client	Week1	Week2	Week3	Week4	Total	Value
6	Smiths Ltd	15	15	15	15	60	=F6*B3
7	Jones and Partner	12	8	10	9	39	
8	Redwoods	13	20	11	7	51	
9	Underhills	13	20	11	2	46	

We will now change the formula to =F6*$B$3 so that we can copy it and still keep the reference to B3, the cell where the hourly rate of £20 is entered.

| PPMT | ▼ | ⋮ | ✕ | ✓ | *fx* | =F6*B |

⊿	A	B	C	D	E	F	G
1	Work bookings						
2							
3	Hourly rate	£20					
4							
5	Client	Week1	Week2	Week3	Week4	Total	Value
6	Smiths Ltd	15	15	15	15	60	=F6*$B$3
7	Jones and Partner	12	8	10	9	39	
8	Redwoods	13	20	11	7	51	
9	Underhills	13	20	11	2	46	

When the formula =F6*$B$3 is then copied to cell G7, you can see on the screen image below that the cell reference has not changed, but remains B3. If the hourly rate changes from £20 to £22, then all you need to do is amend the amount entered in cell B3.

| G7 | ▼ | ⋮ | ✕ | ✓ | *fx* | =F7*$B$3 |

⊿	A	B	C	D	E	F	G
1	Work bookings						
2							
3	Hourly rate	£20					
4							
5	Client	Week1	Week2	Week3	Week4	Total	Value
6	Smiths Ltd	15	15	15	15	60	£1,200
7	Jones and Partner	12	8	10	9	39	£780
8	Redwoods	13	20	11	7	51	
9	Underhills	13	20	11	2	46	

Absolute cell addressing is a very important part of creating formulas within spreadsheets.

As an alternative, you could name the cell B3 which holds the rate, for example **HrlyRate**, and use this name in your formulas.

DATE FUNCTIONS

We often want to include date information in a spreadsheet, and we may want to perform a calculation on the information. For example, in a purchasing department, we might want a spreadsheet to display the expected interval of time between an order being placed with a supplier and the delivery date of the goods.

To enable date-based calculations, a spreadsheet stores all dates as numbers, based on the number of days from 1/1/1900. This is referred to as a **serial number** representation.

The time element of the date/time is also stored numerically as the decimal part of the serial number, for example the serial number 0.5 represents 12:00 noon.

You can see dates displayed as serial numbers, if you enter a date in a cell and the cell is not formatted as a date.

The functions we are going to cover in this section are as follows: **today** and **now**.

TODAY

The **TODAY** function returns the serial number of today's date based on your computer system clock, it does not include the time. The function is:

=TODAY( )

The TODAY function has no arguments (values).

For example, the formula:

= TODAY( ) +14

This would return the current date plus 14 days.

The =TODAY( ) function is useful if you want to have the current date displayed on a worksheet.

Another use would be if you wished to calculate a person's age as of today and you only had their date of birth.

In the example below, we have placed today's date in cell G1. This will change every time we re-open this workbook.

G1	▾	:	✕ ✓ ƒx	=TODAY()			
◢	A	B	C	D	E	F	G
1	Work bookings						01/03/2016
2							
3	Hourly rate	£20					
4							
5	Client	Week1	Week2	Week3	Week4	Total	Value
6	Smiths Ltd	15	15	15	15	60	£1,200
7	Jones and Partner	12	8	10	9	39	£780
8	Redwoods	13	20	11	7	51	
9	Underhills	13	20	11	2	46	

In some instances the result may appear as the serial number. If this happens, change the cell format to be date, as described previously and it will display correctly.

NOW

The **NOW** function returns the serial number of today's date and the current time based on your computer system clock: =NOW ( )

The =NOW( ) function has no arguments (values).

In the example below, we have used the =NOW( ) function in cell G1. The time will change every time the worksheet re-calculates or is re-opened.

	A	B	C	D	E	F	G
1	Work bookings						01/03/2016 09:55
2							
3	Hourly rate	£20					
4							
5	Client	Week1	Week2	Week3	Week4	Total	Value
6	Smiths Ltd	15	15	15	15	60	£1,200
7	Jones and Partner	12	8	10	9	39	£780
8	Redwoods	13	20	11	7	51	
9	Underhills	13	20	11	2	46	

In some instances the result may appear as the serial number. If this happens,

■ change the cell format to **Custom**

■ select format type dd/mm/yyyy hh:mm

and it will display correctly.

TEXT FUNCTIONS

We sometimes want to combine text from two or more different cells and put the result in another cell. To do this we use a function CONCATENATE, for example if we wanted to combine a first name and a surname into one cell.

concatenate

This function returns the combined text of its arguments.

The concatenate function has these arguments:

■ text1 is required

■ text2, text33 . . . are optional

You can specify up to a total of 255 arguments (cells) to be combined.

For example:

= CONCATENATE (C2,C16,C20)

This would return the text from each of these cells combined together in one long text string.

Note: If you want to combine strings, but have them separated by a space, you will have to include a space string (" ") between each string, or similarly you could put a comma (","). Each has to be surrounded by quotes.

For example:

= CONCATENATE (C2," ", C16, ",", C20)

This would combine C2 and C16, with a space between, then add a comma then combine C20.

In the example below we have combined the Client name with the text Total from cell F6.

| G6 | ▾ : | ✕ ✓ _fx_ | =CONCATENATE(A6,F5) |

◢	A	B	C	D	E	F	G	H
1	Work bookings							
2								
3	Hourly rate	£20						
4								
5	Client	Week1	Week2	Week3	Week4	Total		
6	Smiths Ltd	15	15	15	15	60	Smiths LtdTotal	
7	Jones and Partner	12	8	10	9	39		
8	Redwoods	13	20	11	7	51		
9	Underhills	13	20	11	2	46		

In cell G6, looking at the formula you can see we have not included a space in the CONCATENATE function. We now edit the formula to include a space, and make the reference to cell F5 an absolute reference, so that we can easily copy the formula. You can see the difference in cell G6 and how it copies into G7 in the image below:

| G7 | ▾ : | ✕ ✓ _fx_ | =CONCATENATE(A7," ",$F$5) |

◢	A	B	C	D	E	F	G	H
1	Work bookings							
2								
3	Hourly rate	£20						
4								
5	Client	Week1	Week2	Week3	Week4	Total		
6	Smiths Ltd	15	15	15	15	60	Smiths Ltd Total	
7	Jones and Partner	12	8	10	9	39	Jones and Partner Total	
8	Redwoods	13	20	11	7	51		
9	Underhills	13	20	11	2	46		

LOGICAL FUNCTIONS AND OPERATORS

A concept used regularly in spreadsheets is **conditional logic**.

This is a concept where if something is true, then something else happens.

For example:

> *if I swim in the sea **then** I will get wet*

> *if I do no work **then** I will not pass my exams*

Within the spreadsheet environment, we often want to test a cell for a certain value, and

- if it is this value we make one thing happen

- if it is not this value, we want something different to happen

logical operators

We can apply the standard comparison 'operators' to create situations where **conditional logic** can be used. These include:

- equal to (=)

- greater than (>)

- greater than or equal to (>=)

- less than (<)

- less than or equal to(<=)

- not equal to (<>)

For example, a condition could be that cell B10 is greater than 100 which we would express as:

> B10>100

The main logical function which is used in spreadsheets is the **IF( )** function

IF

The **IF** function returns one value if the condition you specify evaluates to TRUE, and another value if that condition evaluates to FALSE.

For example, if you take an exam and the pass mark is 55%, if you get 60% you will pass, and if you get 54% you will fail.

Using the IF function you can use a spreadsheet to work out the 'pass' or 'fail' for you, as we will see in the example on the next page.

The IF function is made up of three parts:

=IF(logical test, value if true, value if false)

These three parts can be explained as follows:

- **logical test**

   This can be any value or expression which can be evaluated to TRUE or FALSE. In the case of the exam pass mark this is:

   =IF(F4>=55% . . . the logical test here is whether the mark in cell F4 is greater than or equal to 55%

- **value if true**

   This is the value which will be returned by the function if the condition evaluates to TRUE . . . if the value is 60% the answer is "PASS"

- **value if false**

   This is the value which will be returned by the function if the condition evaluates to FALSE . . . if the value is 54% (ie less than the pass mark of 55%,) the answer is "FAIL"

Therefore, to recap, the structure of the IF function is as follows:

=IF(logical test, value if true, value if false)

In the example we used to work out exam success or failure on the basis of a 55% pass mark, the IF function will be expressed as follows:

=IF(F4>=55%,"PASS","FAIL")

Note that:

- any text which is to appear in the spreadsheet should be shown in quotes: **"PASS"**

- the third part of the function - ie 'value if false' is optional; if it is not included, no value will be returned if the condition is false

In the example screen on the next page, we have entered formulas in column G, for each person.

The formula in cell G4 for John Smith is:

   =IF(F4>=55%,"PASS","FAIL")

This formula looks at the value in cell F4, and since it more than 55%, this returns a value of PASS in cell G4.

Similarly for Harpret Bhopal, the formula in cell G5 is:

   =IF(F5>=55%,"PASS","FAIL")

This formula returns a value of FAIL because Harpret Bhopal's average is less than 55%.

| G4 | ▼ | : | ✕ ✓ *fx* | =IF(F4>=55%,"PASS","FAIL") | | |

◢	A	B	C	D	E	F	G
1	Midterm exams						
2							
3	**Name**	**Module1**	**Module2**	**Module3**	**Module4**	**Average**	
4	*John Smith*	75%	62%	45%	65%	61.75%	PASS
5	*Harpret Bhopal*	61%	48%			54.50%	FAIL
6	*Wendy Owen*	63%	80%	51%	41%	58.75%	PASS
7	*Mohammed Iqbal*	53%		41%	64%	52.67%	FAIL
8	*Barbara White*	42%	63%	85%	43%	58.25%	PASS

Note: If we wanted to either specify PASS or leave it blank, a blank is "" (empty quote marks), so our formula would be:

=IF(F5>=55%,"PASS","")

Let's look at another example.

Suppose we had a costing sheet containing Budget figures for our expected costs (column B) and Actual figures for each of these costs (column C). In column D we have calculated the Variance (Budget – Actual), as shown in the image below:

◢	A	B	C	D	E	F
1	Costing comparison					
2						
3	**Cost Type**	**Budget**	**Actual**	**Variance**	**Adverse**	**Favourable**
4	Direct Materials	£12,000	£18,500	-£6,500		
5	Direct Labour	£25,000	£24,500	£500		
6	Production Overheads	£15,000	£18,900	-£3,900		
7	Administration Overheads	£6,500	£5,050	£1,450		
8	Selling & Distribution Overheads	£11,000	£12,000	-£1,000		

We could manually identify whether the Actual figure compared to the Budget figure is Adverse (greater than Budget) or Favourable (less than Budget), but we are going to use the IF function to do it for us.

In cell E4, we are going to put the formula: IF(D4<0, D4,0)

This formula equates to:

if the value in D4 is less than zero, ie the variance is less than 0,

put the value of D4 in cell E4,

otherwise, put 0 in E4.

The results are shown in the image on the next page:

| E4 | ▾ | ⋮ | ✕ ✓ *fx* | =IF(D4<0,D4,0) | | | | |

◢	A	B	C	D	E	F
1	Costing comparison					
2						
3	**Cost Type**	**Budget**	**Actual**	**Variance**	**Adverse**	**Favourable**
4	Direct Materials	£12,000	£18,500	-£6,500	-£6,500	
5	Direct Labour	£25,000	£24,500	£500	£0	
6	Production Overheads	£15,000	£18,900	-£3,900	-£3,900	
7	Administration Overheads	£6,500	£5,050	£1,450	£0	
8	Selling & Distribution Overheads	£11,000	£12,000	-£1,000	-£1,000	

Similarly, in the Favourable column, F4 we put the formula:
=IF(D4>0, D4,0)

This formula equates to:
if the value in D4 is greater than zero, ie the variance is greater than 0,
put the value of D4 in cell F4,
otherwise, put 0 in F4.

Again, this can be seen below:

| F4 | ▾ | ⋮ | ✕ ✓ *fx* | =IF(D4>0,D4,0) | | | | |

◢	A	B	C	D	E	F
1	Costing comparison					
2						
3	**Cost Type**	**Budget**	**Actual**	**Variance**	**Adverse**	**Favourable**
4	Direct Materials	£12,000	£18,500	-£6,500	-£6,500	£0
5	Direct Labour	£25,000	£24,500	£500	£0	£500
6	Production Overheads	£15,000	£18,900	-£3,900	-£3,900	£0
7	Administration Overheads	£6,500	£5,050	£1,450	£0	£1,450
8	Selling & Distribution Overheads	£11,000	£12,000	-£1,000	-£1,000	£0

It is a good idea to spend time to familiarise yourself with the IF function. It is used a great deal within spreadsheets and is very powerful.

LOOKUP FUNCTIONS

We can often have large amounts of data within a spreadsheet, and it may not be very easy to find a particular value, so we may wish to use an automated function to do it for us.

There are two built in functions which are regularly used: **HLOOKUP** and **VLOOKUP**.

HLOOKUP

The H in HLOOKUP is to identify that the function searches in a horizontal direction, ie along rows.

The function searches for a value in a particular row, and if found, it returns the matching value in the same column, from a specified row below the row being searched..

=HLOOKUP(lookup value,range,row index,lookup)

The HLOOKUP function has these four arguments:

▪ **lookup value**

This is the value which you want to look for

▪ **range**

This is the horizontal group of cells where you want to look for the value, and should include at least 2 part rows, the row containing the value, and the row holding the values to return, usually referred to as a table of values.

▪ **row index**

This is the value counting rows from the search row as 1, to the row holding the values to return, or the row number within the table.

▪ **lookup**

This is either TRUE or FALSE, and specifies whether or not you want the function to find an exact match to the lookup value, or an approximate match. If TRUE or omitted, an approximate match is returned if an exact match is not found; this requires the lookup cells to be sorted in ascending order.

In our example below, we have a table in rows 6 to 9 which allows us to look up the currency exchange rate for a small selection of countries.

⊿	A	B	C	D	E	F	G
1	Exchange rates			01/03/2016			
2							
3			Country	Exch Rate	Currency		
4			CN	9.18	Yuan		
5							
6	Country	JP	FR	AU	TH	CN	DK
7	Exch rate	158.46	1.29	1.96	49.9	9.18	9.61
8	Currency	Yen	€	$	Baht	Yuan	Krone
9	Full name	Japan	France	Australia	Thailand	China	Denmark

The data in rows 6 to 8 gives the abbreviated country name, the current exchange rate, the name of the currency, and the full country name.

In cell C4, we will select the Country for which we will lookup exchange rate and currency.

To make this easy, we have applied data validation to cell C4, so that we can pick from the list of countries in cells B6 to G6, as shown below.

	A	B	C	D	E	F	G
1	Exchange rates			01/03/2016			
2							
3			Country	Exch Rate	Currency		
4			CN	9.18	Yuan		
5			JP				
6	Country	JP	FR		TH	CN	DK
7	Exch rate	158.46	AU	1.96	49.9	9.18	9.61
8	Currency	Yen	TH		Baht	Yuan	Krone
9	Full name	Japan	CN DK	Australia	Thailand	China	Denmark

In cell D4 we want to display the Exchange rate for the country, specified in C4, we have created the HLOOKUP formula as follows:

=HLOOKUP(C4,B6:G9,2,FALSE)

Cell C4 is the value we want to find.

Cells B6:G9 contain all the information we are wanting to look up; this is effectively a table.

The row containing the value we want to return is effectively the 2nd row (Exch rate) in the block of cells containing the data.

We want to return only an exact match for the country we specify, so the final parameter is FALSE.

D4		:	X ✓ *fx*	=HLOOKUP(C4,B6:G9,2,FALSE)			
	A	B	C	D	E	F	G
1	Exchange rates			01/03/2016			
2							
3			Country	Exch Rate	Currency		
4			CN	9.18	Yuan		
5							
6	Country	JP	FR	AU	TH	CN	DK
7	Exch rate	158.46	1.29	1.96	49.9	9.18	9.61
8	Currency	Yen	€	$	Baht	Yuan	Krone
9	Full name	Japan	France	Australia	Thailand	China	Denmark

Similarly, if we now want to look up the currency, into cell E4, we would create the formula

=HLOOKUP(C4,B6:G9,3,FALSE)

E4	▾ ⋮	✕ ✓	*fx*	=HLOOKUP(C4,B6:G9,3,FALSE)		
	A	B	C	D	E	F	G
1	Exchange rates			01/03/2016			
2							
3			Country	Exch Rate	Currency		
4			CN	9.18	Yuan		
5							
6	Country	JP	FR	AU	TH	CN	DK
7	Exch rate	158.46	1.29	1.96	49.9	9.18	9.61
8	Currency	Yen	€	$	Baht	Yuan	Krone
9	Full name	Japan	France	Australia	Thailand	China	Denmark

If we now change the country in cell C4, the Exchange rate and currency will automatically change too, as you can see below.

	A	B	C	D	E	F	G
1	Exchange rates			01/03/2016			
2							
3			Country	Exch Rate	Currency		
4			FR	▾ 1.29	€		
5							
6	Country	JP	FR	AU	TH	CN	DK
7	Exch rate	158.46	1.29	1.96	49.9	9.18	9.61
8	Currency	Yen	€	$	Baht	Yuan	Krone
9	Full name	Japan	France	Australia	Thailand	China	Denmark

VLOOKUP

The V in VLOOKUP is to identify that the function searches in a vertical direction, ie down columns.

The function searches for a value in a particular column. If the value is found, it returns the matching value in the same row, from a specified column to the right of the column being searched.

=VLOOKUP(lookup value,range,col index,lookup)

The VLOOKUP function syntax has these arguments:

■ **lookup value**

This is the value which you want to look for

- **range**

  This is the horizontal group of cells where you want to look for the value, and should include at least 2 part columns, the column containing the value, and the column holding the values to return, usually referred to as a table of values.

- **col index**

  This is the value counting columns from the search column as 1, to the column holding the values to return, or the column number within the table.

- **lookup**

  This optional argument is either TRUE or FALSE, and specifies whether or not you want the function to find an exact match to the lookup value, or an approximate match. If TRUE or omitted, an approximate match is returned if an exact match is not found; this requires the lookup cells to be sorted in ascending order.

Look at the example below and read the explanatory text that follows.

| PPMT | ▾ | ⋮ | ✕ ✓ ƒx | =VLOOKUP(B3,A6:B17,2,FALSE) |

	A	B	C	D	E
1	Products				
2					
3	Lookup inventory code	P133		Quantity	=VLOOKU
4					
5	Inventory Code	Quantity			
6	A1	12			
7	A3	34			
8	B4	22			
9	A5	1			
10	D6	89			
11	H8	900			
12	K5	31			
13	S9	451			
14	C3	67			
15	P133	76			
16	A112	32			
17	W34	90			

We have entered data in columns A and B giving the inventory (stock) code, and quantity for a group of products.

In cell B3 we have entered an inventory code and we want to look up the quantity held for this Inventory Code.

In cell E3 where we want to display the quantity for this inventory code, we have created the VLOOKUP formula as follows:

=VLOOKUP(B3, A6:B17,2,FALSE)

Here B3 is the value we want to find.

Cells A6:B17 contain all the information we are wanting to look up, effectively a table (only 2 columns).

The column we want to return is effectively the 2nd column (Quantity) in the block of cells containing the data.

We want to return only an exact match for the inventory code we specify, so the final parameter is FALSE.

If you look at the image below, you can see that the formula returns 76, the quantity for inventory code P133.

PPMT ▾ ⋮	✕ ✔ *fx*	=VLOOKUP(B3,A6:B17,2,FALSE)

	A	B	C	D	E
1	Products				
2					
3	Lookup inventory code	P133		Quantity	=VLOOKU
4					
5	Inventory Code	Quantity			
6	A1	12			
7	A3	34			
8	B4	22			
9	A5	1			
10	D6	89			
11	H8	900			
12	K5	31			
13	S9	451			
14	C3	67			
15	P133	76			
16	A112	32			
17	W34	90			

notes on lookups

■ When doing a lookup for a text value, the search does not distinguish between upper and lower case text. They are both regarded as the same.

■ If you want to return an approximate value if an exact match cannot be found, the search data must be in ascending order.

circular references

A **Circular Reference** occurs when a cell containing a formula includes its own cell reference in the formula. A simple example would be if cell B7 held the formula =sum(B2:B7).

When this occurs you will be given a warning, as shown in the image below.

To remove the error, select OK and correct the formula in the cell.

SOME USEFUL SHORTCUTS

To insert a cell reference into a formula

When creating a formula you can click on the cell to include its reference in the formula.

For example, if we were creating a formula to multiply two cells

= B4*B5 :

- in the formula bar enter "="
- click on cell B4
- enter "*" for multiply
- click on cell B5
- press enter

To insert an absolute cell reference into a formula

Using the same multiplication example, but with an absolute cell reference for B4

= $B$4 *B5 :

- in the formula bar enter "="
- click on cell B4
- press the function key F4, and you see B4 becomes $B$4 in the formula bar
- enter "*" for multiply
- click on cell B5
- press enter

To copy a formula

An easy way to copy a formula to adjacent cells in the row or column:

- select the cell containing a formula
- move the cursor to the bottom right corner of the cell, until a plus sign (+) appears
- press down the left mouse key and drag across the adjacent cells

When you release the mouse the new formulas will be inserted.

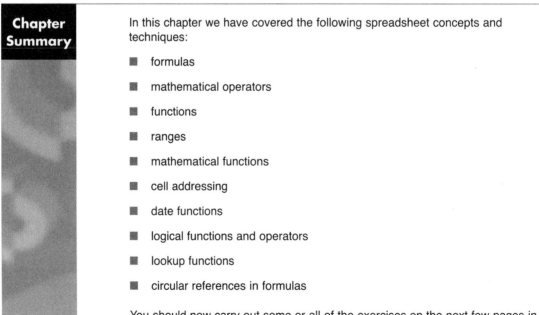

Chapter Summary

In this chapter we have covered the following spreadsheet concepts and techniques:

- formulas
- mathematical operators
- functions
- ranges
- mathematical functions
- cell addressing
- date functions
- logical functions and operators
- lookup functions
- circular references in formulas

You should now carry out some or all of the exercises on the next few pages in order to practise and reinforce your learning.

Activities

Exercise 1 – using formulas and modifying formats

In this first exercise we will open an existing spreadsheet containing some data, introduce some formulas, use the basic operators (+, -, /, *), and make use of ranges and absolute cell references.

To access this spreadsheet visit www.osbornebooks.co.uk ('Products and Resources'), and download **T4investment**.

Stage 1

This stage is about starting to introduce some formulas into our spreadsheet, and using the basic arithmetic operators (+, -, /, *).

1.   Download the workbook **T4investment**.

2.   Open the downloaded file, save the workbook with new name **T4Exercise1**.

The workbook should appear as shown below.

	A	B	C	D	E	F
1	Investment Portfolio					
2						
3					Annual	Weekly
4		Year start	Year end		Growth	Growth
5	Where	Amount	Amount	Growth	Rate	Amount
6		£	£	£	%	£
7	Bank1	500.00	512.50			
8	Bank2	4,000.00	4,100.33			
9	Building Society1	2,000.00	2,100.00			
10	Building Society2	3,000.00	3,099.99			
11	Post Office	100.00	102.95			
12	Bonds1	1,000.00	1,201.54			
13	Bonds2	2,000.00	2,095.00			

3.   The first formula we want to enter is to calculate the growth which has been added to each investment. Enter formulas in column D to calculate the growth. (Taking the Year start amount from the Year end amount.)

4.   Format the growth column (D) to display 2 decimal places, no currency symbol.

5.   We want to calculate the growth rate for each investment. Enter formulas in column E for the growth rate as a decimal. (Take the growth divided by the Year start amount.)

6.   Display Annual Growth Rate as a percentage with 2 decimal places.

7.   We now want to calculate how much growth we were getting weekly. Enter formulas in column F to calculate the weekly amount of growth. (Use the growth column D, and divide it by 52.)

8.   Format the weekly growth column to display with 3 decimal places.

9.   Save the workbook with the same name **T4Exercise1**.

Your spreadsheet should appear as follows:

	A	B	C	D	E	F
1	Investment Portfolio					
2						
3					Annual	Weekly
4		Year start	Year end		Growth	Growth
5	Where	Amount	Amount	Growth	Rate	Amount
6		£	£	£	%	£
7	Bank1	500.00	512.50	12.50	2.50%	0.240
8	Bank2	4,000.00	4,100.33	100.33	2.51%	1.929
9	Building Society1	2,000.00	2,100.00	100.00	5.00%	1.923
10	Building Society2	3,000.00	3,099.99	99.99	3.33%	1.923
11	Post Office	100.00	102.95	2.95	2.95%	0.057
12	Bonds1	1,000.00	1,201.54	201.54	20.15%	3.876
13	Bonds2	2,000.00	2,095.00	95.00	4.75%	1.827

The image below also shows the formulas used to perform the calculations.

	A	B	C	D	E	F
1	Investment Portfolio					
2						
3					Annual	Weekly
4		Year start	Year end		Growth	Growth
5	Where	Amount	Amount	Growth	Rate	Amount
6		£	£	£	%	£
7	Bank1	500	512.5	=C7-B7	=D7/B7	=D7/52
8	Bank2	4000	4100.33	=C8-B8	=D8/B8	=D8/52
9	Building Society1	2000	2100	=C9-B9	=D9/B9	=D9/52
10	Building Society2	3000	3099.99	=C10-B10	=D10/B10	=D10/52
11	Post Office	100	102.95	=C11-B11	=D11/B11	=D11/52
12	Bonds1	1000	1201.54	=C12-B12	=D12/B12	=D12/52
13	Bonds2	2000	2095	=C13-B13	=D13/B13	=D13/52

Stage 2

In this stage, we are going to continue to extend the calculations using autosum, and modify the formatting.

1.   We want to introduce some totals in row 14. In cell A14, enter **Totals**.

2.   Using **AUTOSUM** (if available, if not, just manually use **SUM( )**). Enter a formula in cell B14 to total the year start amounts.

3.   Similarly, again using **AUTOSUM**, total the year end amounts, into cell C14.

4.   Format cells B14 and C14 to display 2 decimal places, no currency symbol and with a border along the bottom of the cells, style thin double line.

5.   Insert a row above row 3.

6.   In cell A3 enter **Average growth**.

7.   In cell B3 enter a formula to calculate the average of the growth rates in the growth rate column.

8.   Display as a percentage, 3 decimal places.

9.   Save your spreadsheet (keeping the same name – **T4Exercise1**).

Your spreadsheet should now appear as shown below:

	A	B	C	D	E	F
1	Investment Portfolio					
2						
3	Average growth	5.885%				
4					Annual	Weekly
5		Year start	Year end		Growth	Growth
6	Where	Amount	Amount	Growth	Rate	Amount
7		£	£	£	%	£
8	Bank1	500.00	512.50	12.50	2.50%	0.240
9	Bank2	4,000.00	4,100.33	100.33	2.51%	1.929
10	Building Society1	2,000.00	2,100.00	100.00	5.00%	1.923
11	Building Society2	3,000.00	3,099.99	99.99	3.33%	1.923
12	Post Office	100.00	102.95	2.95	2.95%	0.057
13	Bonds1	1,000.00	1,201.54	201.54	20.15%	3.876
14	Bonds2	2,000.00	2,095.00	95.00	4.75%	1.827
15	Totals	12,600.00	13,212.31			

Stage 3

We are now going to use ranges, conditional formatting and absolute addressing.

1. Insert a row above the Totals row as follows:

    Special Bonds   1000   1120

2. Enter the appropriate formulae for cells D15, E15, F15 if they do not appear automatically.

3. On the totals row, cell B15, check the formula includes cell B14.

4. Similarly for cell C15, check the formula includes cell C14.

5. Edit the Average growth formula in cell B3 to ensure this new row is included.

6   Apply conditional formatting to display the growth rate in a **bold** and **italic** typeface for all entries where the growth rate is greater than the average growth figure in cell B3 (use automatic addressing).

7. In cell G5, enter **Maximum**.

8. In cell G6 enter **Growth**.

9. In cell G7 enter **£**, aligned in the centre.

10. Create a formula to calculate the maximum growth which would have been earned, if each investment had received the largest growth rate (cell E13) in cell G8, ie year start amount multiplied by this growth rate. Use absolute addressing for cell E13 within the formula.

11. Copy the formula to G9 through to G15.

12. Save your spreadsheet (keeping the same name – **T4Exercise1**).

Your spreadsheet should now look as shown below.

	A	B	C	D	E	F	G
1	Investment Portfolio						
2							
3	Average growth	6.649%					
4					Annual	Weekly	
5		Year start	Year end		Growth	Growth	Maximum
6	Where	Amount	Amount	Growth	Rate	Amount	Growth
7		£	£	£	%	£	£
8	Bank1	500.00	512.50	12.50	2.50%	0.240	100.77
9	Bank2	4,000.00	4,100.33	100.33	2.51%	1.929	806.16
10	Building Society1	2,000.00	2,100.00	100.00	5.00%	1.923	403.08
11	Building Society2	3,000.00	3,099.99	99.99	3.33%	1.923	604.62
12	Post Office	100.00	102.95	2.95	2.95%	0.057	20.154
13	Bonds1	1,000.00	1,201.54	201.54	*20.15%*	3.876	201.54
14	Bonds2	2,000.00	2,095.00	95.00	4.75%	1.827	403.08
15	Special Bonds	1,000.00	1,120.00	120.00	*12.00%*	2.308	201.54
16	Totals	13,600.00	14,332.31				

With formulae as shown below:

	A	B	C	D	E	F	G
1	Investment Portfolio						
2							
3	Average growth	=AVERAGE(E8:E15)					
4					Annual	Weekly	
5		Year start	Year end		Growth	Growth	Maximum
6	Where	Amount	Amount	Growth	Rate	Amount	Growth
7		£	£	£	%	£	£
8	Bank1	500	512.5	=C8-B8	=D8/B8	=D8/52	=B8*$E$13
9	Bank2	4000	4100.33	=C9-B9	=D9/B9	=D9/52	=B9*$E$13
10	Building Society1	2000	2100	=C10-B10	=D10/B10	=D10/52	=B10*$E$13
11	Building Society2	3000	3099.99	=C11-B11	=D11/B11	=D11/52	=B11*$E$13
12	Post Office	100	102.95	=C12-B12	=D12/B12	=D12/52	=B12*$E$13
13	Bonds1	1000	1201.54	=C13-B13	=D13/B13	=D13/52	=B13*$E$13
14	Bonds2	2000	2095	=C14-B14	=D14/B14	=D14/52	=B14*$E$13
15	Special Bonds	1000	1120	=C15-B15	=D15/B15	=D15/52	=B15*$E$13
16	Totals	=SUM(B8:B15)	=SUM(C8:C15)				

You have now completed the first exercise.

Exercise 2 – using numerical and date functions, and conditional logic

In this next exercise we are going to use more of the numerical and date functions, together with some conditional logic (IF statements). We are again going to make use of an existing spreadsheet.

Visit the website www.osbornebooks.co.uk ('Products and Resources') to download the spreadsheet **T4employee**.

Stage 1

This stage is utilising built in functions within a previously created workbook.

1.   Download the workbook **T4employee**.

2.   Open the downloaded file, save the workbook with new name **T4Exercise2**.

3.   The workbook should appear as shown below.

	A	B	C	D	E	F	G
1	Employee records						
2							
3						Calculated	Age
4	Surname	Birth Date	Start Date	Department	Salary	Age	Years
5	Johal	02/03/1975	01/06/2000	Sales	20000		
6	Jones	14/10/1963	01/07/2001	HR	16000		
7	Wakula	03/09/1978	01/07/2002	Sales	20000		
8	White	30/06/1967	03/01/2009	Accounts	15000		
9	Hacek	24/05/1970	01/07/2010	Accounts	18000		
10	Bhopal	12/02/1978	01/07/2010	Sales	20500		
11	Plant	19/03/1976	01/09/2010	Sales	21500		

4.   In cell D1, enter **Date**.

5.   In cell E1, enter a formula to display today's date, in the format dd/mm/yyyy.

6.   In cell F5, we want to create a formula to display the person's age. To do this we will need to use today's date (cell E1), the birth date (cell B5), and convert the difference between the two into years, by dividing by 365. (**Note**: you will need to use brackets to obtain the correct result.)

7.   Once you have created the formula and visually checked that it gives the correct result, edit the formula to make the reference to cell E1 (today's date) an absolute address.

8.   Copy the formula to cells F6 through to F11.

9.   Format cells F5 through to F11 as Number with 2 decimal places.

10. In column G, create a formula, which gives the calculated age (Column F) as a whole number of years only, using the INT function, apply the formula to cells G5 through to G11.

11. Format the column G to display with no decimal places.

12. Save your spreadsheet (keeping the same name – **T4Exercise2**).

Your spreadsheet should now look as shown below:

	A	B	C	D	E	F	G
1	Employee	records		Date	03/03/2016		
2							
3						Calculated	Age
4	Surname	Birth Date	Start Date	Department	Salary	Age	Years
5	Johal	02/03/1975	01/06/2000	Sales	20000	41.03	41
6	Jones	14/10/1963	01/07/2001	HR	16000	52.42	52
7	Wakula	03/09/1978	01/07/2002	Sales	20000	37.52	37
8	White	30/06/1967	03/01/2009	Accounts	15000	48.71	48
9	Hacek	24/05/1970	01/07/2010	Accounts	18000	45.81	45
10	Bhopal	12/02/1978	01/07/2010	Sales	20500	38.08	38
11	Plant	19/03/1976	01/09/2010	Sales	21500	39.98	39

The image below displays the formulas used to perform the calculations.

	A	B	C	D	E	F	G
1	Employee			Date	=TODAY()		
2							
3						Calculated	Age
4	Surname	Birth Date	Start Date	Department	Salary	Age	Years
5	Johal	27455	36678	Sales	20000	=($E$1-B5)/365	=INT(F5)
6	Jones	23298	37073	HR	16000	=($E$1-B6)/365	=INT(F6)
7	Wakula	28736	37438	Sales	20000	=($E$1-B7)/365	=INT(F7)
8	White	24653	39816	Accounts	15000	=($E$1-B8)/365	=INT(F8)
9	Hacek	25712	40360	Accounts	18000	=($E$1-B9)/365	=INT(F9)
10	Bhopal	28533	40360	Sales	20500	=($E$1-B10)/365	=INT(F10)
11	Plant	27838	40422	Sales	21500	=($E$1-B11)/365	=INT(F11)

Stage 2

We are going to make some changes to the format, and enter some more formulas.

1. Format the salary data (column E), so that each value displays with the 1000 separator (,) and no decimal places.

2. Hide columns F and G.

3. Make all text in rows 3 and 4 (our column headings) bold and underlined.

4. Enter **Service**, in cell H4, **Award** in cell H5 (make sure they are bold and underlined).

5. Insert a row between rows 2 and 3.

6. In cell A3, enter **_Award date_** in italics, widen column A so that this text fits within the column.

7. In cell B3, enter 01/01/2005. Ensure it is formatted as a date.

8. We are going to use a formula in column H to calculate whether or not an employee was employed before 1st January 2005, and may receive a service award. You are to use the IF( ) function to do the calculation, and cell B3 (where the date to compare against has been entered).

    For example to calculate H6, IF the value in C6 is before (less than) B3 THEN "yes", OTHERWISE "no").

9. Modify the formula to use the absolute address of cell B3.

10. Once you are happy with the formula in cell H6, copy the formula to cells H7 through to H12.

11. Save the workbook with the name **T4Exercise2**.

Your spreadsheet should appear as follows:

	A	B	C	D	E	H
1	Employee records			Date	03/03/2016	
2						
3	_Award date_	01/01/2005				
4						**Service**
5	**Surname**	**Birth Date**	**Start Date**	**Department**	**Salary**	**Award**
6	Johal	02/03/1975	01/06/2000	Sales	20,000	yes
7	Jones	14/10/1963	01/07/2001	HR	16,000	yes
8	Wakula	03/09/1978	01/07/2002	Sales	20,000	yes
9	White	30/06/1967	03/01/2009	Accounts	15,000	no
10	Hacek	24/05/1970	01/07/2010	Accounts	18,000	no
11	Bhopal	12/02/1978	01/07/2010	Sales	20,500	no
12	Plant	19/03/1976	01/09/2010	Sales	21,500	no

The image on the next page displays the formulas used to perform the calculations.

	A	B	C	D	E	H
1	Employee re			Date	=TODAY()	
2						
3	*Award date*	38353				
4						**Service**
5	**Surname**	**Birth Date**	**Start Date**	**Department**	**Salary**	**Award**
6	Johal	27455	36678	Sales	20000	=IF(C6<$B$3,"yes","no")
7	Jones	23298	37073	HR	16000	=IF(C7<$B$3,"yes","no")
8	Wakula	28736	37438	Sales	20000	=IF(C8<$B$3,"yes","no")
9	White	24653	39816	Accounts	15000	=IF(C9<$B$3,"yes","no")
10	Hacek	25712	40360	Accounts	18000	=IF(C10<$B$3,"yes","no")
11	Bhopal	28533	40360	Sales	20500	=IF(C11<$B$3,"yes","no")
12	Plant	27838	40422	Sales	21500	=IF(C12<$B$3,"yes","no")

Stage 3

We are now going to do some more calculations.

1.   Enter **New**, in cell I4, **Salary** in cell I5 (make sure they are bold and underlined).

2.   We are going to calculate new salaries, to populate column I. All those in the Sales Department are getting a pay rise of £200, all other departments are only going to receive £100. You are to use the IF( ) function to do the calculation.

     For example to calculate I6, IF the value in D6 is "Sales" THEN E6 add £200, OTHERWISE E6 add £100).

3.   Once you are happy with the formula in cell I6, copy the formula to cells I7 through to I12.

4.   Format the new salary data (column I), so that each value displays with the 1000 separator (,) and no decimal places.

5.   Create another column in column J, with **Name** in cell J4, and **Award** in cell J5 (make sure they are bold and underlined).

6.   Enter a formula in cell J6 to combine the surname from cell A6, and the award (yes/no) from cell H6, separated by a comma.

7.   Once you are happy with the formula in cell J6, copy the formula to cells J7 through to J12.

8.   Widen column J so all text fits within the column.

9.   Save the workbook with the name **T4Exercise2**.

Your spreadsheet should appear as shown on the next page.

	A	B	C	D	E	H	I	J
1	Employee records			Date	03/03/2016			
2								
3	*Award date*	01/01/2005						
4						Service	New	Name
5	**Surname**	**Birth Date**	**Start Date**	**Department**	**Salary**	**Award**	**Salary**	**Award**
6	Johal	02/03/1975	01/06/2000	Sales	20,000	yes	20,200	Johal,yes
7	Jones	14/10/1963	01/07/2001	HR	16,000	yes	16,100	Jones,yes
8	Wakula	03/09/1978	01/07/2002	Sales	20,000	yes	20,200	Wakula,yes
9	White	30/06/1967	03/01/2009	Accounts	15,000	no	15,100	White,no
10	Hacek	24/05/1970	01/07/2010	Accounts	18,000	no	18,100	Hacek,no
11	Bhopal	12/02/1978	01/07/2010	Sales	20,500	no	20,700	Bhopal,no
12	Plant	19/03/1976	01/09/2010	Sales	21,500	no	21,700	Plant,no

The image below shows the formulas behind the calculations:

	A	B	C	D	E	H	I	J
1	Employee re			Date	=TODAY()			
2								
3	*Award date*	38353						
4						Service	New	Name
5	**Surname**	**Birth Date**	**Start Date**	**Department**	**Salary**	**Award**	**Salary**	**Award**
6	Johal	27455	36678	Sales	20000	=IF(C6<$B$3,"yes","no")	=IF(D6="sales",E6+200,E6+100)	=CONCATENATE(A6,",",H6)
7	Jones	23298	37073	HR	16000	=IF(C7<$B$3,"yes","no")	=IF(D7="sales",E7+200,E7+100)	=CONCATENATE(A7,",",H7)
8	Wakula	28736	37438	Sales	20000	=IF(C8<$B$3,"yes","no")	=IF(D8="sales",E8+200,E8+100)	=CONCATENATE(A8,",",H8)
9	White	24653	39816	Accounts	15000	=IF(C9<$B$3,"yes","no")	=IF(D9="sales",E9+200,E9+100)	=CONCATENATE(A9,",",H9)
10	Hacek	25712	40360	Accounts	18000	=IF(C10<$B$3,"yes","no")	=IF(D10="sales",E10+200,E10+100)	=CONCATENATE(A10,",",H10)
11	Bhopal	28533	40360	Sales	20500	=IF(C11<$B$3,"yes","no")	=IF(D11="sales",E11+200,E11+100)	=CONCATENATE(A11,",",H11)
12	Plant	27838	40422	Sales	21500	=IF(C12<$B$3,"yes","no")	=IF(D12="sales",E12+200,E12+100)	=CONCATENATE(A12,",",H12)

You have now completed the second exercise.

Exercise 3 – using VLOOKUP

In this next exercise we are going to use the VLOOKUP function. We are again going to make use of an existing spreadsheet.

To access this spreadsheet visit www.osbornebooks.co.uk ('Products and Resources') to download the spreadsheet **T4inventory**.

Stage 1

This stage uses VLOOKUP with a previously created workbook.

Note: if you enter the formula and the cell displays #N/A this means that the value you are trying to find does not exist in the data range through which you are searching – check the formula thoroughly.

1.   Download the workbook **T4inventory**.

2.   Open the downloaded file, save the workbook with new name **T4Exercise3**.

The workbook should appear as shown below.

	A	B	C	D
1	Warehouse information			
2				
3				
4	Code	Bin	Price	
5	ab1	1	£2.00	
6	ab2	2	£30.00	
7	ab3	1	£27.00	
8	ab4	1	£14.00	
9	ab5	3	£21.00	
10	ab6	4	£12.00	
11	ab7	1	£7.00	
12	ab8	2	£24.00	

3.   Use the scroll bars to move up and down the data. You can see that it gets harder to pick out individual items once we start to work with more data. Return to the top of the data.

4.   Insert a row between rows 2 and 3.

5.   In cell A3, enter **Product?**, cell C3 enter **Bin**, E3 enter **Price**.

6.   In Cell B3 enter **fr4**.

7.   In cell D3 enter the formula to lookup the Bin number from the data below, for the product code specified in cell B3.
      (Use VLOOKUP on cell B3, specifying the lookup range to include codes and bin data only.)

8. In cell F3 enter the formula to lookup the price from the data below, for the product code in cell B3. (Use VLOOKUP on cell B3, specifying the lookup range to include codes, bin and price data only.)

9. Format cell F3 to display **Currency (£ pounds** and pence (ie 2 decimal places)).

10. Save the workbook with the name **T4Exercise3**.

The workbook should appear as shown below.

	A	B	C	D	E	F
1	Warehouse information					
2						
3	Product?	fr4	Bin		4 Price	£7.00
4						
5	Code	Bin	Price			
6	ab1		1	£2.00		
7	ab2		2	£30.00		
8	ab3		1	£27.00		
9	ab4		1	£14.00		
10	ab5		3	£21.00		
11	ab6		4	£12.00		

The formulas are shown in the image below.

	A	B	C	D	E	F
1	Warehc					
2						
3	Product?	fr4	Bin	=VLOOKUP(B3,A6:B51,2,FALSE)	Price	=VLOOKUP(B3,A6:C51,3,FALSE)
4						
5	Code	Bin	Price			
6	ab1	1	2			
7	ab2	2	30			
8	ab3	1	27			
9	ab4	1	14			
10	ab5	3	21			
11	ab6	4	12			

Stage 2

We will now make some small modifications to the spreadsheet.

1. Insert 2 rows between row 4 and row 5.

2. In cell A5, enter **Product2?**, cell C5 enter **Bin2**, E5 enter **Price2**.

3. In Cell B5 enter **ab1**.

4. In cell D5 enter the formula to lookup the Bin number from the data below, for the product code specified in cell B5.

    (Use VLOOKUP on cell B5, specifying the lookup range to include codes and bin data only).

5. In cell F5 enter the formula to lookup the price from the data below, for the product code in cell B5.

    (Use VLOOKUP on cell B5, specifying the lookup range to include codes, bin and price data only.)

6. Format cell F5 to display **Currency (£ pounds)**.

7. Modify the first product code to be looked up in B3, change this to be code dd4.

8. Move to cell A1.

9. Save the workbook with the name **T4Exercise3**. The workbook should appear as shown below.

	A	B	C	D	E	F
1	Warehouse information					
2						
3	Product?	dd4	Bin		10	Price	£19.00
4						
5	Product2?	ab1	Bin2		1	Price2	£2.00
6						
7	Code	Bin	Price			
8	ab1		1	£2.00			
9	ab2		2	£30.00			
10	ab3		1	£27.00			
11	ab4		1	£14.00			
12	ab5		3	£21.00			
13	ab6		4	£12.00			

The formulas are shown in the image below.

	A	B	C	D	E	F
1	Wareho					
2						
3	Product?	dd4	Bin	=VLOOKUP(B3,A8:B53,2,FALSE)	Price	=VLOOKUP(B3,A8:C53,3,FALSE)
4						
5	Product2?	ab1	Bin2	=VLOOKUP(B5,A8:B53,2,FALSE)	Price2	=VLOOKUP(B5,A8:C53,3,FALSE)
6						

Exercise 4 – using HLOOKUP

In this next exercise we are going to use the HLOOKUP function. We are going to create the currency spreadsheet used in the text to illustrate HLOOKUP.

Note: if you enter the formula and the cell displays #N/A this means that the value you are trying to find does not exist in the data range through which you are searching – check the formula thoroughly.

Stage 1

1.   Open a new workbook.

2.   Name sheet1 **Exchange**

3.   On worksheet **Exchange**, enter **Exchange rates** in cell A1.

4.   In cell D1 enter the formula to display today's date.

5.   Starting in cell A3, enter the information shown in the table below:

Country	JP	FR	AU	TH	CN	DK
Exch rate	158.46	1.29	1.96	49.9	9.18	9.61
Currency	Yen	€	$	Baht	Yuan	Krone
Full name	Japan	France	Australia	Thailand	China	Denmark

Note: The euro symbol (€) can be found using the **INSERT** menu, **Symbol** and selecting from the symbols displayed.

6.   Add borders to each cell.

7.   Save your workbook as **T4Exercise4.**

The workbook should appear as shown below. (Cell D1 will show the current date.)

▲	A	B	C	D	E	F	G	H
1	Exchange rates			07/03/2016				
2								
3	Country	JP	FR	AU	TH	CN	DK	
4	Exch rate	158.46	1.29	1.96	49.9	9.18	9.61	
5	Currency	Yen	€	$	Baht	Yuan	Krone	
6	Full name	Japan	France	Australia	Thailand	China	Denmark	

Stage 2

We are now going to add the lookup option, using HLOOKUP.

1.   Insert three rows above row 3

2.   Enter **Country, Exch Rate, Currency** in cells C3, D3, E3 respectively.

3.   Make them bold and underlined.

4.   Select cells B6 to G6 and **name** this range **Countries**.

5.   In cell C4 set Data Validation, using a list with acceptable values range **Countries**.

6.   In cell C4, select country **FR** from the list.

7.   In cell D4, enter the HLOOKUP formula to lookup the **exchange rate** for the **country** in cell C4 using the data in rows 6 to 9.

8.   In cell E4, enter the HLOOKUP formula to lookup the **currency** for the country in cell C4 again using the data in rows 6 to 9.

9.   Save your workbook.

The workbook should appear as shown below.

	A	B	C	D	E	F	G
1	Exchange rates			07/03/2016			
2							
3			Country	Exch Rate	Currency		
4			FR	1.29	€		
5							
6	Country	JP	FR	AU	TH	CN	DK
7	Exch rate	158.46	1.29	1.96	49.9	9.18	9.61
8	Currency	Yen	€	$	Baht	Yuan	Krone
9	Full name	Japan	France	Australia	Thailand	China	Denmark

D4 = HLOOKUP(C4,B6:G9,2,FALSE)

Stage 3

We are now going to take this one stage further to create an exchange currency calculator, making changes to the layout, and introducing new formulas.

1. Move the contents of cell C3 and C4 to A3 and A4 respectively.

2. Move the contents of cell D3 and D4 to G3 and G4 respectively.

3. In cells B3 enter **Amount** and C3 enter **Receive**, make them bold and underlined.

4. Enter 100 in cell B4, and name this cell **Amount.**

5. Move the contents of cell E3 and E4 to D3 and D4 respectively.

6. In cell C4 we are going to use the exchange rate to calculate what we would receive, enter the formula to take the **Amount** (cell B4) and multiply by the exchange rate (G4).

7. Select country **TH** in cell A4, see how everything changes.

8. Enter **220** for the amount in cell B4.

Save your workbook.

	A	B	C	D	E	F	G
1	Exchange rates			07/03/2016			
2							
3	Country	Amount	Receive	Currency			Exch Rate
4	TH	220	10978	Baht			49.9
5							
6	Country	JP	FR	AU	TH	CN	DK
7	Exch rate	158.46	1.29	1.96	49.9	9.18	9.61
8	Currency	Yen	€	$	Baht	Yuan	Krone
9	Full name	Japan	France	Australia	Thailand	China	Denmark

5 Sorting, checking and importing data

this chapter covers...

This chapter covers the tools which are regularly available within spreadsheet packages, and shows how you can move data between spreadsheets and other documents. It explains and takes you through the concepts and techniques listed below. By the time you have finished this chapter and carried out the exercises which follow, you should be able to organise your spreadsheet to include subtotals, and be able to transfer information between spreadsheets and other software packages.

The concepts and techniques covered are:

- *formula validation*
- *spell check*
- *find and replace*
- *sorting and filtering data*
- *introducing subtotals*
- *linking, embedding and screenshots*
- *importing and exporting data*

Note that the step-by-step instructions given in this chapter are based on the Microsoft® Excel model, but the concepts and techniques described relate to all spreadsheet packages.

FORMULA AUDITING

We have explained formulas and how to create them earlier in this book. We are now going to explain some of the ways of checking that the formulas we have entered are doing what we expect them to do. The methods which we are going to cover are:

- show formulas
- error checking
- circular references
- trace precedents
- trace dependents

show formulas

This is a simple visual method, where formulas are displayed within the sheet. The example below shows the worksheet displayed in the normal way:

	A	B	C	D	E
1	Bank transactions				
2					
3	Opening balance	£1,500.00			
4	Closing balance	£1,289.05			**Down
5					
6	Date	Debit	Credit	Balance	
7	02/04/2016	95.34	0.00	1,404.66	
8	11/04/2016	0.00	25.50	1,430.16	
9	15/04/2016	0.00	34.78	1,464.94	
10	22/04/2016	67.90	0.00	1,397.04	
11	28/04/2016	107.99	0.00	1,289.05	
12	Totals	271.23	60.28		1,289.05

We then select **Show Formulas** from the FORMULAS menu and the way in which the cells display changes is shown below:

	A	B	C	D	E
1	Bank transactions				
2					
3	Opening balance	1500			
4	Closing balance	=D11			=IF(B4<B3,"**Down","")
5					
6	Date	Debit	Credit	Balance	
7	42462	95.34	0	=B3-B7+C7	
8	42471	0	25.5	=D7-B8+C8	
9	42475	0	34.78	=D8-B9+C9	
10	42482	67.9	0	=D9-B10+C10	
11	42488	107.99	0	=D10-B11+C11	
12	Totals	=SUM(B7:B11)	=SUM(C7:C11)		=B3-B12+C12

In the screen at the bottom of the previous page are displayed the actual data or formulas contained in each cell.

In column A where we have dates, for example, what we now see is the serial number representation of the date (as described previously). Similarly column D shows the mathematical formulas used to calculate the running balance of the bank account.

In a relatively small worksheet, or a particular section of a larger worksheet, it is easy to check that the formulas that have been entered are correct by using the **Show Formulas** option.

It is possible to print the worksheet in this form using the normal print options.

To revert to the normal display we select **Show Formulas** again from the Formulas menu bar and select the appropriate command.

As mentioned, this is a fairly basic way of checking formulas. There is a more automated way using a facility called **error checking**, which is available in most spreadsheet packages.

error checking

The **error checking** facility checks for common errors which occur in formulas. These include:

- formulas that result in an error, such as dividing by zero
- numbers formatted as text, or preceded by an apostrophe (')
- formulas inconsistent with other formulas near them
- formulas which omit cells which are near others which have been included in the formula (eg a range of cells)
- cells containing circular references

Any cells where the formula is in error are flagged with a small green triangle in the upper-left corner of the cell.

In the same way that we can have our word processing package checking for errors as we type, it is possible to set the spreadsheet package options, so that our formulas are checked as we enter them; this is known as **automatic error checking**. Alternatively, we can use the **error checking facility** at any time to check through the whole worksheet.

If we take the Bank transactions spreadsheet shown on the previous page we can modify the formula in cell D9:

from	**=D8-B9+C9**
to	**=D8-B10+C9**

You can see in the image below, that when we have automatic checking on, we get a small triangle in the upper left of the cell D9, indicating a formula error.

	A	B	C	D	E
1	Bank transactions				
2					
3	Opening balance	£1,500.00			
4	Closing balance	£1,221.15			**Down
5					
6	Date	Debit	Credit	Balance	
7	02/04/2016	95.34	0.00	1,404.66	
8	11/04/2016	0.00	25.50	1,430.16	
9	15/04/2016	0.00	34.78	1,397.04	
10	22/04/2016	67.90	0.00	1,329.14	
11	28/04/2016	107.99	0.00	1,221.15	
12	Totals	271.23	60.28		1,289.05

If we then select cell D9 we get an exclamation icon and a description of the error – 'Inconsistent Formula' – which tells us that this formula does not match the pattern of the formulas above and below (or to either side in the same row.) Here cell D9 is inconsistent with the formulas in Column D.

	A	B	C	D	E	F
1	Bank transactions					
2						
3	Opening balance	£1,500.00				
4	Closing balance	£1,221.15			**Down	
5						
6	Date	Debit	Credit	Balance		
7	02/04/2016	95.34	0.00	1,404.66		
8	11/04/2016	0.00	25.50	1,430.16		
9	15/04/2016	0.00	! ▾	1,397.04		
10	22/04/2016	67.90		Inconsistent Formula		
11	28/04/2016	107.99		Copy Formula from Above		
12	Totals	271.23		Help on this error		
13						
14				Ignore Error		
15				Edit in Formula Bar		
16				Error Checking Options...		
17						

To set your choices for error checking:

Either

- Select **Options** from the File menu
- Select **Formulas**

Or, if you have an error, as shown in the example above

■ Select Checking Options from the drop down menu shown by clicking the ! (exclamation mark)

Then

■ Either check or uncheck **Enable background error checking** as required

■ Check or uncheck the **Rules** to configure as you require

Note that if the formula is actually what we want we can instruct the error check to **ignore the error**.

To perform a full worksheet error check:

■ Select **Error check** (or its equivalent) from the menu

The rules will be applied as set up in the Options described on the previous page, and any cells with a formula error will be flagged as shown on the previous page.

circular references

As mentioned previously, this occurs when a cell's formula contains a reference to itself. The **Error Checking** menu displays a drop down list and one of the items in the list is **Circular References**. Clicking this item will cause a list of those cells containing circular references to be displayed. If you click on any of the cells in the list, the cursor will move to that cell and you can edit the formula. When all circular references have been resolved, the list will be empty.

trace precedents

The **Trace Precedents** facility allows you to identify those cells which affect the value of the currently selected cell.

For example, if cell D4 contained the formula

   =A3 + B3

both A3 and B3 would be **precedents** of D4, since they both affect the value of D4.

If we take the Bank transactions worksheet illustrated on the last few pages as an example, if we select cell E12, which holds the formula

   =B3-B12+C12

and then select **Trace Precedents** from the formulas menu, we can see the result as shown on the next page.

◢	A	B	C	D	E
1	Bank transactions				
2					
3	Opening balance	£1,500.00			
4	Closing balance	£1,289.05			**Down
5					
6	Date	Debit	Credit	Balance	
7	02/04/2016	95.34	0.00	1,404.66	
8	11/04/2016	0.00	25.50	1,430.16	
9	15/04/2016	0.00	34.78	1,464.94	
10	22/04/2016	67.90	0.00	1,397.04	
11	28/04/2016	107.99	0.00	1,289.05	
12	Totals	271.23	60.28		1,289.05

From this image you can see that the arrows indicate that cells B3, B12 and C12 all affect (ie are precedents of) the value E12.

If we were to select **Trace Precedents** for a second time without moving from the selected cell, we would see the cells which are precedents for B3, B12 and C12 are added to the picture, as shown below.

E12	▼	⋮	✕ ✓ *fx*	=B3-B12+C12	

◢	A	B	C	D	E
1	Bank transactions				
2					
3	Opening balance	£1,500.00			
4	Closing balance	£1,289.05			**Down
5					
6	Date	Debit	Credit	Balance	
7	02/04/2016	95.34	0.00	1,404.66	
8	11/04/2016	0.00	25.50	1,430.16	
9	15/04/2016	0.00	34.78	1,464.94	
10	22/04/2016	67.90	0.00	1,397.04	
11	28/04/2016	107.99	0.00	1,289.05	
12	Totals	271.23	60.28		1,289.05

The arrows show that B12 utilises the cells B7 through to B11, and similarly C12 utilises the cells C7 through to C11.

This **Trace Precedents** tool is very useful for checking formulas, especially on more complex sheets.

To Trace Precedents for a particular cell:

- Select the required cell
- Select **Trace Precedents** from the menu bar (usually in the formulas section)
- Repeat as required

To remove the arrows generated:

■ Select **Remove Arrows** from the menu bar

trace dependents

The **Trace Dependents** facility allows you to identify those cells which are affected by the value of the currently selected cell.

For example if cell D4 contained the formula

$$=22+F4/20$$

D4 would be a **dependent** of F4, because its value is dependent on the value of F4.

If we return to the Bank transactions worksheet again and select cell B3, the Opening balance value, and then select **Trace Dependents**, the screen will appear as follows:

	A	B	C	D	E
1	Bank transactions				
2					
3	Opening balance	£1,500.00			
4	Closing balance	£1,289.05			Down
5					
6	Date	Debit	Credit	Balance	
7	02/04/2016	95.34	0.00	1,404.66	
8	11/04/2016	0.00	25.50	1,430.16	
9	15/04/2016	0.00	34.78	1,464.94	
10	22/04/2016	67.90	0.00	1,397.04	
11	28/04/2016	107.99	0.00	1,289.05	
12	Totals	271.23	60.28		1,289.05
13					

From this image you can see that the arrows indicate that cell B3 is used in formulas in cells E4, D7 and E12, showing that cells E4, D7, E12 are all **dependent** on B3.

If we were to select **Trace Dependents** for a second time without moving from the selected cell, we would then see any cells affected by E4, D7 and E12 added to the picture, as shown on the next page:

⬢	A	B	C	D	E
1	Bank transactions				
2					
3	Opening balance	£1,500.00			
4	Closing balance	£1,289.05			⬅Down
5					
6	Date	Debit	Credit	Balance	
7	02/04/2016	95.34	0.00	2,404.66	
8	11/04/2016	0.00	25.50	1,430.16	
9	15/04/2016	0.00	34.78	1,464.94	
10	22/04/2016	67.90	0.00	1,397.04	
11	28/04/2016	107.99	0.00	1,289.05	
12	Totals	271.23	60.28		1,289.05
13					

On this screen only cell D8 is affected by these cells, since it is dependent on D7, so we see one additional small arrow, showing this dependency.

To Trace Dependents for a particular cell:

■ Select the required cell

■ Select **Trace Dependents** from the menu bar (usually in the formulas section)

■ Repeat as required

To remove the arrows generated:

■ Select **Remove Arrows** from the menu bar

SPELL CHECK

Spreadsheet packages usually provide built-in **Spell checking** tools to check the text in your worksheets.

For our example, we will use a modified version of our expenditure forecast worksheet, which now contains several typing mistakes. This is illustrated on the next page:

A1	▾	⋮	✕	✓	fx	Expenditure forecsat		

▲	A	B	C	D	E	F	G	H
1	Expenditure forecsat							
2								
3								
4		January	February	March	April	May	June	Average
5	Salaries	£80,000	£80,000	£80,000	£90,000	£90,000	£90,000	£85,000
6	Insurance	£1,000	£500	£0	£0	£0	£500	£333
7	Accountanci	£270	£0	£270	£0	£270	£0	£135
8	Advertising	£0	£1,500	£0	£0	£0	£1,800	£550
9	Psotage	£95	£190	£95	£80	£95	£150	£118
10	Rent	£3,500	£3,500	£3,500	£3,500	£3,500	£3,500	£3,500
11	Stationery	£57	£90	£0	£90	£0	£90	£55
12	Totals	£84,922	£85,780	£83,865	£93,670	£93,865	£96,040	

If we select **Spelling** from the Review menu, the first text to be identified will be in cell A1, where we have spelt forecast incorrectly:

Spelling: English (United Kingdom)	? ✕
Not in Dictionary:	
forecsat	Ignore Once
	Ignore All
	Add to Dictionary
Suggestions:	
forecast	Change
	Change All
	AutoCorrect
Dictionary language: English (United Kingdom)	
Options...	Undo Last Cancel

Once identified, you can choose how you want to proceed from the options given, as shown above. The tool can step through and check the spelling in all cells on the worksheet.

Within the spellcheck tool options, you can choose rules which you want to apply when performing a spell check – for example, to ignore words that are all uppercase.

To set your rule choices for Spell check:

■ Select **Options** from the appropriate menu

■ Select **Proofing**

■ Check or uncheck the rules to configure as you require

You can request **Spell check** on just one cell or a **group of cells**.

To perform Spell check on a cell or group of cells:

■ Select the required cell(s)

■ Select **Spelling** from the menu

The rules will be applied as set up in the Options/Proofing described above, and any cells with a spelling error will be highlighted and suggestions for revised spellings offered.

To perform a full worksheet Spell check:

■ Select **Spelling** from the menu

■ Confirm that you wish to check the whole sheet

FIND AND REPLACE

find

Another powerful facility is the **Find** tool which can be used to find a specific value or text within the worksheet.

To use **Find**, select the **Find and Select** icon, select **Find** from the menu. As shown in the screen below, you then specify:

Find what – this will be the value or text which is to be found (known as the **search string**):

If you chose **Find All**, all occurrences will be displayed together with their cell references allowing you to move to any one of them.

Find Next will find the first occurrence of the search string. You then click **Find Next** again to find the next one, and so on until there are no more to be found.

replace

The **Replace** tool enables you to find and replace specific text or values. To use this tool, select **Replace** from the **Find and Select** menu.

As you can see in the image below, you specify the value or text you want to find, and then the value or text which you want to replace it with (known as the **replacement string**):

Find and Replace	?	✕

Find **Replace**

Find what: sometext

Replace with: new text

Options >>

Replace All   Replace   Find All   Find Next   Close

If you chose **Replace All**, all occurrences of the **search string** will automatically be replaced with the **replacement string**.

Sometimes, you may only want to replace certain occurrences of the search string, in which case, you would select **Find Next**, until you find one which you want to change, and then you select **Replace** and then **Find Next** again until you have made all the changes you require.

Look at the Work bookings example sheet below.

	A	B	C	D	E	F
1	Work bookings					
2						
3	Hourly rate	£20				
4						
5	Client	Week1	Week2	Week3	Week4	Client Total
6	Smiths Ltd	15	5	15	6	41
7	Jones and Partner	12	8	10	6	36
8	Redwoods	13	20	11	6	50

We could use **Find and Replace** to change the column titles from Week1, Week2 etc to be Month1, Month2 and so on. To do this:

- Select **Find and Replace** from the menu

- Find what – enter **Week**

- Replace with – enter **Month**

- Click **Replace All**

This is shown in the image below.

A message will be displayed indicating how many occurrences of the search string have been found and changed.

You can see the results in the screen below.

SORTING DATA

If we look at worksheet Weekly Pay data shown in the image below, we can see that the employee names are not in alphabetical order.

	A	B	C	D	E	F
1	Weekly Pay data					
2						
3	Std weekly hours	38				
4	Hourly Rate	£8.60				
5	Overtime Rate	£10.75				
6						
7	Employee	Hours worked	Overtime hours	Basic pay	Overtime pay	Total pay
8	Johal	40	2	£326.80	£21.50	£348.30
9	Bhopal	49	11	£326.80	£118.25	£445.05
10	Wakula	50	12	£326.80	£129.00	£455.80
11	Hacek	38	0	£326.80	£0.00	£326.80
12	Young	39.5	1.5	£326.80	£16.13	£342.93
13	White	52	14	£326.80	£150.50	£477.30
14	Jones	38	0	£326.80	£0.00	£326.80
15	Plant	39.5	1.5	£326.80	£16.13	£342.93

Alphabetical sorting is very simple, using a built-in **sort tool**, which allows us to sort data alphabetically A to Z, or reversely Z to A. Numeric data, can also be sorted in ascending or descending order.

When we are doing a sort we have to identify and select the data which is to be sorted. It is very important that we include any associated data in the nearby columns within our selection.

In the example above, because the data in the hours and pay columns is specific to the individual employee, if we change the order of the employees, we must also change the order of the other data in the same way. This will happen automatically if we include the associated columns in our selection, before we select sort.

In the image on the next page, the data in all six columns is selected, from row 8 downwards.

	A	B	C	D	E	F
1	Weekly Pay data					
2						
3	Std weekly hours	38				
4	Hourly Rate	£8.60				
5	Overtime Rate	£10.75				
6						
7	Employee	Hours worked	Overtime hours	Basic pay	Overtime pay	Total pay
8	Johal	40	2	£326.80	£21.50	£348.30
9	Bhopal	49	11	£326.80	£118.25	£445.05
10	Wakula	50	12	£326.80	£129.00	£455.80
11	Hacek	38	0	£326.80	£0.00	£326.80
12	Young	39.5	1.5	£326.80	£16.13	£342.93
13	White	52	14	£326.80	£150.50	£477.30
14	Jones	38	0	£326.80	£0.00	£326.80
15	Plant	39.5	1.5	£326.80	£16.13	£342.93

We then select **Sort and Filter** from the Home menu, choose Sort A to Z to order alphabetically A to Z and get the results below.

	A	B	C	D	E	F
1	Weekly Pay data					
2						
3	Std weekly hours	38				
4	Hourly Rate	£8.60				
5	Overtime Rate	£10.75				
6						
7	Employee	Hours worked	Overtime hours	Basic pay	Overtime pay	Total pay
8	Bhopal	49	11	£326.80	£118.25	£445.05
9	Hacek	38	0	£326.80	£0.00	£326.80
10	Johal	40	2	£326.80	£21.50	£348.30
11	Jones	38	0	£326.80	£0.00	£326.80
12	Plant	39.5	1.5	£326.80	£16.13	£342.93
13	Wakula	50	12	£326.80	£129.00	£455.80
14	White	52	14	£326.80	£150.50	£477.30
15	Young	39.5	1.5	£326.80	£16.13	£342.93

The selected data has been sorted by the first column on the left – Employee, and you can see that all the data has moved with the individual employee name and remains correct.

The data will always be sorted by the first column on the left, unless you use **Custom Sort**, and specifically choose a different column. SORT is also available from the Data menu, this leads directly into a Custom Sort.

When doing a **sort** to a column containing text, we could choose reverse order Z to A if required.

Columns containing numbers can be sorted in **Ascending** (increasing) or **Descending** (decreasing) order.

Our headings in row 5 are recognised as column headings or names, so when we select **Custom Sort**, these column names are displayed for us to choose from, as shown below. (The **My data has headers** box is checked to indicate this.)

Within Custom Sort, you can chose the column to sort by.

What you want to sort on.

And the order you want to sort by.

If we had chosen to sort by Total pay, a numeric column, we can then select order Smallest to Largest, or Largest to Smallest, as shown on the next page.

We would have the rows of data sorted as shown below.

	A	B	C	D	E	F
1	Weekly Pay data					
2						
3	Std weekly hours	38				
4	Hourly Rate	£8.60				
5	Overtime Rate	£10.75				
6						
7	Employee	Hours worked	Overtime hours	Basic pay	Overtime pay	Total pay
8	White	52	14	£326.80	£150.50	£477.30
9	Wakula	50	12	£326.80	£129.00	£455.80
10	Bhopal	49	11	£326.80	£118.25	£445.05
11	Johal	40	2	£326.80	£21.50	£348.30
12	Plant	39.5	1.5	£326.80	£16.13	£342.93
13	Young	39.5	1.5	£326.80	£16.13	£342.93
14	Hacek	38	0	£326.80	£0.00	£326.80
15	Jones	38	0	£326.80	£0.00	£326.80

As we have two rows with the same total pay, we might want to sort rows with the same value by another level, for example employee name. To do this, in custom sort we would add a level, and specify the column, sort on and the order, as shown in the example on the next page.

Sort						? ✕
⁺ᴬ⌄ **Add Level**	✕ **Delete Level**	🗅 **Copy Level**	▲ ▼	**Options...**		☑ My data has **headers**

Column		Sort On		Order	
Sort by	Total pay ⌄	Values ⌄		Largest to Smallest	⌄
Then by	⌄	Values ⌄		A to Z	⌄

			OK	Cancel

Selecting as shown below.

Sort						? ✕
⁺ᴬ⌄ **Add Level**	✕ **Delete Level**	🗅 **Copy Level**	▲ ▼	**Options...**		☑ My data has **headers**

Column		Sort On		Order	
Sort by	Total pay ⌄	Values ⌄		Largest to Smallest	⌄
Then by	Employee ⌄	Values ⌄		Z to A	⌄

			OK	Cancel

Would give the data sorted as follows:

	A	B	C	D	E	F
1	**Weekly Pay data**					
2						
3	Std weekly hours	38				
4	Hourly Rate	£8.60				
5	Overtime Rate	£10.75				
6						
7	**Employee**	**Hours worked**	**Overtime hours**	**Basic pay**	**Overtime pay**	**Total pay**
8	White	52	14	£326.80	£150.50	£477.30
9	Wakula	50	12	£326.80	£129.00	£455.80
10	Bhopal	49	11	£326.80	£118.25	£445.05
11	Johal	40	2	£326.80	£21.50	£348.30
12	Young	39.5	1.5	£326.80	£16.13	£342.93
13	Plant	39.5	1.5	£326.80	£16.13	£342.93
14	Jones	38	0	£326.80	£0.00	£326.80
15	Hacek	38	0	£326.80	£0.00	£326.80

Employees Young and Plant have the same total pay. Young now appears above Plant since we have ordered by Total pay, and then by Employees name, going from Z to A.

To remove a level within the custom sort:

■ Select the sort level to be deleted

■ Click **Delete Level**

In summary, to sort data:

■ **Select** the data which we want to sort (including any associated data)

■ Select **Sort and Filter** from the menu

Either

■ Choose **Sort** (A to Z, Z to A, Ascending or Descending) as appropriate

Or

■ Select Custom sort and make your choices, as described above

filter

If you have a spreadsheet containing a large amount of data as in the example below (which shows sales by month), the **Filter** facility allows you to filter the data so that you only see rows which contain certain values or combinations of values. For example, **Filter** could show just those rows where Region=North West or a combination such as Region=North West and Manufacturer=Ford (see illustration below).

	A	B	C	D	E
1	Year	Month	Manufacturer	Region	Quantity
2	2016	Jan	Mercedes	South West	220
3	2016	Mar	BMW	North West	155
4	2016	Feb	Toyota	North West	35
5	2016	Jun	VW	South	125
6	2016	Jul	Ford	East	126
7	2016	Jul	Skoda	East	1,345
8	2016	Apr	VW	South West	56
9	2016	Aug	Mercedes	South	68
10	2016	Aug	Toyota	South	100
11	2015	Feb	Ford	South	1,500
12	2015	Feb	Seat	East	220
13	2015	Mar	Seat	South West	155
14	2015	Apr	VW	North West	35
15	2015	Mar	Mercedes	North West	125
16	2015	Jan	Skoda	South	1,260
17	2015	Mar	Toyota	East	45
18	2015	Jul	VW	South West	56
19	2015	Feb	Ford	South West	68

To **Filter** data:

- Place the cursor in the cell containing the leftmost heading text

- Select **Filter** from the **Sort and Filter** menu.

You will see something similar to the image below.

	A	B	C	D	E
1	Year	Month	Manufacturer	Region	Quantit
2	2016	Jan	Mercedes	South West	220
3	2016	Mar	BMW	North West	155
4	2016	Feb	Toyota	North West	35
5	2016	Jun	VW	South	125
6	2016	Jul	Ford	East	126
7	2016	Jul	Skoda	East	1,345
8	2016	Apr	VW	South West	56
9	2016	Aug	Mercedes	South	68
10	2016	Aug	Toyota	South	100
11	2015	Feb	Ford	South	1,500
12	2015	Feb	Seat	East	220
13	2015	Mar	Seat	South West	155

You can now choose how you want to filter the data:

- Click on the drop down arrow on a column

- Select the required values which you wish to analyse from the drop down menu

- Repeat on other columns as required to refine the rows displayed

In the image below, you can see the rows which would be displayed when a filter of Region=North West is applied to the sales data. The funnel symbol next to Region indicates that a filter has been applied to that column.

	A	B	C	D	E
1	Year	Month	Manufacturer	Region	Quantit
3	2016	Mar	BMW	North West	155
4	2016	Feb	Toyota	North West	35
14	2015	Apr	VW	North West	35
15	2015	Mar	Mercedes	North West	125
25	2014	Apr	Ford	North West	56
26	2014	Nov	Seat	North West	125
33	2015	Dec	Ford	North West	34
35	2015	Dec	VW	North West	1,500
36	2015	Nov	Mercedes	North West	220

If we applied a further filter to the Manufacturer, looking only for Ford, we would get only those rows displayed where Region=North West and Manufacturer=Ford, as can be seen on the next page:

⊿	A	B	C	D	E
1	Year ▾	Month ▾	Manufacturer ⊤	Region ⊤	Quanti ▾
25	2014	Apr	Ford	North West	56
33	2015	Dec	Ford	North West	34

When filtering is active, to **Turn off** the active filter on a column:

■ click on the Filter symbol on the column

■ select clear filters

To **Remove all Filters**:

■ select **Filter** from the **Sort and Filter** menu

(The filter icon will be highlighted in the menu, showing filtering is active.)

SUB TOTALS

There are usually facilities within the spreadsheet package to calculate subtotals or totals for sections of data within your worksheet.

For example, if we look at the car sales worksheet, we might want to total the sales for each manufacturer.

The first step is to order/sort the data, so that it is arranged by the column for which we want subtotals. For example, if we want subtotals by manufacturer we will sort the data by that column, if we want subtotals by Region, we would sort the data by that column.

⊿	A	B	C	D	E
1	Year	Month	Manufacturer	Region	Quantity
2	2016	Mar	BMW	North West	155
3	2014	Sep	BMW	East	1,460
4	2014	Sep	BMW	South West	34
5	2015	Oct	BMW	South West	68
6	2015	Nov	BMW	East	56
7	2015	Oct	BMW	South West	35
8	2015	Dec	BMW	South West	125
9	2016	Jul	Ford	East	126
10	2015	Feb	Ford	South	1,500
11	2015	Feb	Ford	South West	68
12	2014	Apr	Ford	North West	56
13	2015	Dec	Ford	North West	34
14	2016	Jan	Mercedes	South West	220
15	2016	Aug	Mercedes	South	68
16	2015	Mar	Mercedes	North West	125
17	2014	Dec	Mercedes	South West	56

Let us assume we want to create **Sub totals** by **manufacturer**, ie we want to know how many cars each manufacturer has sold. We will first sort the data as shown below, using Custom Sort, and selecting the **manufacturer column**. The data is then shown in alphabetical order by **manufacturer**.

The next step is to select all the data including our column headings, and select **Subtotal** from the **Data** menu bar.

The Subtotal options then appear, and we have to make some choices:

1 The first choice is the column for which we need a subtotal.

The default choice is the column on the left – the 'Year' column.

Because we want to create a Subtotal for each manufacturer, we use the 'Manufacturer' column. For **At each change in** we select 'Manufacturer'.

2 The next choice is the **function** we want to use.

We select **SUM**, because we want to total the number of cars sold by each manufacturer.

3   The final choice is the column we are adding up and the column to which we want to add a Subtotal.

We select the Quantity column.

4   You should keep the defaults for the remaining options.

The results are shown in the screen below.

	A	B	C	D	E
1	Year	Month	Manufacturer	Region	Quantity
2	2016	Mar	BMW	North West	155
3	2014	Sep	BMW	East	1,460
4	2014	Sep	BMW	South West	34
5	2015	Oct	BMW	South West	68
6	2015	Nov	BMW	East	56
7	2015	Oct	BMW	South West	35
8	2015	Dec	BMW	South West	125
9			**BMW Total**		1,932
10	2016	Jul	Ford	East	126
11	2015	Feb	Ford	South	1,500
12	2015	Feb	Ford	South West	68
13	2014	Apr	Ford	North West	56
14	2015	Dec	Ford	North West	34
15			**Ford Total**		1,784
16	2016	Jan	Mercedes	South West	220
17	2016	Aug	Mercedes	South	68
18	2015	Mar	Mercedes	North West	125
19	2014	Dec	Mercedes	South West	56
20	2015	Nov	Mercedes	North West	220
21			**Mercedes Total**		689

Looking at the image on the previous page, on the left hand side, you can see minus (-) symbols and lines, these are known as outlines, which allow us to see all the detail rows making up the subtotals.

We can chose to just see the summary of subtotals in outline, either by selecting individual minus (-) symbols on the left or selecting all the data, and then **Hide Detail** from the **DATA** menu, the red minus symbol, (found to the right of the Subtotal option) or by selecting 1, 2, or 3 from the symbols shown on the top left, indicating levels of detail to be displayed. As shown in the image below, you can see that the minus signs are now replaced by plus signs (+).

1 2 3		A	B	C	D	E
	1	Year	Month	Manufacturer	Region	Quantity
+	9			BMW Total		1,932
+	15			Ford Total		1,784
+	21			Mercedes Total		689
+	28			Seat Total		2,185
+	31			Skoda Total		2,605
+	37			Toyota Total		434
+	46			VW Total		4,777
−	47			Grand Total		14,406

If we had wanted Average number of cars sold by each manufacturer, we would have just chosen the **average** function within the subtotal options, as shown below.

Subtotal dialog:

At each change in: Manufacturer

Use function: Average

Sum, Count, Average, Max, Min, Product

☑ Quantity

☑ Replace current subtotals
☐ Page break between groups
☑ Summary below data

Remove All — OK — Cancel

Which would give us the following:

1 2 3		A	B	C	D	E	
	1	Year	Month	Manufacturer	Region	Quantity	
	2	2016	Mar	BMW	North West	155	
	3	2014	Sep	BMW	East	1,460	
	4	2014	Sep	BMW	South West	34	
	5	2015	Oct	BMW	South West	68	
	6	2015	Nov	BMW	East	56	
	7	2015	Oct	BMW	South West	35	
	8	2015	Dec	BMW	South West	125	
	9			**BMW Average**		276	
	10	2016	Jul	Ford	East	126	
	11	2015	Feb	Ford	South	1,500	
	12	2015	Feb	Ford	South West	68	
	13	2014	Apr	Ford	North West	56	
	14	2015	Dec	Ford	North West	34	
	15			**Ford Average**		357	

Alternatively, we could use subtotal to give us the Count, Max or Min for each manufacturer.

As you can see from the screens on the previous page and above, the Subtotal function is extremely useful when we have large amounts of data, and only want to look at a summary.

If you need to revert to full detail, either select individual plus signs (+), or select all the data and then show detail from the menu, or by selecting 3 from the symbols shown on the top left, indicating levels of detail to be displayed.

To remove the subtotals:

■ select **Subtotal** from the Data menu

■ click on **Remove All**

LINKING, EMBEDDING AND SCREENSHOTS

The terms **linking and embedding** – also known as **OLE** (Object Linking and Embedding) – are used to describe a technique where data created by one software package is inserted into a file created by another software package.

For example, we might want to **place data from a spreadsheet into a word processing document**.

There are several ways of doing this:

■ simple **Copy and Paste**

■ **Embedding**

■ **Linking**

copy and paste

Copy and Paste would just put a copy of the spreadsheet data in the word processing document, but if anything changed in the original spreadsheet, the data would not change in the document.

embedding

If we **Embed** the data in the word processing document, it creates a static copy of the spreadsheet data as a table in the word processing document, so if anything changed in the original spreadsheet, the data would not change in the document. This can be useful if you don't want the document to reflect changes in the spreadsheet.

If you select to edit this table of spreadsheet data within the word processing document (usually by DOUBLE CLICK), it will automatically open up the spreadsheet software and display the data ready to be changed.

To insert spreadsheet data as embedded:

Select and copy the data in the original spreadsheet, switch to the word processing package with the document open, select **Paste Special**, and paste as a worksheet object.

linking

If the spreadsheet data were **linked** in the word processing document, then if it changed in the original spreadsheet, it would automatically update in the word processing document the next time the word processing document was opened, or if it were open when the original spreadsheet were changed.

To link data:

First select the data in the original worksheet to copy, switch to the word processing package with a document open, select **Paste Special**, paste as a worksheet object, and select **Paste Link**.

This is an area where you should experiment with your software packages, since detailed key strokes will vary from package to package.

screenshots

There are several ways to create a screenshot:

■ Select Illustrations from the Insert menu

■ Select Screenshot

Either

■ Choose from one of the windows displayed

Or

■ Use the clipping tool to clip the area you want to include

The window or clipped image will be inserted into you spreadsheet.

Alternatively, if you wish to create a screenshot of your spreadsheet to insert into another package:

■ Select the appropriate spreadsheet window

■ Press ALT and PrintScreen buttons together

■ Select the application window where you want to place the screenshot

■ Select PASTE, or press CTRL and V

EXPORT AND IMPORT

In this section we will be looking at the concepts of importing and exporting files.

Historically, if you wanted to move data from one software package to another, and the software packages were produced by different companies, you would take the data out of the first package – **export** – into a text file format, and then load or **import** the data as a text file into the second package.

The need to export and import has greatly reduced as software packages have become more sophisticated; however you may still need to do it.

There are two commonly used text files formats:

■ **Delimited text files** (.txt), in which the TAB character typically separates each field of text.

■ **Comma separated values** text files (.csv), in which the comma character (,) typically separates each field of text.

An example csv file based on part of the car sales spreadsheet is shown below.

```
CarSales.csv ✕

Year,Month,Manufacturer,Region,Quantity,,
2016,Mar,BMW,North West,155,,
2014,Sep,BMW,East,"1,460",,
2014,Sep,BMW,South West,34,,
2015,Oct,BMW,South West,68,,
2015,Nov,BMW,East,56,,
2015,Oct,BMW,South West,35,,
2015,Dec,BMW,South West,125,,
2016,Jul,Ford,East,126,,
2015,Feb,Ford,South,"1,500",,
2015,Feb,Ford,South West,68,,
2014,Apr,Ford,North West,56,,
2015,Dec,Ford,North West,34,,
2016,Jan,Mercedes,South West,220,,
2016,Aug,Mercedes,South,68,,
2015,Mar,Mercedes,North West,125,,
```

You can see each cell of data is separated by a comma, and each row of data is output on a fresh line. The lines with no data, just commas, are our blank lines within the spreadsheet, and are included for consistency.

To export data from a spreadsheet as a text file:

■ Select **Save as** from the File menu

■ From the **Format** or **Save as type** select **Text** (tab delimited), or **CSV** (comma separated)

Or

■ Select Export from the File menu

■ Select Change File Type

■ Select Text or CSV from the list of file types

then

■ Select the folder and specify the file name which you wish to use for the file

Note that only the current worksheet will be exported from a workbook, and formatting will not be carried through into the text file.

To import the data to create a spreadsheet:

■ Select **Open** from the menu

■ From the **Files of type** select **Text** files

■ Select the folder and the file name to import

■ Save the file using **Save as** from the File menu and select a **File type of Excel workbook** from the drop-down list of file types.

Alternatively you may wish to create a PDF file copy of your spreadsheet to share with other people.

To export your spreadsheet as a pdf file:

Either

■ Select **Save as** from the File menu

■ From the **Save as type** select **PDF**

Or

■ Select **Export** from the File menu

■ Select **Create PDF/XPS** document

■ Click on **Create PDF/XPS** button

Then

■ Select the folder and specify the file name for the new file

■ Click on **Publish**

The file will automically be displayed in Adobe reader if the application is present.

If you wished to save your file as a web page (HTML):

■ Select **Save as** from the File menu

■ From the **Save as type** select **Web Page**

■ Select the folder and specify the file name for the new file

The **Save as** option offers a variety of different formats. We will not be covering them all here, but you should experiment with the different outputs available.

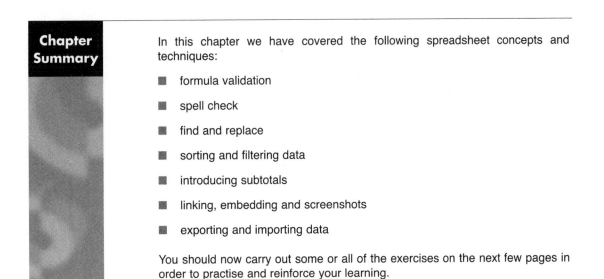

Chapter Summary

In this chapter we have covered the following spreadsheet concepts and techniques:

■ formula validation

■ spell check

■ find and replace

■ sorting and filtering data

■ introducing subtotals

■ linking, embedding and screenshots

■ exporting and importing data

You should now carry out some or all of the exercises on the next few pages in order to practise and reinforce your learning.

Activities

Exercise 1 – validating formulas and spell check

In this first exercise we are going to practise using the tools available for validating formulas and checking the spelling of our text, using a spreadsheet already created. We will then create a new spreadsheet.

To download the spreadsheet which has already been created visit www.osbornebooks.co.uk ('Products and Resources'). The filename is **T5investcheck.** This spreadsheet sets out the interest (or gain) and the growth obtained from a variety of investments over different time periods.

Stage 1

This stage covers checking the formulas in our spreadsheet.

1. From the **File** menu, select **Options, Formulas**. Change if necessary so that background error checking is off. (This is useful for this stage of the exercise.)

2. Download the workbook **T5investcheck.**

3. Open the downloaded file, **Save** the workbook with new name **T5Exercise1.**

The workbook should be familiar from the exercises in Topic 4; it should appear as shown below.

	A	B	C	D	E	F	G
1	Investment Portfolio						
2					Annual	Weekly	
3		Year start	Year end	Interest or	Growth	Growth	Maximum
4	Where	Amount	Amount	Gain	Rate	Amount	Growth
5		£	£	£	%	£	£
6	Bank1	500.00	512.50	12.50	2.50%	0.24	100.77
7	Bank2	4,000.00	4,100.33	100.33	2.51%	1.93	403.08
8	Building Society1	2,000.00	2,100.00	100.00	5.00%	1.92	403.08
9	Building Society2	3,000.00	3,099.99	99.99	3.33%	1.92	604.62
10	Post Office	100.00	102.95	2.95	2.95%	0.06	20.15
11	Stocks & shares	1,000.00	1,201.54	201.54	20.15%	3.88	33.33
12	Totals	9,600.00	9,915.77				

4. As a first step to validation, select **Show Formulas** from the menu bar. See if you can see any errors in the formulas – do not make any changes.

5. Move from formula to formula and you will see the cells making up that formula highlighted. Where you think there may be an error, change the font to show red, but do not change the formula yet.

6. Select **Show Formulas** again, so the formulas are now hidden.

7.   Select **Options, Formulas**, and change **Background Error Checking** to **On**. You should now see some green error triangles appear in the top left-hand corner of those cells which may contain an error. These should coincide with those cells which you changed to a red font.

8.   Select **Error Checking** from the menu bar. Follow the process as it steps through each cell. Where it identifies a possible error, change as appropriate. (As shown in the example below.)

Error Checking	? ×
Error in cell G7	Copy Formula from Above
=B8*$E$11	
Inconsistent Formula	Help on this error
The formula in this cell differs from the formulas in this area of the spreadsheet.	Ignore Error
	Edit in Formula Bar
Options...	Previous Next

9.   Save the workbook with the same name **T5Exercise1.**

It should have the same values as the image shown below.

	A	B	C	D	E	F	G
1	Investment Portfolio						
2					Annual	Weekly	
3		Year start	Year end	Interest or	Growth	Growth	Maximum
4	Where	Amount	Amount	Gain	Rate	Amount	Growth
5		£	£	£	%	£	£
6	Bank1	500.00	512.50	12.50	2.50%	0.24	100.77
7	Bank2	4,000.00	4,100.33	100.33	2.51%	1.93	806.16
8	Building Society1	2,000.00	2,100.00	100.00	5.00%	1.92	403.08
9	Building Society2	3,000.00	3,099.99	99.99	3.33%	1.92	604.62
10	Post Office	100.00	102.95	2.95	2.95%	0.06	20.15
11	Stocks & shares	1,000.00	1,201.54	201.54	20.15%	3.88	33.33
12	Totals	10,600.00	11,117.31				

10.   Check that your values match. If they do not, you should step through the error checking routine again and correct formulas as appropriate.

11.   Select **Show Formulas** so that all formulas are displayed. The corrected worksheet should look as shown at the top of the next page. (The columns have been narrowed for the purpose of the illustration.)

	A	B	C	D	E	F	G
1	Investment Portfc						
2					Annual	Weekly	
3		Year start	Year end	Interest or	Growth	Growth	Maximum
4	Where	Amount	Amount	Gain	Rate	Amount	Growth
5		£	£	£	%	£	£
6	Bank1	500	512.5	=C6-B6	=D6/B6	=D6/52	=B6*$E$11
7	Bank2	4000	4100.33	=C7-B7	=D7/B7	=D7/52	=B7*$E$11
8	Building Society1	2000	2100	=C8-B8	=D8/B8	=D8/52	=B8*$E$11
9	Building Society2	3000	3099.99	=C9-B9	=D9/B9	=D9/52	=B9*$E$11
10	Post Office	100	102.95	=C10-B10	=D10/B10	=D10/52	=B10*$E$11
11	Stocks & shares	1000	1201.54	=C11-B11	=D11/B11	=D11/52	=B11*E9
12	Totals	=SUM(B6:B11)	=SUM(C6:C11)				

Stage 2

In this stage, we are going to continue checking the formulas in the Investment Portfolio spreadsheet.

1. Change the value in cell C9 to £3,300.

2. Look how this affects the Maximum Growth (cell G11) for Stocks & shares.

3. Select cell G11, select **Trace Precedents**.

4. Select G6, select **Trace Precedents**.

5. Select G7, select **Trace Precedents**.

6. Select G8, select **Trace Precedents**.

You can see from this that a pattern emerges:

Cells G6, G7, G8 all use cell E11 in their formula, but cell G11 does not. This is an error which was not picked up by the error checking facility, although it did find several other errors as we saw earlier. The process is not foolproof.

The worksheet should look as shown in the image below.

	A	B	C	D	E	F	G
1	Investment Portfolio						
2					Annual	Weekly	
3		Year start	Year end	Interest or	Growth	Growth	Maximum
4	Where	Amount	Amount	Gain	Rate	Amount	Growth
5		£	£	£	%	£	£
6	Bank1	500.00	512.50	12.50	2.50%	0.24	100.77
7	Bank2	4,000.00	4,100.33	100.33	2.51%	1.93	806.16
8	Building Society1	2,000.00	2,100.00	100.00	5.00%	1.92	403.08
9	Building Society2	3,000.00	3,300.00	300.00	10.00%	5.77	604.62
10	Post Office	100.00	102.95	2.95	2.95%	0.06	20.15
11	Stocks & shares	1,000.00	1,201.54	201.54	20.15%	3.88	100.00
12	Totals	10,600.00	11,317.32				

7.   Select **Remove Arrows**, to clear all arrows from the worksheet.

8.   Select cell E11, select **Trace Dependents**.

9.   Select cell E9, select **Trace Dependents**.

    You can see from the arrows, as shown in the image below, that the formula in cell G11 is incorrectly dependent on cell E9.

▲	A	B	C	D	E	F	G
1	Investment Portfolio						
2					Annual	Weekly	
3		Year start	Year end	Interest or	Growth	Growth	Maximum
4	Where	Amount	Amount	Gain	Rate	Amount	Growth
5		£	£	£	%	£	£
6	Bank1	500.00	512.50	12.50	2.50%	0.24	100.77
7	Bank2	4,000.00	4,100.33	100.33	2.51%	1.93	806.16
8	Building Society1	2,000.00	2,100.00	100.00	5.00%	1.92	403.08
9	Building Society2	3,000.00	3,300.00	300.00	10.00%	5.77	604.62
10	Post Office	100.00	102.95	2.95	2.95%	0.06	20.15
11	Stocks & shares	1,000.00	1,201.54	201.54	20.15%	3.88	100.00
12	Totals	10,600.00	11,317.32				

10.   Correct the formula in cell G11.

11.   Select cell D11, select **Trace Precedents**.

    You will receive an error message to say that this cell does not contain a formula. This highlights that there is something wrong, because it should contain a formula.

12.   Enter £1,350 in cell C11. See how cell D11 does not change. Enter the appropriate formula in D11 and see how all the values in column G now update.

Your spreadsheet should now look as shown below.

▲	A	B	C	D	E	F	G
1	Investment Portfolio						
2					Annual	Weekly	
3		Year start	Year end	Interest or	Growth	Growth	Maximum
4	Where	Amount	Amount	Gain	Rate	Amount	Growth
5		£	£	£	%	£	£
6	Bank1	500.00	512.50	12.50	2.50%	0.24	175.00
7	Bank2	4,000.00	4,100.33	100.33	2.51%	1.93	1,400.00
8	Building Society1	2,000.00	2,100.00	100.00	5.00%	1.92	700.00
9	Building Society2	3,000.00	3,300.00	300.00	10.00%	5.77	1,050.00
10	Post Office	100.00	102.95	2.95	2.95%	0.06	35.00
11	Stocks & shares	1,000.00	1,350.00	350.00	35.00%	6.73	350.00
12	Totals	10,600.00	11,465.78				

Exercise 2 – using spell check and search and replace

In this next exercise we are going to use the built in spell check facility and search and replace to make corrections and changes to text within our worksheet. We are again going to make use of an existing spreadsheet which contains data relating to international sales of fashion items.

This spreadsheet contains nearly 40 rows of data relating to sales information: the month of the sale, the category of product, the value, the sales rep that made the sale and the country to which the sale was made. Not all 40 rows will be visible at the same time on the screen images in this book.

To download this sales spreadsheet visit www.osbornebooks.co.uk ('Products and Resources'). The filename is **T5sales**.

Stage 1

This stage uses the built in spell check tool within a previously created workbook.

1.   Download the workbook **T5sales**.

2.   Open the downloaded file, save the workbook with new name **T5Exercise2**. The workbook should appear as shown below.

◢	A	B	C	D	E
1	Sales				
2					
3	Month	Product	Value	Sales Rep	Country
4	Jan	Acessories	£125.75	TP	UK
5	Jan	Footwear	£99.95	SM	UK
6	Jan	Lugage	£220.00	py	ger
7	Feb	Jewelery	£1,500.00	TP	UK
8	Feb	Footwear	£220.00	py	Fr
9	Feb	Jewelery	£67.75	IO	ger
10	Feb	Clothing	£34.90	SM	Sp
11	Mar	Footwear	£154.50	py	ger
12	Mar	Lugage	£124.60	SM	Sp
13	Mar	Clothing	£44.75	py	Fr

3.   Select cells B4 to B10 in the Product column.

4.   Select the **Spelling** option from the **REVIEW** menu.

5.   Step through the individual checks, making corrections as appropriate, choosing the correct spelling from the choices offered as illustrated on the next page.

6.   Select the whole of column B (using the column header).

7.   Select the **Spelling** option from the menu.

8.   Step through the individual checks, choosing the correct spelling from the choices offered, and this time select **Change All**, to correct all occurrences in column B which are spelt incorrectly.

9.   Save the workbook with the name **T5Exercise2**.

Your spreadsheet should now look as shown below:

	A	B	C	D	E
1	Sales				
2					
3	Month	Product	Value	Sales Rep	Country
4	Jan	Accessories	£125.75	TP	UK
5	Jan	Footwear	£99.95	SM	UK
6	Jan	Luggage	£220.00	py	ger
7	Feb	Jewellery	£1,500.00	TP	UK
8	Feb	Footwear	£220.00	py	Fr
9	Feb	Jewellery	£67.75	IO	ger
10	Feb	Clothing	£34.90	SM	Sp
11	Mar	Footwear	£154.50	py	ger
12	Mar	Luggage	£124.60	SM	Sp
13	Mar	Clothing	£44.75	py	Fr

Stage 2

We are going to use the **Find** facility to locate some specific values, and also the **Find and Replace** to make some more changes to the data.

1.   In the Value column (column C) we have a query regarding a sale of value £67.75 where Country (column E) is UK. Use the **Find** facility to find this entry, selecting next until you find the required row, and change the text font style to Italics for this row of data.

2.   Use the **Find** facility to find the month Nov (column A), where Product (column B) is **Other**. Change the text font style to Bold for this row of data. Note that this entry may not initially be visible on your screen due to the number of rows of data in this worksheet.

3.   Use the **Find and Replace** facility to change all occurrences of py in the Sales Rep column (column D) to all capitals – PY.

4.   Use the **Find and Replace** facility to change all occurrences of Fr in the Country column (column E) to all capitals – FR.

5.   Again, in the Country column (column E), change all occurrences of ger, and Sp to all capitals GER and SP.

6.   Save the workbook with the name **T5Exercise2**.

Your spreadsheet should appear as shown in the image below.

	A	B	C	D	E
1	Sales				
2					
3	Month	Product	Value	Sales Rep	Country
4	Jan	Accessories	£125.75	TP	UK
5	Jan	Footwear	£99.95	SM	UK
6	Jan	Luggage	£220.00	PY	GER
7	Feb	Jewellery	£1,500.00	TP	UK
8	Feb	Footwear	£220.00	PY	FR
9	Feb	Jewellery	£67.75	IO	GER
10	Feb	Clothing	£34.90	SM	SP
11	Mar	Footwear	£154.50	PY	GER
12	Mar	Luggage	£124.60	SM	SP
13	Mar	Clothing	£44.75	PY	FR

The image on the next page shows the rows with the different font styles.

Note that Row 27 is now in italics and Row 38 is in Bold.

	A	B	C	D	E
26	Aug	Other	£1,500.00	PY	FR
27	*Aug*	*Luggage*	*£67.75*	*SM*	*UK*
28	Aug	Clothing	£99.95	TP	UK
29	Aug	Other	£1,460.40	PY	FR
30	Sep	Accessories	£1,460.40	PY	FR
31	Sep	Accessories	£34.00	PY	GER
32	Sep	Clothing	£154.50	SM	UK
33	Oct	Accessories	£67.75	IO	GER
34	Oct	Clothing	£99.95	SM	UK
35	Oct	Accessories	£34.90	PY	GER
36	Nov	Footwear	£124.60	SM	SP
37	Nov	Footwear	£125.75	TP	UK
38	**Nov**	**Other**	**£44.75**	**PY**	**FR**
39	Nov	Accessories	£56.00	PY	FR

You have now completed the second exercise.

Exercise 3 – using subtotals, sorting and filtering

In this next exercise we are going to use sorting and introduce some Subtotals. We will use the workbook from the previous exercise.

This workbook can be downloaded from www.osbornebooks.co.uk ('Products and Resources'), filename **T5sort**.

Stage 1

In this stage we are going to use the **Sort** facility.

>	**Note**: one facility which you may need to make use of, which is common to all packages, is the **Undo** button or option. This will allow you to revert the data back a step at a time, undoing your changes or edits. This is particularly useful when doing a sort, since if you sort incorrectly and mix up the data, there is no other easy way to get back to where you were before you started to sort the data.

1.	Download the workbook **T5sort**.

2.	Save the workbook with new name **T5Exercise3**.

The workbook should look as shown below:

	A	B	C	D	E
1	Sales				
2					
3	Month	Product	Value	Sales Rep	Country
4	Jan	Accessories	£125.75	TP	UK
5	Jan	Footwear	£99.95	SM	UK
6	Jan	Luggage	£220.00	PY	GER
7	Feb	Jewellery	£1,500.00	TP	UK
8	Feb	Footwear	£220.00	PY	FR
9	Feb	Jewellery	£67.75	IO	GER
10	Feb	Clothing	£34.90	SM	SP
11	Mar	Footwear	£154.50	PY	GER
12	Mar	Luggage	£124.60	SM	SP
13	Mar	Clothing	£44.75	PY	FR

3. We are going to sort the data by Product (column B). Select all the data and **Sort** alphabetically A -> Z.

Your spreadsheet should appear like the screen image below.

	A	B	C	D	E
1	Sales				
2					
3	Month	Product	Value	Sales Rep	Country
4	Jan	Accessories	£125.75	TP	UK
5	Mar	Accessories	£154.50	IO	SP
6	May	Accessories	£144.50	IO	SP
7	Jul	Accessories	£44.75	IO	GER
8	Sep	Accessories	£1,460.40	PY	FR
9	Sep	Accessories	£34.00	PY	GER
10	Oct	Accessories	£67.75	IO	GER
11	Oct	Accessories	£34.90	PY	GER
12	Nov	Accessories	£56.00	PY	FR
13	Dec	Accessories	£124.60	MP	GER
14	Feb	Clothing	£34.90	SM	SP
15	Mar	Clothing	£44.75	PY	FR

4.   Within each product, we now want to sort by the **value** (column C) in descending order (largest to smallest), by adding another level to the sort.

	A	B	C	D	E
1	Sales				
2					
3	Month	Product	Value	Sales Rep	Country
4	Sep	Accessories	£1,460.40	PY	FR
5	Mar	Accessories	£154.50	IO	SP
6	May	Accessories	£144.50	IO	SP
7	Jan	Accessories	£125.75	TP	UK
8	Dec	Accessories	£124.60	MP	GER
9	Oct	Accessories	£67.75	IO	GER
10	Nov	Accessories	£56.00	PY	FR
11	Jul	Accessories	£44.75	IO	GER
12	Oct	Accessories	£34.90	PY	GER
13	Sep	Accessories	£34.00	PY	GER
14	Jun	Clothing	£1,124.60	TP	UK
15	Sep	Clothing	£154.50	SM	UK
16	Aug	Clothing	£99.95	TP	UK

In the image below, you can see the settings within the sort facility.

5. Save the workbook with the name **T5Exercise3**.

Stage 2

We are now going to introduce some subtotals. We want to subtotal the value of sales by Sales Rep.

1.   **Sort** the data by the Sales Rep (column D). **Sort** alphabetically A -> Z.

(**Note** you will need to delete the sort level for Value, and change the first sort level to be Sales Rep), as illustrated below).

2.   Using the **Subtotal** facility, we want to subtotal at each change of Sales Rep. Use function **SUM**, add subtotal to **Value**, **Replace** current subtotals (yes), summary below data (yes), as illustrated below.

3.   Select the **Hide Detail** option from the menu bar.

4.   Widen the value column so that all data displays in full.

5.   Save the workbook with the name **T5Exercise3a**.

Your spreadsheet should appear as shown in the image below.

1 2 3		A	B	C	D	E
	1	Sales				
	2					
	3	Month	Product	Value	Sales Rep	Country
+	17			£2,803.80	IO Total	
+	20			£158.60	MP Total	
+	33			£5,355.45	PY Total	
+	41			£706.25	SM Total	
+	49			£4,561.05	TP Total	
−	50			£13,585.15	Grand Total	

6.   Select the IO total row (row 17), and either click on the plus sign (+) to the left of the row, or select the **Show Detail** option from the menu bar.

Your spreadsheet should appear as shown in the image below.

1 2 3		A	B	C	D	E
	1	Sales				
	2					
	3	Month	Product	Value	Sales Rep	Country
	4	Mar	Accessories	£154.50	IO	SP
	5	May	Accessories	£144.50	IO	SP
	6	Oct	Accessories	£67.75	IO	GER
	7	Jul	Accessories	£44.75	IO	GER
	8	Feb	Jewellery	£67.75	IO	GER
	9	Apr	Jewellery	£56.00	IO	SP
	10	Nov	Luggage	£220.00	IO	SP
	11	Dec	Luggage	£56.25	IO	GER
	12	Dec	Other	£1,500.00	IO	FR
	13	May	Other	£344.90	IO	SP
	14	Apr	Other	£56.25	IO	GER
	15	Jul	Other	£56.25	IO	GER
	16	Apr	Other	£34.90	IO	SP
−	17			£2,803.80	IO Total	
+	20			£158.60	MP Total	
+	33			£5,355.45	PY Total	
+	41			£706.25	SM Total	
+	49			£4,561.05	TP Total	
−	50			£13,585.15	Grand Total	

Stage 3

We are now going to use this same data to practise using the **Filter** tool.

1.   Open the workbook which you saved with the name **T5Exercise3**.

2.   Remove all the subtotals.

3.   Select all data, then select the **filter** tool to apply a filter.

4.   On the Country column, apply a filter so that you can only see rows where Country is GER.

The workbook should look as shown below.

3	Month ▼	Product ▼	Value ▼	Sales R ▼	Countr ▼
6	Oct	Accessories	£67.75	IO	GER
7	Jul	Accessories	£44.75	IO	GER
8	Feb	Jewellery	£67.75	IO	GER
11	Dec	Luggage	£56.25	IO	GER
14	Apr	Other	£56.25	IO	GER
15	Jul	Other	£56.25	IO	GER
17	Dec	Accessories	£124.60	MP	GER
21	Oct	Accessories	£34.90	PY	GER
22	Sep	Accessories	£34.00	PY	GER
25	Mar	Footwear	£154.50	PY	GER
27	Jan	Luggage	£220.00	PY	GER

5.   Apply an additional filter to the rows, using the product column, so that only the rows for Product = Accessories and Country = GER are to be shown.

The workbook should look as shown below.

	A	B	C	D	E
1	Sales				
2					
3	Month ▼	Product ▼	Value ▼	Sales R ▼	Countr ▼
6	Oct	Accessories	£67.75	IO	GER
7	Jul	Accessories	£44.75	IO	GER
17	Dec	Accessories	£124.60	MP	GER
21	Oct	Accessories	£34.90	PY	GER
22	Sep	Accessories	£34.00	PY	GER

This completes Exercise 3.

Exercise 4 – embedding, linking, importing and exporting data

In this exercise we are going to practise linking and embedding, and explore the import and export facilities. We will be using a word processing document, and a workbook containing the required spreadsheet data.

The following files can be downloaded from www.osbornebooks.co.uk ('Products and Resources'): filename **T5embed** (the workbook), and **T5word** (a word processing document in Microsoft® Word format).

Stage 1

This stage uses **embedding** with a previously created workbook.

1.   Open **T5embed** in your spreadsheet program, and **T5word** in your word processing package.

The word processing file should look as shown below:

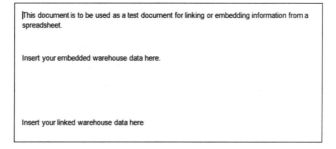

The workbook should appear as follows:

	A	B	C
1	**Warehouse information**		
2			
3			
4	**Code**	**Bin**	**Price**
5	ab1	1	£2.00
6	ab2	2	£30.00
7	ab3	1	£27.00
8	ab4	1	£14.00
9	ab5	3	£21.00
10	ab6	4	£12.00
11	ab7	1	£7.00
12	ab8	2	£24.00
13	ab9	1	£27.00
14	ab10	5	£50.00

2. Within the open worksheet, select all cells in the range A4:C14. Select **Copy** from the Edit menu, or use **CTRL** and **C** to copy the data.

3. Turning to the word processing package, move down the document, so that the cursor is below the text relating to embedding the data. Select **Paste Special**, and paste as worksheet object.

This is illustrated below.

Paste Special		? ☓
Source:	Microsoft Excel Worksheet	
	Sheet1!R4C1:R14C3	

As:

◉ Paste: | Microsoft Excel Worksheet Object | ☐ Display as icon
○ Paste link: | Formatted Text (RTF)
| Unformatted Text
| Bitmap
| Picture (Enhanced Metafile)
| HTML Format
| Unformatted Unicode Text

Result

Inserts the contents of the Clipboard into your document so that you can edit it using Microsoft Excel Worksheet.

| OK | Cancel |

The document should appear as follows:

Insert your embedded warehouse data here.

Code	Bin	Price
ab1	1	£2.00
ab2	2	£30.00
ab3	1	£27.00
ab4	1	£14.00
ab5	3	£21.00
ab6	4	£12.00
ab7	1	£7.00
ab8	2	£24.00
ab9	1	£27.00
ab10	5	£50.00

4. Stay in the word processing package, double click on the inserted data, and change the price for **ab1** to **£2.50**. Click lower down in the word processing document, to move away from the embedded data.

5. Save the word processing document as **T5word5.**

Stage 2

This stage uses linking to connect a word processing file with a previously created workbook.

1. If the files are not already open, open the word processing package, with file **T5word5**, and open the spreadsheet with workbook **T5embed**.

2. Within the open worksheet, select all cells in the range A4:C14, select **Copy** from the Edit menu, or use **CTRL** and **C** to copy the data.

3. Turning to the word processing package, move down the document, so that the cursor is below the text relating to linking the data, select **Paste Special**, **Paste as Worksheet Object**, and click the **Paste Link** button.

Paste Special   ?   ✕

Source: Microsoft Excel Worksheet
         Sheet1!R4C1:R14C3

As:

○ **P**aste: | Microsoft Excel Worksheet Object | ☐ **D**isplay as icon
● Paste **l**ink: | Formatted Text (RTF) |
                   | Unformatted Text |
                   | Picture (Windows Metafile) |
                   | Bitmap |
                   | Word Hyperlink |
                   | HTML Format |
                   | Unformatted Unicode Text |

Result

Inserts the contents of the Clipboard as a picture.

Paste Link creates a shortcut to the source file. Changes to the source file will be reflected in your document.

[OK]   [Cancel]

The document should appear as shown on the right.

Insert your linked warehouse data here

Code	Bin	Price
ab1	1	£2.00
ab2	2	£30.00
ab3	1	£27.00
ab4	1	£14.00
ab5	3	£21.00
ab6	4	£12.00
ab7	1	£7.00
ab8	2	£24.00
ab9	1	£27.00
ab10	5	£50.00

4. Remain in the word processing package, double click on the inserted data, which will take you to the spreadsheet package, change the price for ab1 to £2.50, swap back to the word processing package, right click on the linked data table, and select **Update Link**, if it has not automatically updated.

5. Swap to the spreadsheet package, change cell C8 to **£16**, swap back to the word processing document, right click on the linked data table, and select **Update Link** if it has not automatically updated.

6. Save the word processing document as **T5word5**.

The document should appear as shown below.

Insert your linked warehouse data here

Code	Bin	Price
ab1	1	£2.50
ab2	2	£30.00
ab3	1	£27.00
ab4	1	£16.00
ab5	3	£21.00
ab6	4	£12.00
ab7	1	£7.00
ab8	2	£24.00
ab9	1	£27.00
ab10	5	£50.00

You can see in the linked data section of this word processing document that the prices for **ab1** and **ab4** which have been changed in the spreadsheet have now been updated in the word document, without you having to edit them.

Stage 3

In this stage we will use the **Save As** facility within the spreadsheet package to allow us to take an existing worksheet and **export** it to produce a text file containing the spreadsheet data, in the form of a .TXT, .CSV or PDF file.

The file **T5export** can be downloaded from www.osbornebooks.co.uk.

1.   Download and open **T5export** in your spreadsheet program.

The workbook should appear as shown below.

	A	B	C
1	Code	Bin	Price
2	ab1	1	£2.50
3	ab2	2	£30.00
4	ab3	1	£27.00
5	ab4	1	£16.00
6	ab5	3	£21.00
7	ab6	4	£12.00
8	ab7	1	£7.00
9	ab8	2	£24.00
10	ab9	1	£27.00
11	ab10	5	£50.00

2.   **Export** the spreadsheet as a Text (Tab delimited file), with name **T5txt**. Close the spreadsheet.

3.   Open the file **T5txt** in Microsoft® Notepad (found from the **Start Menu**, under **All Programs, Accessories, Notepad**) or equivalent file.

The file should appear as shown at the top of the next page.

4.   Re-open the spreadsheet **T5Export**, and **Export** the spreadsheet as a CSV (Comma delimited file), with name **T5csv**. Close the spreadsheet.

5.   Open the file **T5csv** in Microsoft® Notepad. You will need to select **File Type – all files**.

The file should appear as shown in the second image down on the next page.

```
text (tab delimited) file

Code        Bin        Price
ab1         1          £2.50
ab2         2          £30.00
ab3         1          £27.00
ab4         1          £16.00
ab5         3          £21.00
ab6         4          £12.00
ab7         1          £7.00
ab8         2          £24.00
ab9         1          £27.00
ab10        5          £50.00
```

```
CSV file

Code,Bin,Price
ab1,1,£2.50
ab2,2,£30.00
ab3,1,£27.00
ab4,1,£16.00
ab5,3,£21.00
ab6,4,£12.00
ab7,1,£7.00
ab8,2,£24.00
ab9,1,£27.00
ab10,5,£50.00
```

6. Re-open the spreadsheet **T5Export**, and **Export** the spreadsheet as a **PDF** with name T5pdf.

The file complete with formatting will be displayed in Adobe Reader, if present.

Stage 4

In this stage we will **import** the spreadsheet data held in the text file which we have previously exported in Stage 3, and use it to create a new copy of the original spreadsheet.

1. Open your spreadsheet program.

2. Select **File, Open**, change **Files of Type** to **All Files**, select the file **T5txt**.

3. Step through the import options, shown on the next page.

Text Import Wizard - Step 1 of 3   ?   ✕

The Text Wizard has determined that your data is Delimited.

If this is correct, choose Next, or choose the data type that best describes your data.

Original data type

Choose the file type that best describes your data:

◉ Delimited   - Characters such as commas or tabs separate each field.

○ Fixed width   - Fields are aligned in columns with spaces between each field.

Start import at row: | 1 | ⬍ | File origin: | Windows (ANSI) | ⌄ |

☑ My data has headers.

Preview of file C:\Users\Wendy\Documents\Osborne books\AAT level 3 Jan 2016 revisi...\T5txt.txt.

```
1 CodeBinPrice
2 ab11£2.50
3 ab22£30.00
4 ab31£27.00
5 ab41£16.00
```

                        Cancel   < Back   Next >   Finish

On step 1, make sure the **File Origin** is **Windows (ANSI)**, check **My data has headers**. On Step 2 of 3, the Delimiters, make sure the Tab box is checked.

The workbook should appear as shown below.

	A	B	C
1	Code	Bin	Price
2	ab1	1	£2.50
3	ab2	2	£30.00
4	ab3	1	£27.00
5	ab4	1	£16.00
6	ab5	3	£21.00
7	ab6	4	£12.00
8	ab7	1	£7.00
9	ab8	2	£24.00
10	ab9	1	£27.00
11	ab10	5	£50.00

Note how all the formatting we had for our column headings has been stripped out of the data.

4. Save the spreadsheet data which is displayed, as **type Excel Workbook**, and name it **T5ex4txt**

5. Still with the spreadsheet package open, select **File, Open**, change **Files of Type** to **All Files**. Select the file **T5csv**.

   There are no import options this time, but you can see that the formatting has again been stripped out of the data, but the results are exactly the same.

6. Save the spreadsheet data which is below, as **type Excel Workbook**, and name it **T5ex4csv**.

	A	B	C
1	Code	Bin	Price
2	ab1	1	£2.50
3	ab2	2	£30.00
4	ab3	1	£27.00
5	ab4	1	£16.00
6	ab5	3	£21.00
7	ab6	4	£12.00
8	ab7	1	£7.00
9	ab8	2	£24.00
10	ab9	1	£27.00
11	ab10	5	£50.00

This concludes the exercises for chapter 5.

6 Statistical functions

this chapter covers...

This chapter covers the use of statistical formulas. It explains and takes you through the concepts and techniques listed below.

By the time you have finished this chapter and carried out the exercises which follow, you should be able to produce spreadsheets which perform a variety of statistical calculations.

The concepts and techniques covered are:

■ *simple statistical functions*

■ *analysis tools*

■ *remove duplicates*

■ *comments*

Note that the step-by-step instructions given in this chapter are based on the Microsoft® Excel model, but the concepts and techniques described generally relate to all spreadsheet packages. The one exception to this is coverage of the Excel Data Analysis Toolpack in the section 'Analysis Tools'.

STATISTICAL FUNCTIONS

The functions we are going to cover in this chapter are as follows:
- COUNT
- COUNTA
- MAX
- MIN
- AVERAGE
- COUNTIF
- SUMIF

count

The **COUNT** function counts **the number of cells that contain numbers** within a group of cells specified by the user. The formula is:

=COUNT(value1,[value2],....)

The COUNT function has these arguments:

- **value1**

    This is required and can be the first item, cell reference, or range within which you want to count numbers

- **value2**

    This is optional

You can specify up to 255 arguments. Each 'argument' can be either a number, cell reference, or range of cells.

Here are some examples:

=COUNT(B1:B16)

This would tell us how many cells in the range B1 to B16 contain numbers.

=COUNT(B1:B16,C20:C36)

This would return the total of how many cells in the range B1 to B16, and C20 to C36 contain numbers.

A simple illustration of customer sales is shown in the screen image on the next page, where we are counting out of the six months, how many months the customers bought something, and record the result in column H.

We use the formula **=COUNT(B4:G4)** entered in cell H4 to tell us how many months Farmhouse Foods made a purchase. This formula can then be copied to the remaining customer rows.

H4		▼ ⋮ ✕ ✓ *fx*	=COUNT(B4:G4)					
◢	A	B	C	D	E	F	G	H
1				**Monthly Sales Value**				
2								**Months made**
3	**Customer Name**	**Month1**	**Month2**	**Month3**	**Month4**	**Month5**	**Month6**	**a purchase**
4	*Farmhouse Foods*		£112				£26	2
5	*Engineering Services*					£67		1
6	*Another Food Service*				£58	£116		2
7	*Top Quality Supplies*		£56					1
8	*Halal Foods*							0
9	*Edwards Farm*					£40		1
10	*Allen and co*	£45	£68	£231	£0	£331	£37	6
11	*Ahmed and son*							0

COUNTA

The **COUNTA** function counts the number of cells that are not empty within a group of cells specified by the user. The formula is:

=COUNTA(value1,[value2],...)

The COUNTA function has these arguments:

■ **value1**

This is required and can be the first item, cell reference, or range within which you want to count numbers

■ **value2**

This is optional

You can specify up to 255 arguments. Each 'argument' can be either a number, cell reference, or range of cells.

Very similar to COUNT,

=COUNTA(B1:B16)

would tell us how many cells in the range B1 to B16 are not empty.

=COUNTA(B1:B16,C20:C36)

would return how many cells in the range B1 to B16, and C20 to C36 are not empty.

We have an example on the next page, with the list of customers and sales, together with their postcode, we can use the COUNTA function to tell us how many customers have the postcode specified, using formula =COUNTA(B4:B15) as shown in cell B16.

B16	▼	:	✕	✓	*fx*	=COUNTA(B4:B15)				

	A	B	C	D	E	F	G	H	I
1					Monthly Sales Value				
2									Months made
3	Customer Name	Postcode	Month1	Month2	Month3	Month4	Month5	Month6	a purchase
4	Farmhouse Foods	WR15 2AA		£112				£26	2
5	Engineering Services	SR12 T12					£67		1
6	Another Food Service					£58	£116		2
7	Top Quality Supplies	TH2 J11		£56					1
8	Halal Foods	KL1 C34							0
9	Edwards Farm	LM1 6LL					£40		1
10	Allen and co		£45	£68	£231	£0	£331	£37	6
11	Ahmed and son	L11 5GG							0
12	Green & Sons Wholesalers	MN12 1RT	£700		£104				2
13	Higginbottom and son								0
14	W B Meats	WW1 3HH		£45					1
15	The Halal Centre	DD12 3DF			£50			£0	2
16	Postcode Specified	9							

MAX

'MAX' is an abbreviation of 'maximum'. The **MAX** function returns the maximum (largest) number within a group of cells specified by the user.

The formula is:

=MAX(number1,number2,...)

The **MAX** function has these arguments:

■ **number1** – this is required

■ **number2** – this is optional

You can specify up to 255 arguments for which you want to find the maximum value. Each argument can be either a number, cell reference, or range.

Here are some examples:

=MAX(B1:B6)

This would return the largest of the numbers in the range B1 to B6.

=MAX(B1:B6,80)

This would return the largest of the numbers in the range B1 to B6, and 80, ie if none of the numbers within the range is greater than 80 it would return a value of 80.

In the customer sales spreadsheet shown on the next page, we have setup column H to show the maximum (highest) monthly spend by each customer, the formula is put in H4, and copied to H5 through to H15.

H4	▾	⋮	✕	✓	*fx*	=MAX(B4:G4)		

	A	B	C	D	E	F	G	H
1					**Monthly Sales Value**			
2								**Max**
3	**Customer Name**	**Month1**	**Month2**	**Month3**	**Month4**	**Month5**	**Month6**	**Purchase**
4	*Farmhouse Foods*		£112				£26	£112
5	*Engineering Services*					£67		£67
6	*Another Food Service*				£58	£116		£116
7	*Top Quality Supplies*		£56					£56
8	*Halal Foods*							£0
9	*Edwards Farm*					£40		£40
10	*Allen and co*	£45	£68	£231	£0	£331	£37	£331
11	*Ahmed and son*							£0
12	*Green & Sons Wholesalers*	£700		£104				£700
13	*Higginbottom and son*							£0
14	*W B Meats*		£45					£45
15	*The Halal Centre*			£50			£0	£50

MIN

'MIN' is an abbreviation of 'minimum'. The **MIN** function returns the smallest number within a group of cells specified by the user.

The formula is:

=MIN(number1,number2,...)

The **MIN** function has these arguments:

- **number1** – this is required

- **number2** – this is optional

You can specify up to 255 arguments for which you want to find the minimum value. Each argument can be either a number, or cell reference, or range.

Here are some examples:

=MIN(C2:C16)

This would return the smallest of the numbers in the range C2 to C16.

=MIN(C2:C16,10)

This would return the smallest of the numbers in the range C2 to C16, and 10, ie if none of the numbers within the range is smaller than 10 it would return a value of 10.

In the customer sales spreadsheet shown on the next page, we have this time setup column H to show the minimum (lowest) monthly purchase for each customer. The formula has been input in cell H4 and copied to H5 through to H15.

H4	▼	:	✕	✓	*fx*	=MIN(B4:G4)		

⊿	A	B	C	D	E	F	G	H
1				**Monthly Sales Value**				
2								Min
3	**Customer Name**	**Month1**	**Month2**	**Month3**	**Month4**	**Month5**	**Month6**	**Purchase**
4	*Farmhouse Foods*		£112				£26	£26
5	*Engineering Services*					£67		£67
6	*Another Food Service*				£58	£116		£58
7	*Top Quality Supplies*		£56					£56
8	*Halal Foods*							£0
9	*Edwards Farm*					£40		£40
10	*Allen and co*	£45	£68	£231	£0	£331	£37	£0
11	*Ahmed and son*							£0
12	*Green & Sons Wholesalers*	£700		£104				£104
13	*Higginbottom and son*							£0
14	*W B Meats*		£45					£45
15	*The Halal Centre*			£50			£0	£0

AVERAGE

The **AVERAGE** function returns the average (arithmetic mean) of a group of cells specified by the user.

The formula is:

=AVERAGE(number1,number2,...)

The **AVERAGE** function has these arguments:

■ **number1** – this is required

■ **number2** – this is optional

You can specify up to 255 arguments for which you want to find the **AVERAGE** value. Each argument can be either a number, or cell reference, or range.

Here are some examples:

= AVERAGE (C2:C16)

This would return the average of the numbers in the cell range C2 to C16.

= AVERAGE (C2:C16,10)

This would return the average of the numbers in the cell range C2 to C16 and 10.

In the example on the next page, we have calculated the average spent by each customer over the six months. The formula used for row 4 is =AVERAGE(B4:G4)

| H4 | ▼ | ⋮ | ✕ | ✓ | *fx* | =AVERAGE(B4:G4) |

◢	A	B	C	D	E	F	G	H
1				**Monthly Sales Value**				
2								Average
3	**Customer Name**	**Month1**	**Month2**	**Month3**	**Month4**	**Month5**	**Month6**	**Purchase**
4	Farmhouse Foods		£112				£26	£69
5	Engineering Services					£67		
6	Another Food Service				£58	£116		
7	Top Quality Supplies		£56					
8	Halal Foods							
9	Edwards Farm					£40		
10	Allen and co	£45	£68	£231	£0	£331	£37	
11	Ahmed and son							
12	Green & Sons Wholesalers	£700		£104				
13	Higginbottom and son							
14	W B Meats		£45					
15	The Halal Centre			£50			£0	

Notice what happens when this formula is copied to the other rows:

◢	A	B	C	D	E	F	G	H
1				**Monthly Sales Value**				
2								Average
3	**Customer Name**	**Month1**	**Month2**	**Month3**	**Month4**	**Month5**	**Month6**	**Purchase**
4	Farmhouse Foods		£112				£26	£69
5	Engineering Services					£67		£67
6	Another Food Service				£58	£116		£87
7	Top Quality Supplies		£56					£56
8	Halal Foods							#DIV/0!
9	Edwards Farm					£40		£40
10	Allen and co	£45	£68	£231	£0	£331	£37	£119
11	Ahmed and son							#DIV/0!
12	Green & Sons Wholesalers	£700		£104				£402
13	Higginbottom and son							#DIV/0!
14	W B Meats		£45					£45
15	The Halal Centre			£50			£0	£25

We get errors in those rows where the customer has not made any purchases over the six months.

This can be corrected by changing our formula to only calculate the average, if the customer has made a purchase in the six months, ie use an IF statement, together with the COUNT function to see if there are any values greater than 0 in the 6 months. This is illustrated in the image on the next page.

H4	▾ : ✕ ✓ *fx*		=IF(COUNT(B4:G4)>0,AVERAGE(B4:G4),0)				

▲	A	B	C	D	E	F	G	H
1				**Monthly Sales Value**				
2								**Average**
3	**Customer Name**	**Month1**	**Month2**	**Month3**	**Month4**	**Month5**	**Month6**	**Purchase**
4	*Farmhouse Foods*		£112				£26	£69
5	*Engineering Services*					£67		£67
6	*Another Food Service*				£58	£116		£87
7	*Top Quality Supplies*		£56					£56
8	*Halal Foods*							£0
9	*Edwards Farm*					£40		£40
10	*Allen and co*	£45	£68	£231	£0	£331	£37	£119
11	*Ahmed and son*							£0
12	*Green & Sons Wholesalers*	£700		£104				£402
13	*Higginbottom and son*							£0
14	*W B Meats*		£45					£45
15	*The Halal Centre*			£50			£0	£25

COUNTIF

The COUNTIF function counts the number of cells within a group of cells specified by the user which meet certain criteria. The formula is:

=COUNTIF(range, criteria)

The COUNTIF function has these arguments:

■ range

This is required, it is the range within which you want to count, e.g B4:B15

■ criteria

defines the condition that tells the function which cells to count. It can be a number, text, cell reference or expression.

=COUNTIF(B1:B16, 10)

would tell us how many cells in the range B1 to B16 have the value 10.

=COUNTIF(B1:B16, ">10")

would return how many cells in the range B1 to B16, are bigger than 10.

=COUNTIF(B1:B16, A1)

would return how many cells in the range B1 to B16 contain the value held in cell A1.

In the customers sales example on the next page, we have identified new customers with a Y, we can use the COUNTIF function to tell us how many customers are new, using the formula

=COUNTIF(B4:B15,"Y")

as shown in cell B16

B16	▾ ⋮	✕ ✓ *fx*	=COUNTIF(B4:B15,"Y")					

◢	A	B	C	D	E	F	G	H
1				**Monthly Sales Value**				
2		**New**						
3	**Customer Name**	**Customer**	**Month1**	**Month2**	**Month3**	**Month4**	**Month5**	**Month6**
4	*Farmhouse Foods*	*Y*		£112				£26
5	*Engineering Services*	*N*					£67	
6	*Another Food Service*	*N*				£58	£116	
7	*Top Quality Supplies*	*N*		£56				
8	*Halal Foods*	*N*						
9	*Edwards Farm*	*Y*					£40	
10	*Allen and co*	*N*	£45	£68	£231	£0	£331	£37
11	*Ahmed and son*	*N*						
12	*Green & Sons Wholesalers*	*Y*	£700		£104			
13	*Higginbottom and son*	*N*						
14	*W B Meats*	*Y*		£45				
15	*The Halal Centre*	*Y*			£50			£0
16	**New Customers**	5						

SUMIF

The SUMIF function totals the cells within a group of cells specified by the user which meet certain criteria. The formula is:

=SUMIF(range, criteria,[sum_range])

The SUMIF function has these arguments:

■ range

This is required, it is the range within which you want to count, eg B4:B15

■ criteria

defines the condition that tells the function which cells to include in the total. It can be a number, text, cell reference or expression.

■ sum_range

this is optional, and defines the actual cells to add, if you want to add cells other than those specified in the *range* argument. If the *sum_range* argument is omitted, the cells that are specified in the *range* argument (the same cells to which the criteria is applied) are added together.

=**SUMIF(C1:C16, ">50")**

would add together those cells in the range C1 to C16 which have a value greater than 50.

=**SUMIF(B1:B16, "Y",C1:C16)**

would add together those cells in the range C1 to C16 where the corresponding value in column B is Y. ie if the value in B1 is Y, C1 would be included in the total.

Similarly if the value in B2 is Y, C2 would be included, and so on.

In the customers sales example below, we have identified new customers with a Y, we can use the SUMIF function to create a monthly total for each month for new customers

=**SUMIF(B4:B15,"Y", C4:C15)**

as shown in cell B16

C16	▾	:	✕	✓	f_x	=SUMIF(B4:B15,"Y",C4:C15)		
	A		B	C	D	E	F	G	H

	A	B	C	D	E	F	G	H
1				**Monthly Sales Value**				
2		**New**						
3	**Customer Name**	**Customer**	**Month1**	**Month2**	**Month3**	**Month4**	**Month5**	**Month6**
4	Farmhouse Foods	Y		£112				£26
5	Engineering Services	N					£67	
6	Another Food Service	N				£58	£116	
7	Top Quality Supplies	N		£56				
8	Halal Foods	N						
9	Edwards Farm	Y					£40	
10	Allen and co	N	£45	£68	£231	£0	£331	£37
11	Ahmed and son	N						
12	Green & Sons Wholesalers	Y	£700		£104			
13	Higginbottom and son	N						
14	W B Meats	Y		£45				
15	The Halal Centre	Y			£50			£0
16	**New Customers Monthly Total**		£700					

If we just copy the formula in cell C16 into D16, we would get the formula

=**SUMIF(C4:C15,"Y",D4:D15)**

Which isn't want we want, we need to use absolute addressing, so that we are always comparing the values in column B:-

=**SUMIF($B$4:$B$15,"Y",C4:C15)**

This will now copy across to the other cells to produce the required result, as can be seen on the next page.

D16	▾	:	✕ ✔ *fx*	=SUMIF($B$4:$B$15,"Y",D4:D15)				

▲	A	B	C	D	E	F	G	H
1				**Monthly Sales Value**				
2		**New**						
3	**Customer Name**	**Customer**	**Month1**	**Month2**	**Month3**	**Month4**	**Month5**	**Month6**
4	Farmhouse Foods	Y		£112				£26
5	Engineering Services	N					£67	
6	Another Food Service	N				£58	£116	
7	Top Quality Supplies	N		£56				
8	Halal Foods	N						
9	Edwards Farm	Y					£40	
10	Allen and co	N	£45	£68	£231	£0	£331	£37
11	Ahmed and son	N						
12	Green & Sons Wholesalers	Y	£700		£104			
13	Higginbottom and son	N						
14	W B Meats	Y		£45				
15	The Halal Centre	Y			£50			£0
16	**New Customers Monthly Total**		£700	£157	£154	£0	£40	£26

ANALYSIS TOOLS

Tools for detailed statistical analysis may be provided within the spreadsheet program or package that you are using. The features will vary greatly from package to package. In this section we are going to describe and explain some of the tools available within the Microsoft® Excel **Data Analysis Toolpak.**

We are not going to cover the statistical theory which underlies these tools, but will concentrate on how to use the functions provided by the tools.

We are going to describe:

▨ Rank and percentile

▨ Moving averages

▨ Histograms

The first step is to ensure that the Excel **Analysis Toolpak** has been loaded and is available. It is not loaded automatically by default at installation time.

To do this:

▨ select the **File** menu

▨ select **Options**

▨ select **Add-Ins**

▨ click on **Manage Add-Ins**

The screen should look similar to that shown below.

Excel Options   ?   ✕

General	⬚ View and manage Microsoft Office Add-ins.
Formulas	
Proofing	**Add-ins**
Save	
Language	
Advanced	
Customize Ribbon	
Quick Access Toolbar	
Add-Ins	
Trust Center	

Name ⌃	Location	Type	
Active Application Add-ins			
No Active Application Add-ins			
Inactive Application Add-ins			
Analysis ToolPak	C:\...\Library\Analysis\analys32.xll	Excel Add-in	
Analysis ToolPak - VBA	C:\...ry\Analysis\ATPVBAEN.XLAM	Excel Add-in	
Date (XML)	C:\... Shared\Smart Tag\MOFL.DLL	Action	
Euro Currency Tools	C:\...15\Library\EUROTOOL.XLAM	Excel Add-in	

Add-in:	Analysis ToolPak
Publisher:	Microsoft Corporation
Compatibility:	No compatibility information available
Location:	C:\Program Files\Microsoft Office 15\root\office15\Library\Analysis\analys32.xll
Description:	Provides data analysis tools for statistical and engineering analysis

Manage: Excel Add-ins ⌄   Go...

OK   Cancel

- click on **Go**
- ensure the box next to **Analysis ToolPak** is ticked by clicking in the box

If you cannot see **Analysis ToolPak** in the list of available Add-Ins, you will need to consult your system supervisor.

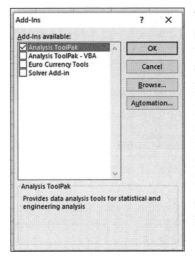

The list of available Add-Ins may look something like the image on the left, but will vary from computer to computer depending on what other software packages you have installed.

If **Analysis ToolPak** is not listed in the active Add-ins, or not 'ticked' in the list that appears, follow the installation steps for your particular version of Excel to install the **Analysis Toolpak**.

Once installation is complete, the tools can be accessed from the **Data** menu.

rank and percentile

The **rank and percentile** analysis tool produces a table that contains the **ordinal** and **percentage rank** of each value in a data set.

The **ordinal** is the ranking of each piece of data or number within the group of data, so the largest number within the group would be ranked 1, the second largest 2 and so on.

The **percentage** rank tells us what percentage of the remaining data values are less than this value. Therefore the value ranked 1 (the highest), will have a percentage rank of 100% since all other values are smaller than this one, and so on down the values order in descending order.

The best way to see how to use this tool is through an example. We are going to use a sales example, where we the value of sales by country, as shown in the image below, and we are going to rank the sales values by percentile.

	A	B
1		**Sales**
2	**Country**	**Value €**
3	France	350000
4	UK	423400
5	Germany	121500
6	China	60000
7	Japan	110900
8	India	45090
9	Australia	689090
10	South Africa	97080

We now select **Data Analysis**, and the list of tools available in the Toolpak is shown, as seen in the image below.

We select **Rank and Percentile**, and then specify our data range to analyse, which in this case is B2:B10, and we check the box that indicates a column label in our first row of data.

We want the output to start in column D, with the headings in row 2 on the same worksheet.

You can see the choices in the image below.

Once we have entered our choices, the output is displayed in a table starting in column D as requested. This is shown in the image below in the highlighted section of the worksheet.

⊿	A	B	C	D	E	F	G
1		**Sales**					
2	**Country**	**Value €**		*Point*	*Value €*	*Rank*	*Percent*
3	France	350000		7	689090	1	100.00%
4	UK	423400		2	423400	2	85.70%
5	Germany	121500		1	350000	3	71.40%
6	China	60000		3	121500	4	57.10%
7	Japan	110900		5	110900	5	42.80%
8	India	45090		8	97080	6	28.50%
9	Australia	689090		4	60000	7	14.20%
10	South Africa	97080		6	45090	8	0.00%

As you can see, the original data is **Ranked** in descending order by value. The **Point** column gives the position of the data value in the original list, **Value** is the data value, **Rank** is its relative position in the ranking, 1 being the highest. The **Percent** column, shows what percentage of values are smaller than this value.

Just to make it a little clearer, we take our original data, and sort it by sales value in ascending order, as shown on the next page.

	A	B
1		**Sales**
2	**Country**	**Value €**
3	Australia	689090
4	UK	423400
5	France	350000
6	Germany	121500
7	Japan	110900
8	South Africa	97080
9	China	60000
10	India	45090

If we now create a rank and percentile for this data, selecting the same options as previously, we can see how the rank and percentile order now matches exactly the order of our sales value, highest to lowest.

	A	B	C	D	E	F	G
1		**Sales**					
2	**Country**	**Value €**		*Point*	*Value €*	*Rank*	*Percent*
3	Australia	689090		1	689090	1	100.00%
4	UK	423400		2	423400	2	85.70%
5	France	350000		3	350000	3	71.40%
6	Germany	121500		4	121500	4	57.10%
7	Japan	110900		5	110900	5	42.80%
8	South Africa	97080		6	97080	6	28.50%
9	China	60000		7	60000	7	14.20%
10	India	45090		8	45090	8	0.00%

If the data set (list of values) includes duplicate values, these are given the same rank.

If changes are made to the data values, the **Rank and Percentile** tool needs to be selected again, to update the analysis table.

moving averages

A moving average is a technique used to show trends in sets of data over a time period, for example the price of stocks and shares or sales figures. It is often used to 'smooth out' fluctuations and provide a more helpful trend line which can then be used to make a forecast of future values.

The **Moving Average** analysis tool calculates values over a given time period, based on the average value of the data over a specific number of preceding periods (the **interval**).

The **interval** is the number of data points used to calculate the moving average. The larger the interval, the smoother the moving average line; the smaller the interval, the more the moving average is affected by individual data point fluctuations.

For example, if we were looking at a 12 month period, the first value calculated might be the average for January, February, and March; the second would then be the average for February, March, and April; the third would be the average of March, April and May; and so on.

The example shown below presents sales figures data which can be analysed to create a **moving average** to help project future sales levels using a trend line.

	A	B	C	D	E	F	G	H
1	Sales forecast							
2								
3		January	February	March	April	May	June	*July*
4	Actual sales	£84,922	£85,780	£83,865	£93,670	£93,865	£96,040	
5								
6	*Forecast sales*							

You can see from the above example that we have actual sales figures for a six month period, which is not perhaps a very long time span in practice, but will be useful in helping to explain how a moving average can be produced and provide a guide for forecasting future sales.

The first step is to select **Data Analysis**, and then select the **Moving Average** tool:

	A	B	C	D	E	F	G	H
1	Sales forecast							
2								
3		January	February	March	April	May	June	*July*
4	Actual sales	£84,922	£85,780	£83,865	£93,670	£93,865	£96,040	
5								
6	*Forecast sales*							
7								
8								
9								
10								
11								
12								
13								
14								

Data Analysis   ?   ✕

Analysis Tools

Correlation
Covariance
Descriptive Statistics
Exponential Smoothing
F-Test Two-Sample for Variances
Fourier Analysis
Histogram
Moving Average
Random Number Generation
Rank and Percentile

OK

Cancel

Help

We then select our **Input** range, to include all of our data and the cell for July, for which we want a forecast value.

We leave the interval blank, which will cause the function to use the default of 3, hence calculating the moving average over 3 data points.

Similarly we define our **Output** range, where we want the calculated moving average values to be placed.

We can also select the **Chart Output** tick box to create a chart to give a visual impression of the values.

This selection process is illustrated in the first screen image below.

When we have entered our choices, the moving average values are calculated and output in the specified range, as can be seen in the second image.

	A	B	C	D	E	F	G	H
1	Sales forecast							
2								
3		January	February	March	April	May	June	July
4	Actual sales	£84,922	£85,780	£83,865	£93,670	£93,865	£96,040	
5								
6	Forecast sales							

Moving Average ? ✕

Input

Input Range: `$B$4:$G$4`

☐ Labels in First Row

Interval:

Output options

Output Range: `$C$6:$H$6`

New Worksheet Ply:

New Workbook

☑ Chart Output   ☐ Standard Errors

OK
Cancel
Help

D6   =AVERAGE(B4:D4)

	A	B	C	D	E	F	G	H
1	Sales forecast							
2								
3		January	February	March	April	May	June	July
4	Actual sales	£84,922	£85,780	£83,865	£93,670	£93,865	£96,040	
5								
6	Forecast sales	#N/A	#N/A	£84,856	£87,772	£90,467	£94,525	

Moving Average

We can see in the second screen that values have been calculated in Row 6 for March through to July (cell H6) which helps the business to forecast sales for July, ie a projected increase to £94,953.

Cells B6 and C6 contain N/A (Not Applicable), since they cannot be calculated. As we are using an interval of 3 (in this case months), these cells do not have enough data values preceding them to enable the software to carry out the moving average calculation. Cell D6 contains the AVERAGE of cells B4, C4, D4.

You can see the Forecast trend line in the chart is much smoother than the actual data points trend line, which is the smoothing effect of using a moving average.

An **important point to note** is that if you are using **Excel** software, the value produced by a three month moving average is recorded in the third (last) month, whereas in your accounting studies you may be used to seeing the average allocated to the second (middle) month. So if a three month moving average is calculated on the basis of the figures for January, February and March, Excel will record the figure in March rather than in February (as in the screen opposite, below).

histogram

When looking at a set of values, it is sometimes necessary to quantify how many values fall within certain categories, for example the ages of people in a class:

- up to and including 16
- between 17 and 30
- between 31 and 60

and so on . . .

or alternatively looking at invoice values, and seeing how many fall within each band:

- up to and including £500
- between £501 and £1000
- between £1001 and £1500

etc.

In histogram terms, these categories are known as **bins**. These are often shown as a series of rectangles, like a series of tower blocks of varying height, the area of which is equal to the **frequency** (the number) of the data items. In the example of the class, if it were a secondary school, there would be a far larger frequency and bin for the 'up to and including 16' age group whereas an adult class would have larger bins for the older age groups.

The **Histogram analysis** tool takes a list of data values (such as ages), and calculates how many of these values fall within the boundaries of each of the specified bins. This gives individual **frequencies** for the data bins from the set of data values.

In the image below we have details of some purchase invoices, with gross values in column C, and we have defined our levels or bins, in columns F and G. We have defined 6 bins:

- **Bin 1** invoice values less than or equal to 1500

- **Bin 2** invoice values greater than 1500 and less than or equal to 2500

- **Bin 3** invoice values greater than 2500 and less than or equal to 3500

- **Bin 4** invoice values greater than 3500 and less than or equal to 4500

- **Bin 5** invoice values greater than 4500 and less than or equal to 5500

- **Bin 6** invoice values greater than 5500 and less than or equal to 6500

Any values exceeding the final bin will be gathered under a bin of 'other'. Bin values should be specified in ascending order.

	A	B	C	E	F	G
1	Purchase invoices					
2						
3	Invoice date	Supplier ref	Gross value			
4	28/04/2016	SUPV5	979			Gross
5	18/04/2016	CSUP11	6,045			Value
6	06/04/2016	ASUP6	562		Bin 1	1500
7	13/04/2016	CSUP6	2,183		Bin 2	2500
8	14/04/2016	CSUP7	6,224		Bin 3	3500
9	09/04/2016	ASUP9	4,519		Bin 4	4500
10	21/04/2016	CSUP14	5,687		Bin 5	5500
11	07/05/2016	ASUP7	4,291		Bin 6	6500

To perform this analysis in our spreadsheet we should select Data Analysis, and select the Histogram tool.

	A	B	C	E	F	G	H	I	J	K	L	M
1	Purchase invoices											
2												
3	Invoice date	Supplier ref	Gross value									
4	28/04/2016	SUPV5	979			Gross						
5	18/04/2016	CSUP11	6,045			Value						
6	06/04/2016	ASUP6	562		Bin 1	1500						
7	13/04/2016	CSUP6	2,183		Bin 2	2500						
8	14/04/2016	CSUP7	6,224		Bin 3	3500						
9	09/04/2016	ASUP9	4,519		Bin 4	4500						
10	21/04/2016	CSUP14	5,687		Bin 5	5500						
11	07/05/2016	ASUP7	4,291		Bin 6	6500						

Data Analysis ? ✕

Analysis Tools

Anova: Single Factor
Anova: Two-Factor With Replication
Anova: Two-Factor Without Replication
Correlation
Covariance
Descriptive Statistics
Exponential Smoothing
F-Test Two-Sample for Variances
Fourier Analysis
Histogram

OK
Cancel
Help

We select our **Input range**, to include all of our data in column C (this in fact includes 32 data values, the first 8 of which are shown in the previous image).

We select cells G5 to G11 as the range holding for our bin definitions including a label in cell G5.

We define our **Output** range, where we want the frequency table to be placed.

We can also choose to create a **chart** of the frequency distribution of the data values.

This is done as follows:

Once we have entered our choices, the frequency values are calculated and output in the specified range, and the histogram chart created as can be seen in the image on the next page.

In the image you can see from the frequency table that:

- 4 of our values are less than or equal to 1500

- 2 are greater than 1500 and less than or equal to 2500

- 3 are greater than 2500 and less than or equal to 3500

- 9 are greater than 3500 and less than or equal to 4500

- 4 are greater than 4500 and less than or equal to 5500

- 6 are greater than 5500 and less than or equal to 6500

- 3 are greater than 6500

	A	B	C	E	F	G	H	I	J
1	Purchase invoices								
2									
3	Invoice date	Supplier ref	Gross value						
4	28/04/2016	SUPV5	979			Gross			
5	18/04/2016	CSUP11	6,045			Value		Value	Frequency
6	06/04/2016	ASUP6	562		Bin 1	1500		1500	4
7	13/04/2016	CSUP6	2,183		Bin 2	2500		2500	2
8	14/04/2016	CSUP7	6,224		Bin 3	3500		3500	3
9	09/04/2016	ASUP9	4,519		Bin 4	4500		4500	9
10	21/04/2016	CSUP14	5,687		Bin 5	5500		5500	4
11	07/05/2016	ASUP7	4,291		Bin 6	6500		6500	6
12	12/05/2016	ASUP12	4,162					More	3
13	15/05/2016	CSUP8	4,599						
14	27/05/2016	SUPV4	3,761						
15	11/05/2016	ASUP11	4,444						
16	25/05/2016	SUPV2	4,357						
17	15/06/2016	CSUP9	3,933						
18	21/06/2016	CSUP15	5,671						
19	02/06/2016	ASUP3	855						
20	16/06/2016	CSUP10	5,195						
21	09/06/2016	ASUP10	3,030						
22	19/06/2016	CSUP13	4,207						
23	22/06/2016	CSUP16	1,316						

To **move** a chart created by the Moving Average or Histogram tools:

- click on the chart to select it
- click and drag the chart to its new position

To **delete** a chart created by the Moving Average or Histogram tools:

- click on the chart to select it
- press **delete**

As you saw when you selected the above tools from the **Analysis Toolpak**, there are numerous other tools which will not be covered in this book.

REMOVE DUPLICATES

If the data within our spreadsheet has come from another program, perhaps via Import, it is possible that some of the rows of data may be repeated. Alternatively, we may have rows which repeat just some values. There is a tool available to **Remove duplicate** rows, or rows containing duplicate values.

The **Remove Duplicates** tool is found in the **DATA** menu.

If we look at an example, where we have a list of purchase invoices as shown below:

▲	A	B	C	E
1	**Purchase invoices**			
2				
3	**Invoice date**	**Supplier ref**	**Gross value**	
4	28/04/2016	SUPV5	979	
5	18/04/2016	CSUP11	6,045	
6	06/04/2016	ASUP6	562	
7	13/04/2016	CSUP6	2,183	
8	14/04/2016	CSUP7	6,045	
9	09/04/2016	ASUP9	4,519	
10	21/04/2016	CSUP14	5,687	
11	07/05/2016	ASUP7	4,291	
12	18/04/2016	CSUP11	6,045	
13	06/04/2016	ASUP6	562	
14	13/04/2016	CSUP6	2,183	

This is the list of purchase invoices used previously, but if we look more closely we can see it has changed, and the entries on rows 5, 6 and 7 appear identical to those on 12, 13 and 14. Somehow the data has been duplicated, we will use the **Remove duplicates** tool to clean the data.

■ select the data in rows 4 to 14

■ select Remove duplicates from the DATA menu

If we select ok, those rows with identical values in all 3 columns will be deleted.

	A	B	C	E	F	G	H	I	J	K
1	Purchase invoices									
2										
3	Invoice date	Supplier ref	Gross value							
4	28/04/2016	SUPV5	979							
5	18/04/2016	CSUP11	6,045							
6	06/04/2016	ASUP6	562							
7	13/04/2016	CSUP6	2,183							
8	14/04/2016	CSUP7	6,045							
9	09/04/2016	ASUP9	4,519							
10	21/04/2016	CSUP14	5,687							
11	07/05/2016	ASUP7	4,291							
12										
13										

Microsoft Excel ✕

ⓘ 3 duplicate values found and removed; 8 unique values remain.

OK

Alternatively we may wish to only delete those with identical values in a certain column, or column(s).

If we just wanted to delete those rows with the same Gross value, we would select only the Gross value column in the Remove Duplicates options, as shown below:

	A	B	C	E	F	G	H	I	J	K
1	Purchase invoices									
2										
3	Invoice date	Supplier ref	Gross value							
4	28/04/2016	SUPV5	979							
5	18/04/2016	CSUP11	6,045							
6	06/04/2016	ASUP6	562							
7	13/04/2016	CSUP6	2,183							
8	14/04/2016	CSUP7	6,045							
9	09/04/2016	ASUP9	4,519							
10	21/04/2016	CSUP14	5,687							
11	07/05/2016	ASUP7	4,291							
12	18/04/2016	CSUP11	6,045							
13	06/04/2016	ASUP6	562							
14	13/04/2016	CSUP6	2,183							

Remove Duplicates ? ✕

To delete duplicate values, select one or more columns that contain duplicates.

⬚ Select All ⬚ Unselect All ☑ My data has headers

Columns
☐ Invoice date
☐ Supplier ref
☑ Gross value

OK Cancel

This removes 4 duplicate values, as can be seen on the next page:

	A	B	C	E	F	G	H	I	J	K
1	Purchase invoices									
2										
3	Invoice date	Supplier ref	Gross value							
4	28/04/2016	SUPV5	979							
5	18/04/2016	CSUP11	6,045							
6	06/04/2016	ASUP6	562							
7	13/04/2016	CSUP6	2,183							
8	09/04/2016	ASUP9	4,519							
9	21/04/2016	CSUP14	5,687							
10	07/05/2016	ASUP7	4,291							
11										
12										
13										
14										

Microsoft Excel

4 duplicate values found and removed; 7 unique values remain.

OK

One more row was deleted than previously, since row 8 matched on value, but not on Invoice date or Supplier.

Note: If you wish to put the rows back into your data, clicking UNDO straight after clicking OK will UNDO the deletions.

COMMENTS

It is possible to add a **note** to a cell. This is called a **comment**, it is a useful way of recording a note which relates to the cell content, perhaps when it was last changed or noting its previous value.

Any cell which has a comment attached to it will display a red indicator in the top right corner of the cell, as can be seen on cell C8 below.

	A	B	C	E	F	G
1	Purchase invoices					
2						
3	Invoice date	Supplier ref	Gross value			
4	28/04/2016	SUPV5	979			
5	18/04/2016	CSUP11	6,045			
6	06/04/2016	ASUP6	562			
7	13/04/2016	CSUP6	2,183			
8	14/04/2016	CSUP7	6,045			
9	09/04/2016	ASUP9	4,519			
10	21/04/2016	CSUP14	5,687			
11	07/05/2016	ASUP7	4,291			

Wendy:
Is this value correct?

When the cursor is on the cell with the red indicator, the comment will be displayed.

It is also possible to adjust the size of the comment box, this is described below.

To ADD a comment

Either

- Right mouse click on the required cell
- Select Insert Comment

Or

- select the cell
- select New comment from the REVIEW menu

Then

- enter your text
- click away from the comment box when you have finished

To EDIT a comment

Either

- Right mouse click on the required cell
- Select Edit Comment

Or

- select the cell
- select Edit comment from the REVIEW menu

Then

- modify your text
- click away from the comment box when you have finished

To RESIZE the comment box

- Right mouse click on the required cell
- Select Edit Comment

The sizing handles appear.

- Drag the handles on the sides or corners of the box to adjust it's size

To MOVE the comment box

- click on the required cell
- move the cursor to the edge of the comment box
- when the four headed arrow symbol appears, drag the comment box to its new position.

To DELETE a comment

Either

■ Right mouse click on the required cell

■ Select Delete Comment

Or

■ select the cell

■ select Delete from the Comments section of the REVIEW menu

To Show All Comments

■ select the Show All Comments option in the REVIEW menu

To stop Show All Comments

■ de-select the Show All Comments option in the REVIEW menu

Chapter Summary

This concludes the text of this chapter, which has covered:

■ simple statistical functions

■ analysis tools

■ remove duplicates

■ comments

You should now carry out some or all of the exercises on the next few pages in order to practise and reinforce your learning.

Activities

Before starting these exercises, check that the **Analysis Toolpak** is available in your spreadsheet software, as described previously in this chapter. If it is not available, you may be able to install it yourself, guided by the instructions provided. Alternatively, you may not have the necessary authority, and may need to refer to your technical support.

Exercise 1 – using statistical functions and rank and percentile

In this first exercise we will open an existing spreadsheet containing some data, add some further data, to practise using the simple statistical functions and some data analysis tools.

To obtain this spreadsheet visit www.osbornebooks.co.uk ('Products and Resources') and download filename **T6expenses**.

Stage 1

This stage is about starting to introduce some simple statistical formulas into our spreadsheet which records monthly expenses.

1. Download the workbook **T6expenses**.

2. Open the downloaded file, save the workbook with new name **T6Exercise1**.

The workbook should appear as shown below.

	A	B	C	D	E	F	G
1	Company Expenses						
2				£			
3		Jan	Feb	Mar	Apr	May	Jun
4	Wages and salaries	25090	25000	60000	25010	30900	24000
5	Motor Expenses	13200	6150	3900	1530	1504	16090
6	Postage	1000	1500	2500	1000	1000	2000
7	Insurance	1200	2800	4000		2130	1770
8	Advertising	7000		25600	9230		11800
9	Rent and rates	22000	22000	22000	22000	22000	22000
10	Heat and light	3200	3200	3200	3200	3200	3200

3. Insert the following additional row between Motor Expenses and Postage (rows 5 and 6).

	Jan	Feb	Mar	Apr	May	Jun
Accountancy	500	500	2340		500	500

4. Merge cells H2, and I2, enter the text *Average*, in bold and italics aligned in the centre.

5. In cell H3, enter *3 month* in bold and italics.

6. In cell I3 enter *6 month* in bold and italics.

7. Format the cells in row 3, so that the text is aligned to the right of the cells, and the font style is bold and italics.

8. In cell H4, enter a formula to calculate the Average for February, April and June.

9. Copy this formula to cells H5 through to H10.

10. In cell I4, enter a formula to calculate the average over all 6 months.

11. Copy this formula to cells I5 through to I10.

12. Format all numeric cells to include a comma (,) to represent thousands, and no decimal places.

13. Save the workbook with the same name **T6Exercise1**.

Your spreadsheet should now look as shown in the image below.

	A	B	C	D	E	F	G	H	I
1	Company Expenses								
2				£					*Average*
3		*Jan*	*Feb*	*Mar*	*Apr*	*May*	*Jun*	*3 month*	*6 month*
4	Wages and salaries	25,090	25,000	60,000	25,010	30,900	24,000	24,670	31,667
5	Motor Expenses	13,200	6,150	3,900	1,530	1,504	16,090	7,923	7,062
6	Accountancy	500	500	2,340		500	500	500	868
7	Postage	1,000	1,500	2,500	1,000	1,000	2,000	1,500	1,500
8	Insurance	1,200	2,800	4,000		2,130	1,770	2,285	2,380
9	Advertising	7,000		25,600	9,230		11,800	10,515	13,408
10	Rent and rates	22,000	22,000	22,000	22,000	22,000	22,000	22,000	22,000
11	Heat and light	3,200	3,200	3,200	3,200	3,200	3,200	3,200	3,200

14. Select show formulas, and you should see the formulas as shown in the image below.

	A	B	C	D	E	F	G	H	I
1	Company Expe								
2				£				*Average*	
3		*Jan*	*Feb*	*Mar*	*Apr*	*May*	*Jun*	*3 month*	*6 month*
4	Wages and salaries	25090	25000	60000	25010	30900	24000	=AVERAGE(C4,E4,G4)	=AVERAGE(B4:G4)
5	Motor Expenses	13200	6150	3900	1530	1504	16090	=AVERAGE(C5,E5,G5)	=AVERAGE(B5:G5)
6	Accountancy	500	500	2340		500	500	=AVERAGE(C6,E6,G6)	=AVERAGE(B6:G6)
7	Postage	1000	1500	2500	1000	1000	2000	=AVERAGE(C7,E7,G7)	=AVERAGE(B7:G7)
8	Insurance	1200	2800	4000		2130	1770	=AVERAGE(C8,E8,G8)	=AVERAGE(B8:G8)
9	Advertising	7000		25600	9230		11800	=AVERAGE(C9,E9,G9)	=AVERAGE(B9:G9)
10	Rent and rates	22000	22000	22000	22000	22000	22000	=AVERAGE(C10,E10,G10)	=AVERAGE(B10:G10)
11	Heat and light	3200	3200	3200	3200	3200	3200	=AVERAGE(C11,E11,G11)	=AVERAGE(B11:G11)

Stage 2

In this stage we are going to add further calculations to the expenses spreadsheet.

1.   Insert 2 rows between rows 1 and 2.

2.   Make sure the font size for row 3 is 11, and in cell A3, enter the text *Max*, in bold and italics, aligned right.

3.   In cell B3, enter a formula to calculate the maximum figure from all the monthly values, using the MAX function.

4.   In cell C3, enter the text *Min*, in bold and italics, aligned right.

5.   In cell D3, enter a formula to calculate the minimum figure from all the monthly values, using the MIN function.

6.   In cell E3, enter the text *Count (row 10)*, in bold and italics, apply wordwrap, aligned left.

7.   In cell F3, enter a formula to calculate how many numeric monthly values there are in the data in columns B to G, row 10, using the COUNT function.

8.   Save your spreadsheet (keeping the same name – **T6Exercise1**).

Your spreadsheet should now appear as shown below.

	A	B	C	D	E	F	G	H	I
1	Company Expenses								
2									
3	*Max*	60,000	*Min*	500	*Count (row 10)*	5			
4					£				*Average*
5		*Jan*	*Feb*	*Mar*	*Apr*	*May*	*Jun*	*3 month*	*6 month*
6	Wages and salaries	25,090	25,000	60,000	25,010	30,900	24,000	24,670	31,667
7	Motor Expenses	13,200	6,150	3,900	1,530	1,504	16,090	7,923	7,062
8	Accountancy	500	500	2,340		500	500	500	868
9	Postage	1,000	1,500	2,500	1,000	1,000	2,000	1,500	1,500
10	Insurance	1,200	2,800	4,000		2,130	1,770	2,285	2,380
11	Advertising	7,000		25,600	9,230		11,800	10,515	13,408
12	Rent and rates	22,000	22,000	22,000	22,000	22,000	22,000	22,000	22,000
13	Heat and light	3,200	3,200	3,200	3,200	3,200	3,200	3,200	3,200

Stage 3

In this stage we are going to look at the ranking and percentile for the values for the month of January.

Continuing with with workbook **T6Exercise1**.

1.   Select **Data Analysis** from the Data or Tools menu, select **Rank and Percentile**.

2.   Either enter the **input range** of data B5 to B13 using absolute cell references, or select the range using the mouse.

3.   Since the data is all in one column, **Grouped by** should be **Columns.**

4.   Check the box **Labels in first row**.

5.   Select **Output range** (rather than new worksheet), enter or select cell K5, (absolute reference $K$5), so that the table will start output in cell K5, as shown in the image below.

Rank and Percentile		? ✕
Input		
Input Range:	$B$5:$B$13	OK
Grouped By:	⦿ Columns	Cancel
	○ Rows	Help
☑ Labels in first row		
Output options		
⦿ Output Range:	$K$5	
○ New Worksheet Ply:		
○ New Workbook		

6.   The Rank and Percentile table will be displayed.

7.   Hide columns C through to I.

8.   Save your spreadsheet (keeping the same name – **T6Exercise1**).

Your spreadsheet should now appear as shown below.

	A	B	J	K	L	M	N
1	Company Expenses						
2							
3	*Max*	60,000					
4		£					
5		*Jan*		*Point*	*Jan*	*Rank*	*Percent*
6	Wages and salaries	25,090		1	25,090	1	100.00%
7	Motor Expenses	13,200		7	22,000	2	85.70%
8	Accountancy	500		2	13,200	3	71.40%
9	Postage	1,000		6	7,000	4	57.10%
10	Insurance	1,200		8	3,200	5	42.80%
11	Advertising	7,000		5	1,200	6	28.50%
12	Rent and rates	22,000		4	1,000	7	14.20%
13	Heat and light	3,200		3	500	8	0.00%

9. We are now going to remove the rank and percentile table from our sheet, either delete columns K to N or clear the contents and remove the borders for cells K5 through to N13.

10. Unhide columns C to I.

11. The spreadsheet should now look as follows:

	A	B	C	D	E	F	G	H	I
1	Company Expenses								
2									
3	Max	60,000	Min	500	Count (row 10)	5			
4					£				Average
5		Jan	Feb	Mar	Apr	May	Jun	3 month	6 month
6	Wages and salaries	25,090	25,000	60,000	25,010	30,900	24,000	24,670	31,667
7	Motor Expenses	13,200	6,150	3,900	1,530	1,504	16,090	7,923	7,062
8	Accountancy	500	500	2,340		500	500	500	868
9	Postage	1,000	1,500	2,500	1,000	1,000	2,000	1,500	1,500
10	Insurance	1,200	2,800	4,000		2,130	1,770	2,285	2,380
11	Advertising	7,000	500	25,600	9,230		11,800	7,177	10,826
12	Rent and rates	22,000	22,000	22,000	22,000	22,000	22,000	22,000	22,000
13	Heat and light	3,200	3,200	3,200	3,200	3,200	3,200	3,200	3,200

Exercise 2 – using COUNTIF, SUMIF and more of the analysis toolpak

In this next exercise we are going to use the Histogram tool found in the Analysis Toolpak (Excel only). We are going to make use of the purchase invoice spreadsheet we saw earlier in the chapter.

To obtain this spreadsheet visit www.osbornebooks.co.uk ('Products and Resources') and download filename **T6purchaseinv**.

Stage 1

We are now going to make use of the data to create a histogram, to analyse the frequency of different numbers in our data.

1. Download the workbook **T6purchaseinv**.

2. Open the downloaded file, save the workbook with new name **T6Exercise2**.

The workbook should appear as shown on the right.

We want to create a histogram to analyse the values of our purchase invoices.

The first step is to get some idea of the spread of gross values.

	A	B	C	D	E
1	Purchase invoices				
2					
3	Invoice date	Supplier ref	Gross value	Date paid	
4	28/04/2016	SUPV5	979	01/06/2016	
5	18/04/2016	CSUP11	6,045	01/06/2016	
6	06/04/2016	ASUP6	562	01/06/2016	
7	13/04/2016	CSUP6	2,183	01/06/2016	
8	14/04/2016	CSUP7	10,045	01/06/2016	
9	09/04/2016	ASUP9	4,519	01/06/2016	
10	21/04/2016	CSUP14	5,687		
11	07/05/2016	ASUP7	4,291	01/07/2016	
12	18/04/2016	CSUP11	6,045	01/06/2016	
13	06/04/2016	ASUP6	562	01/06/2016	
14	13/04/2016	CSUP6	2,183	01/06/2016	
15	12/05/2016	ASUP12	4,162	01/07/2016	
16	15/05/2016	CSUP8	580	01/07/2016	

Since we are going to use the same set of values multiple times, we will define a name for the group of cells holding the gross values.

3. Define a name **GrossValue** for cells C4 through to C38.

4. In cell D2 enter the text **Min value** and in cell E2 enter a formula to calculate the minimum of the Gross values using the range name **GrossValue**, this will give us our smallest value.

5. In cell F2 enter the text **Range of values,** wrap the text, and in cell G2 enter a formula to calculate the difference between the maximum and the minimum of the Gross values.

Your spreadsheet should look as follows:

G2			f_x	=MAX(GrossValue)-MIN(GrossValue)			
	A	B	C	D	E	F	G
1	Purchase invoices						
2				Min value	320	Range of values	9,725
3	Invoice date	Supplier ref	Gross value	Date paid			
4	28/04/2016	SUPV5	979	01/06/2016			
5	18/04/2016	CSUP11	6,045	01/06/2016			
6	06/04/2016	ASUP6	562	01/06/2016			
7	13/04/2016	CSUP6	2,183	01/06/2016			
8	14/04/2016	CSUP7	10,045	01/06/2016			
9	09/04/2016	ASUP9	4,519	01/06/2016			

Note: the formula in G2 could also be =MAX(GrossValue)-E2

From this information, we could decide to have 4 bins, spaced every 2000.

6. In cell G4 enter the **Value**, make it bold.

7. In cell F5 enter the text **Bin1**, and cell G5 enter **2000**

8. In cell F6 enter the text **Bin2**, and cell G6 enter **4000**

9. In cell F7 enter the text **Bin3**, and cell G7 enter **6000**

10. In cell F8 enter the text **Bin4**, and cell G8 enter **8000**

    We will let the values above 8000 go into Other.

11. Select **Data Analysis** from the Data menu, and then select **Histogram**.

12. Either enter the **Input range** of data name GrossValue, or select the range using the mouse.

13. Either enter the **Bin range** of data G4 to G8 using absolute cell references, or select the range using the mouse.

14. Ensure the **labels** box is checked.

15. Select **Output range** (rather than new worksheet), enter or select cell I4, so that the table will start output in cell I4.

16. Select **Chart Output**, as shown on the next page:

The histogram frequency table and the chart will be displayed.

17.   Select and move the chart to be positioned under the bins and frequency tables.

18.   Save your spreadsheet (keeping the same name – **T6Exercise2**).

Your spreadsheet should now look as shown below.

	A	B	C	D	E	F	G	H	I	J
1	Purchase invoices									
2				Min value		320	Range of values	9,725		
3	Invoice date	Supplier ref	Gross value	Date paid						
4	28/04/2016	SUPV5	979	01/06/2016			Value		Value	Frequency
5	18/04/2016	CSUP11	6,045	01/06/2016		Bin 1	2000		2000	9
6	06/04/2016	ASUP6	562	01/06/2016		Bin 2	4000		4000	10
7	13/04/2016	CSUP6	2,183	01/06/2016		Bin 3	6000		6000	10
8	14/04/2016	CSUP7	10,045	01/06/2016		Bin 4	8000		8000	4
9	09/04/2016	ASUP9	4,519	01/06/2016					More	1
10	21/04/2016	CSUP14	5,687							
11	07/05/2016	ASUP7	4,291	01/07/2016						
12	18/04/2016	CSUP11	6,045	01/06/2016						
13	06/04/2016	ASUP6	562	01/06/2016						
14	13/04/2016	CSUP6	2,183	01/06/2016						
15	12/05/2016	ASUP12	4,162	01/07/2016						
16	15/05/2016	CSUP8	580	01/07/2016						
17	27/05/2016	SUPV4	3,761							
18	11/05/2016	ASUP11	4,444	01/07/2016						
19	25/05/2016	SUPV2	4,357	01/07/2016						
20	15/06/2016	CSUP9	3,933							

Stage 2

We are going to do some further analysis on this data.

1.   Add a second sheet to your workbook, name it Invoice copy

2.   Copy all data in columns A to D on the Purchases worksheet to the Invoice copy worksheet, using normal copy and paste.

3.   Clear cell D2.

4.   In cell F3 enter the text **Total invoices**, in cell F4 enter a formula using **COUNT** on the **Value column** to identify how many invoices are listed.

5.   In cell G3 enter the text **Invoices with ref**, in cell G4 enter a formula using COUNTA to identify how many invoices have a supplier reference.

6.   In cell H3 enter the text **Missing suppliers**, enter the formula which uses both the COUNT and COUNTA functions to calculate how many invoices are missing suppliers.

7.   Select show formulas.

8.   Save your workbook.

Your workbook should look similar to below:

	A	B	C	D	E	F	G	H
1	Purchase							
2								
3	Invoice date	Supplier ref	Gross value	Date paid		Total invoices	Invoices with ref	Missing suppliers
4	42488	SUPV5	979	42522		=COUNT(C4:C38)	=COUNTA(B4:B38)	=COUNT(C4:C38)-COUNTA(B4:B38)
5	42478	CSUP11	6045	42522				
6	42466	ASUP6	562	42522				
7	42473	CSUP6	2183	42522				
8	42474	CSUP7	10045	42522				
9	42469	ASUP9	4519	42522				
10	42481	CSUP14	5687					
11	42497	ASUP7	4291	42552				

Notice how all the date values are displayed as numbers in Show Formulas.

Note: We could easily have made the formula for missing suppliers in cell H4 =F4 – G4 but it is useful to practise combining several functions in one formula.

9.   In cell I3, enter the text **Invoices paid**, and in cell I4, enter a formula to count how many invoices have been paid, using **COUNTIF**. (All those paid will have a value >0)

10.   In cell J3, enter the text **Invoices not paid**, and in cell J4, again entering a formula to count how many invoices have not been paid, using **COUNTIF**. (All those not paid will have a blank value "")

11.   Save your workbook.

The results are shown in the image on the next page:

◢	A	B	C	D	E	F	G	H	I	J
1	Purchase invoices									
2										
3	Invoice date	Supplier ref	Gross value	Date paid		Total invoices	Invoices with Ref	Missing suppliers	Invoices paid	Invoices not paid
4	28/04/2016	SUPV5	979	01/06/2016		35	32	3	17	18
5	18/04/2016	CSUP11	6,045	01/06/2016						
6	06/04/2016	ASUP6	562	01/06/2016						
7	13/04/2016	CSUP6	2,183	01/06/2016						
8	14/04/2016	CSUP7	10,045	01/06/2016						
9	09/04/2016	ASUP9	4,519	01/06/2016						

With the formulae as shown below:

F	G	H	I	J
Total invoices	Invoices with Ref	Missing suppliers	Invoices paid	Invoices not paid
=COUNT(C4:C38)	=COUNTA(B4:B38)	=COUNT(C4:C38)-COUNTA(B4:B38)	=COUNTIF(D4:D38,">0")	=COUNTIF(D4:D38,"")

Stage 3

The final steps are to calculate some total values for the paid and unpaid invoices using the SUMIF function.

1. On the Purchases worksheet, select cells C4 to C38 (all the values), and you will see the name GrossValue appear in the Name box.

2. Move to the Invoice Copy worksheet, select cells C4 to C38, no name appears because the range name only applies to the cells on the Purchases worksheet, assign the name GrossCopy to these cells. We will use this range throughout the following steps.

    The first total we want is for those invoices which have been paid, ie those which have a date in column D, because dates are saved as numbers, which we see when we do show formulas, we can use the criteria >0

3. In cell F8 enter text **Invoices paid**, make it bold, and merge and center with cell G8.

4. In cell H8, enter the formula using **SUMIF** to total all the invoice values (column C) which have **been paid**.

    The second total is for those invoices which have not been paid, ie those which have nothing in column D, we can use the criteria "" (double quotes with nothing between, indicating blank).

5. In cell F10 enter text **Invoices not paid**, make it bold, and merge and center with cell G10.

6. In cell H10, enter the formula using **SUMIF** to total all the invoice values (column C) which have **not been paid**.

    The final total, will be those invoices where we have a supplier.

7. In cell F12 enter text **Invoices no supplier**, make it bold, and merge and center with cell G12.

8. In cell H12, enter the formula using **SUMIF** to total all the invoice values (column C) where there is a supplier ref in column B. ie not equal to blank "<>"

9. Format H8, H10, H12 to display as a number, with no decimal places, and with a comma for thousands.

10. Save your workbook.

It should appear as shown below.

	A	B	C	D	E	F	G	H	I	J
1	Purchase invoices									
2										
3	Invoice date	Supplier ref	Gross value	Date paid		Total invoices	Invoices with Ref	Missing suppliers	Invoices paid	Invoices not paid
4	28/04/2016	SUPV5	979	01/06/2016		35	32	3	17	18
5	18/04/2016	CSUP11	6,045	01/06/2016						
6	06/04/2016	ASUP6	562	01/06/2016						
7	13/04/2016	CSUP6	2,183	01/06/2016						
8	14/04/2016	CSUP7	10,045	01/06/2016		Invoices paid		56,502		
9	09/04/2016	ASUP9	4,519	01/06/2016						
10	21/04/2016	CSUP14	5,687			Invoices not paid		61,912		
11	07/05/2016	ASUP7	4,291	01/07/2016						
12	18/04/2016	CSUP11	6,045	01/06/2016		Invoices no supplier		104,689		
13	06/04/2016	ASUP6	562	01/06/2016						
14	13/04/2016	CSUP6	2,183	01/06/2016						
15	12/05/2016	ASUP12	4,162	01/07/2016						
16	15/05/2016	CSUP8	580	01/07/2016						

With formulas:

F	G	H	I	J
Total invoices	Invoices with Ref	Missing suppliers	Invoices paid	Invoices not paid
=COUNT(C4:C38)	=COUNTA(B4:B38)	=COUNT(C4:C38)-COUNTA(B4:B38)	=COUNTIF(D4:D38,">0")	=COUNTIF(D4:D38,"")
Invoices paid		=SUMIF(D4:D38,">0",GrossCopy)		
Invoices not paid		=SUMIF(D4:D38,"",GrossCopy)		
Invoices no supplier		=SUMIF(B4:B38,"<>",GrossCopy)		

Exercise 3 – removing duplicates, adding comments and create a moving average chart

In this final exercise we will practise removing duplicates, adding comments and create a moving average chart utilising an existing spreadsheet and creating a new spreadsheet.

To obtain this spreadsheet visit www.osbornebooks.co.uk ('Products and Resources') and download filename **T6salesexport** which is a csv file.

Stage 1

This stage is about loading a CSV file produced from another system, and cleaning the data.

1. Open the downloaded file **T6salesexport,** save as **T6Exercise3** (note this file will automatically save as a CSV file unless you use Save As, and change the filetype).

It should look as shown below:

◢	A	B	C	D	E	F	G
1	Sales invoices						
2							
3	Customer	Invoice da	Net value	Tax		Gross valu	Due date
4	ACUST6	########	468	94		562	########
5		########	1,819	364		2,183	########
6	CCUST7	########	8,371	1,674		10,045	########
7	ACUST9	########	3,766	753		4,519	########
8	ACUST11	########	3,703	741		4,444	########
9	CUSTV2	########	3,631	726		4,357	########
10	CCUST9	########	3,278	655		3,933	########
11	CCUST15	########	4,726	945		5,671	########
12	ACUST3	########	713	142		855	########
13		########	4,329	866		5,195	########
14	ACUST10	########	2,525	505		3,030	########
15	CCUST13	########	3,506	701		4,207	########
16	CCUST16	########	1,097	219		1,316	########

2. Widen columns B and F so that the data can be seen correctly, and apply wrap text to all column headings.

    If we scroll down, we can see some references are missing in the Supplier ref column.

    We know that all the blank suppliers should have reference CCUST6.

3. Using **Find and Replace**, change all the blank supplier references to CCUST6.

    Hint: leave the Find what: blank, and put the missing ref CCUST6 in Replace with:.

Your worksheet should now look as shown at the top of the next page:

	A	B	C	D	E	F	G
1	Sales invoices						
2							
3	Customer ref	Invoice date	Net value	Tax	Gross value	Due date	
4	ACUST6	06/04/2016	468	94	562	01/06/2016	
5	CCUST6	13/04/2016	1,819	364	2,183	01/06/2016	
6	CCUST7	14/04/2016	8,371	1,674	10,045	01/06/2016	
7	ACUST9	09/04/2016	3,766	753	4,519	01/06/2016	
8	ACUST11	11/05/2016	3,703	741	4,444	01/07/2016	
9	CUSTV2	25/05/2016	3,631	726	4,357	01/07/2016	
10	CCUST9	15/06/2016	3,278	655	3,933	01/07/2016	
11	CCUST15	21/06/2016	4,726	945	5,671	01/07/2016	
12	ACUST3	02/06/2016	713	142	855	01/07/2016	
13	CCUST6	16/06/2016	4,329	866	5,195	01/07/2016	
14	ACUST10	09/06/2016	2,525	505	3,030	01/07/2016	

We are now going to remove any duplicate records, but before we do that, we are going to have a closer look at what invoice records we have using SORT.

4.   SORT all the data by:

Customer ref (A to Z), then add a levels

to sort by **Invoice date (Oldest to Newest)**,

then by **Net value (Smallest to Largest)**,

then by **Tax (Smallest to Largest)**,

then by **Gross value (Smallest to Largest)**,

and finally by **Due date (Oldest to Newest)**.

This sort will put all duplicate records next to each other.

If you glance down the data you can see duplicates, eg rows 7 and 8.

5.   Using Remove Duplicates, delete all rows with a duplicate Gross value.

The message:

should appear and the last row of the data should now be row 33.

This isn't really what we need, since some rows have been deleted with the same values but different customers.

6. Click UNDO to return the rows.

    The last row should be row 51.

7. Now use **Remove duplicates** again, to delete any invoice records which match across each of the 6 columns.

    The message:

    should appear and the data should now look as shown below, with the last row being row 35.

	A	B	C	D	E	F	G	H
1	Sales invoices							
2								
3	Customer	Invoice date	Net value	Tax		Gross valu	Due date	
4	ACUST1	30/06/2016	2,983	596		3,579	01/08/2016	
5	ACUST10	09/06/2016	2,525	505		3,030	01/07/2016	
6	ACUST11	11/05/2016	3,703	741		4,444	01/07/2016	
7	ACUST12	12/05/2016	3,468	694		4,162	01/07/2016	
8	ACUST2	01/07/2016	542	108		650	01/08/2016	
9	ACUST3	02/06/2016	713	142		855	01/07/2016	
10	ACUST4	03/07/2016	1,750	350		2,100	01/08/2016	
11	ACUST5	04/07/2016	1,023	205		1,228	01/08/2016	
12	ACUST5	29/07/2016	5,610	1,122		6,732	01/08/2016	
13	ACUST6	06/04/2016	468	94		562	01/06/2016	
14	ACUST7	07/05/2016	3,576	715		4,291	01/07/2016	
15	ACUST9	09/04/2016	3,766	753		4,519	01/06/2016	
16	CCUST11	18/04/2016	5,038	1,007		6,045	01/06/2016	
17	CCUST12	18/07/2016	2.117	423		2.540	01/08/2016	

8. Save your spreadsheet (keeping the same name – **T6Exercise3**).

Stage 2

We are going to create a new worksheet, where we will enter some data values which we will use to create a Moving average.

1. Check that you have a second worksheet in the workbook you have open, if not add a new worksheet and name it **Turnover**.

2. Select worksheet **Turnover**, enter the data and format as shown below.

	A	B	C	D	E	F	G	H	I	J	K	L
1	Company ABC Ltd											
2					£ (million)							
3		2006	2007	2008	2009	2010	2011	2012	2013	2014	2015	2016
4	Turnover	2.1	2.3	2.9	2.4	3.2	3.5	1.9	3.4	2.6	4.1	

3. In cell A5, enter text Moving average (3 yr).

4. Widen column A to fit all text.

5. Select **Data Analysis** from the Data or Tools menu, select **Moving average**.

6. Either enter the **Input range** of data B4 to L4 using absolute cell references, or select the range using the mouse.

Note: if we did not include the cell L4, we would not get a forecast value for 2016.

7. Leave **Labels in first row** unchecked.

8. Enter 3 in **Interval** (the normal default).

9. Select **Output** range, enter B5 to L5 using absolute cell references, or select the range using the mouse.

10. Select **Chart output**.

As shown below:

11. The **moving average values** will be created in row 5, showing a forecast value for 2016, and the moving average chart will be displayed, comparing the actual values against the forecast.

12. If necessary, move the chart to be positioned under data.

13. Save your spreadsheet (keeping the same name – **T6Exercise3**).

Your spreadsheet should now appear as shown below. Note that the first average figure is recorded in the third year rather than in the second year.

	A	B	C	D	E	F	G	H	I	J	K	L
1	Company ABC Ltd											
2					£ (million)							
3		2006	2007	2008	2009	2010	2011	2012	2013	2014	2015	2016
4	Turnover	2.1	2.3	2.9	2.4	3.2	3.5	1.9	3.4	2.6	4.1	
5	Moving Average 3 yr	#N/A	#N/A	2.433333	2.533333	2.833333	3.033333	2.866667	2.933333	2.633333	3.366667	3.35
6												
7												

Moving Average chart

Stage 3

We are going to calculate the 6 yearly moving average, and add some comments.

1. Continuing with T6Exercise3.

2. In cell A6 enter text **Moving Average 6 yr.**

3. Click on the existing chart, and drag it so that the top corner is in cell A7.

4. Using the Moving Average tool, create the 6 yearly moving average for the turnover in cells B6 to L6, together with a chart.

You will see that there are no data values on the chart until the 6th data point – year 2011.

5. Drag the 6 year chart next to the 3 year chart.

Your worksheet should look something like that shown at the top of the next page:

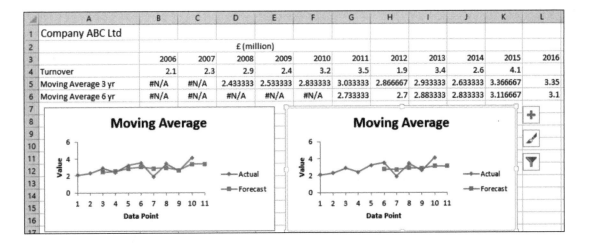

6.   Delete both charts.

7.   Add a comment to cell L5, 3 year forecast.

8.   Add a comment to cell L6, 6 year forecast.

9.   Move the comment attached to L6 to below L6.

10. Select Show all comments.

11. Save your workbook.

It should look as shown below.

	A	B	C	D	E	F	G	H	I	J	K	L	M	N	O
1	Company ABC Ltd														
2				£ (million)											
3		2006	2007	2008	2009	2010	2011	2012	2013	2014	2015	2016			
4	Turnover	2.1	2.3	2.9	2.4	3.2	3.5	1.9	3.4	2.6	4.1				
5	Moving Average 3 yr	#N/A	#N/A	2.433333	2.533333	2.833333	3.033333	2.866667	2.933333	2.633333	3.366667	3.35	Wendy: 3 year forecast		
6	Moving Average 6 yr	#N/A	#N/A	#N/A	#N/A	#N/A	2.733333	2.7	2.883333	2.833333	3.116667	3.1			
7															
8															
9												Wendy: 6 year forecast		
10															
11															

You have now completed the exercises for chapter 6.

7 Charts

this chapter covers...

This chapter covers creating and modifying charts. It explains and takes you through the concepts and techniques listed below.

By the time you have finished this chapter and carried out the exercises which follow, you should be able to produce spreadsheets which contain appropriate charts to illustrate worksheet data.

The concepts and techniques covered are:

■ *types of charts*

■ *creating charts*

■ *modification of charts*

■ *chart printing*

Note that the step-by-step instructions given in this chapter are based on the Microsoft® Excel model, but the concepts and techniques described generally relate to all spreadsheet packages.

TYPES OF CHARTS

Within spreadsheet packages, there are a variety of different chart types available for the visual representation of data. In this section we are going to illustrate the following types of chart. Instructions for the creation of charts will follow in a separate section at the end of this chapter.

- Bar or column
- Line
- Pie
- Scatter
- Doughnut
- Bubble

barchart

The bar chart is probably the most commonly used chart, and can be applied to data that is arranged in columns or rows on a worksheet. In the image below, you can see that we have taken six months of sales data, represented as a **vertical** bar chart, also known as **column** chart, showing how the value of sales has changed over the period of six months.

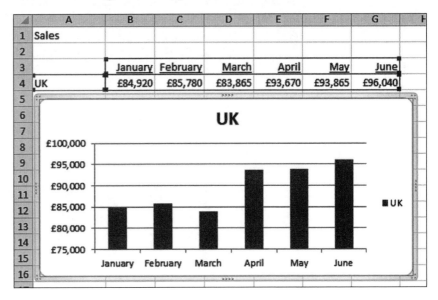

This is a bar chart in its simplest form, with only one set of data values. With two sets of data, sales in the UK and sales in China, we can show the values side by side; this is known as **Clustered**.

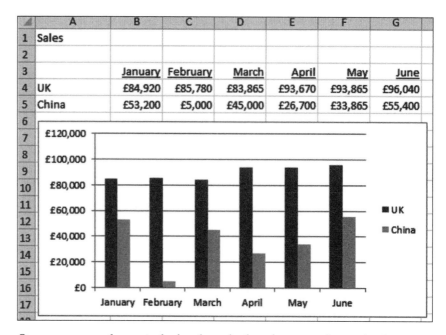

Or we can see them stacked, where both values are shown in the same column, as illustrated below:

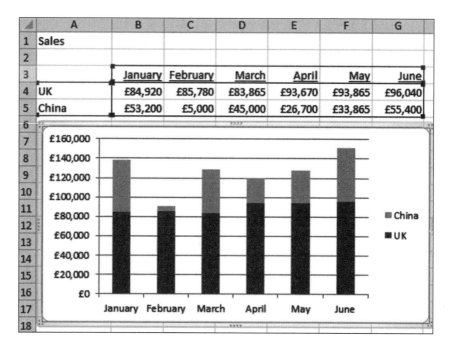

We are also able to **switch the row and column** axis over so that instead of the x axis being the months, and the series being UK and China, the x axis becomes UK and China, and the series becomes the months. This is illustrated on the next page.

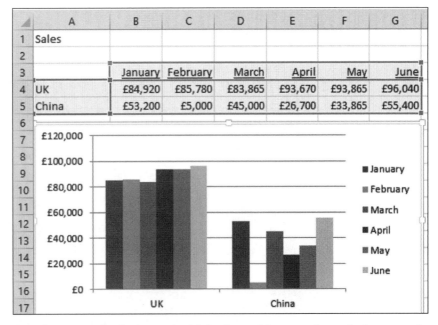

Bar charts can also be created with horizontal bars, as shown in the example below:

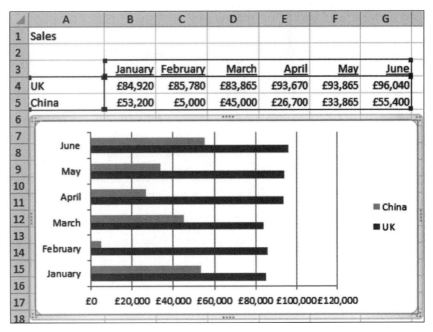

Note: Within the **chart** menu, **Column** is used to create vertical bar charts, and **Bar** to create horizontal bar charts.

Both **column** and **bar** type charts can also be created in 3D (3 dimensional), by selecting the appropriate style from the choices available.

line chart

An example of a **line chart** using some daily Share Price data is shown below.

The line chart below is showing the price of the share over a period of 20 days.

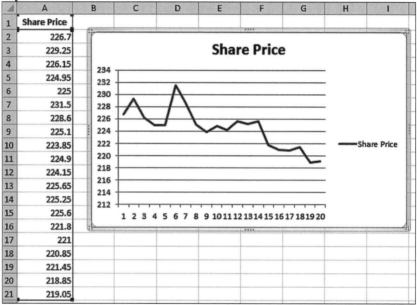

pie chart

A **pie chart** can be produced for only one set of data values, arranged in one column or row on a worksheet. It is known as a 'pie chart' because it looks like a pie divided into a number of 'slices'.

Pie charts show the data values relative to the total of the values. Each data value is shown in a pie chart as a percentage or proportion of the whole 'pie'.

A pie chart can be used when:

- you only have one set of data values that you want to plot
- none of the values that you want to plot is negative
- very few of the values that you want to plot are zero
- you do not have more than seven values
- the data values represent all the parts of the whole

In the image on the next page you can see an example of a pie chart where the value represent sales in China for each of the six months:

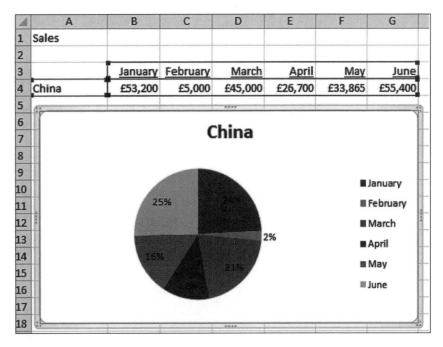

Each value is also shown as a percentage of the whole, which would be the total sales for the six months.

To make the pie chart more visual, it is possible to select a **3D** chart and the slices will be shown as three dimensional, or **exploded** where the individual slices are separated. These options can add to a chart's clarity.

The China sales data is shown as an exploded pie chart in the image below.

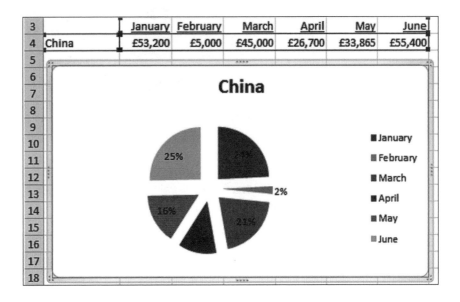

doughnut

A **doughnut chart** is a variation of a pie chart. It can be produced for one or more sets of data values, which are arranged in columns or rows on a worksheet. Whereas a pie is a solid circle cut into a slices, a doughnut appears in the form of a series of concentric rings – ie rings grouped around the same centre.

Each ring of the doughnut represents a different data series, and each ring shows the data values relative to the total of the values for that series. This can be seen in the illustration below, utilising Sales in UK and China.

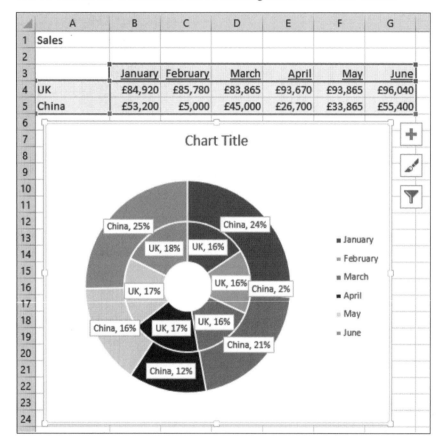

scatter chart

A **scatter chart** can be produced for numeric data values that are arranged on a worksheet as adjacent rows or columns.

The two groups of numbers are plotted as one series of xy coordinates.

To use data on a worksheet for a scatter chart, you should have the x values in one row or column, and then the corresponding y values in the adjacent row or column.

Scatter charts are often used for displaying and comparing numeric values, such as scientific, statistical, and engineering data to show the relationships among several sets of numeric values.

An example of a scatter chart is shown in the image below. The data in columns A and B shows the price of coffee and the price of oil at the same points in time. This gives us a series of values which can be plotted as a scatter diagram. Each point on the diagram represents one pair of prices.

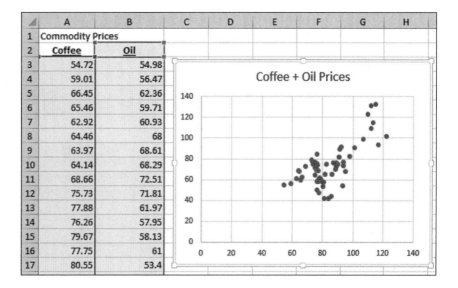

scatter chart with trendline

It is very simple to introduce a **trend line** onto the scatter chart. To do this:

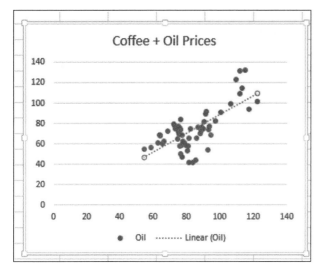

- select the scatter chart (double click within the data points on the chart)

- Right click on the chart

- select **Add Trendline** from the drop down menu

- select the required Trendline options

An example is shown on the left.

bubble

A **bubble chart** is a variation of a scatter chart in which the individual values are replaced with bubbles, and an additional dimension of the data is represented in the size of the bubbles. A bubble chart plots x values, y values, and z (size) values. You can see an example in the image below, where the three data series on the worksheet are represented on the bubble chart.

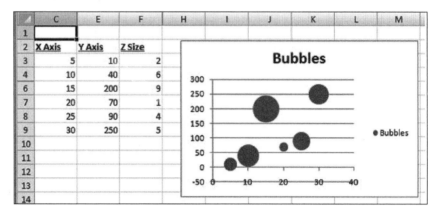

CREATING CHARTS

We have seen that there are numerous chart types available to use. However the basic steps which can be used to create a chart from a worksheet are applicable to most chart types:

- select the data and headings on the worksheet to be presented in the chart
- select INSERT
- select the **chart type** required, either from Recommended charts, the appropriate icon, or the list of all charts
- select a chart style
- select a layout, this can be from QUICK LAYOUT to add default title and axis labels as required
- select set a chart title
- label the 'y' axis
- label the 'x' axis

  to reflect the data shown

These steps are described and illustrated on the next page, using the sales data for UK and China.

◢	A	B	C	D	E	F	G
1	Sales						
2							
3		January	February	March	April	May	June
4	UK	£84,920	£85,780	£83,865	£93,670	£93,865	£96,040
5	China	£53,200	£5,000	£45,000	£26,700	£33,865	£55,400

You may wish to create a spreadsheet, and enter this data yourself, so that you can follow the steps through.

Step 1 – select the data

Select the data, including the text which relates to the data. We are going to select both rows of data, since we want to compare the two rows of sales values. These are known as the **data series**, each row of data represents one data series. The data can be selected as shown below:

◢	A	B	C	D	E	F	G
1	Sales						
2							
3		January	February	March	April	May	June
4	UK	£84,920	£85,780	£83,865	£93,670	£93,865	£96,040
5	China	£53,200	£5,000	£45,000	£26,700	£33,865	£55,400

Note that in some versions of software, you may be taken through the chart creation by a 'help wizard', and may need to specify the range of your data.

This can be done by either moving to the data and selecting as shown in the image above, or manually specifying the range, in this case $A$3:$G$5, always using absolute cell addresses.

Step 2 – create the chart:

■ Select **INSERT** from the menu

■ Select the **Chart type** required

A chart will be created representing your data.

With the chart still selected:

■ Select the **chart style**, which determines the visual effects.

(If you move the cursor over each of the styles, you will see how each style looks.)

From **Quick Layout**:

■ select a layout which has the axes labels, title, and key (**legend**) positioning, which you require.

The **Legend** identifies which line on the graph represents which series of data.

In our example we are going to create a line chart to represent both rows of data.

A chart is created on the same worksheet by default.

In the image below, we have created a line chart, and placed it below our rows of data, as previously mentioned, each row of data is known as a **series**.

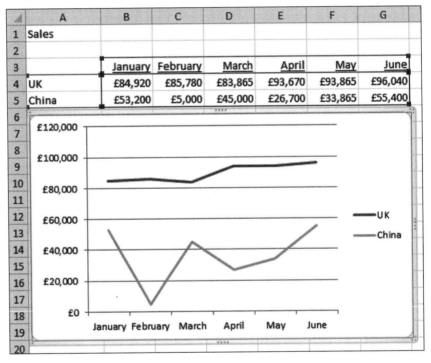

Step 3 – add or change the chart title

The chart axes are automatically created with scales based on the ranges of values in the data. We have chosen to display the **legend**, to the right.

To introduce a title for the chart if you don't already have one:

- select the chart (single or double click)
- from the **CHART TOOLS menu**, select the **Design** tab
- select **Add Chart Element**
- select **Chart title**
- at present this will show none, so select **Above chart**

The text **Chart Title** appears above the chart, as shown on the next page:

	A	B	C	D	E	F	G
1	Sales						
2							
3		January	February	March	April	May	June
4	UK	£84,920	£85,780	£83,865	£93,670	£93,865	£96,040
5	China	£53,200	£5,000	£45,000	£26,700	£33,865	£55,400
6							
7				**Chart Title**			
8							
9	£120,000						

To change the title for the chart

It is very simple to change this text, by clicking the title text and entering the required title.

We will enter the title 'Sales figures'.

Step 4 – dealing with the 'y' axis (vertical axis)

The chart layout we have used does not include an axis label for the y axis.

To add this manually:

- select the chart (single or double click)
- from the **CHART TOOLS menu**, select the **Design** tab
- select **Add Chart Element**
- select **Axis Titles**, **Primary Vertical Axis**
- edit the 'y' axis label as required – here 'Sales Value' is the chosen axis title

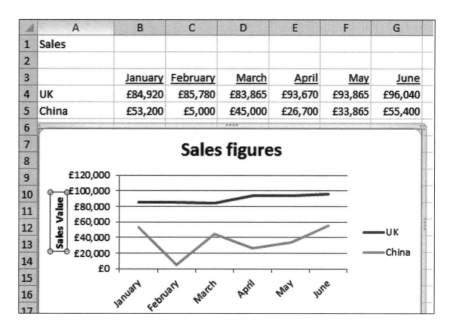

Step 5 – dealing with the 'x' axis (horizontal axis)

The layout we have used does not include an axis label for the x axis. To add this manually:

■ select the chart (single or double click)

■ from the **CHART TOOLS menu**, select the Design tab

■ select **Add Chart Element**

■ select **Axis Titles**, **Primary Horizontal Axis**

■ edit the 'x' axis label as required – here 'Month' is the chosen axis title

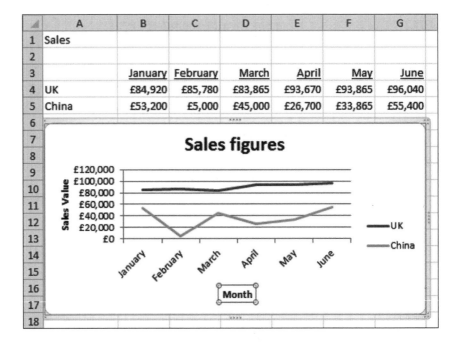

	A	B	C	D	E	F	G
1	Sales						
2							
3		January	February	March	April	May	June
4	UK	£84,920	£85,780	£83,865	£93,670	£93,865	£96,040
5	China	£53,200	£5,000	£45,000	£26,700	£33,865	£55,400

Step 6 – dealing with the chart legend

The legend lists the name and the colour used to represent each data series in the chart. It is usually automatically added to the chart when the chart is created. It is possible to choose whether or not a legend should be displayed and if so, where it should be positioned within the chart.

To manipulate the chart legend:

■ select the chart (single or double click)

■ RIGHT click on the existing **Legend**

■ select Format Legend

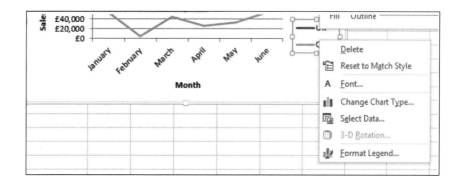

Format Legend will provide you with options which allow to change the position and appearance.

In the earlier image, you can see the legend is positioned on the right of the chart, and in the image below, it is positioned to the left of the chart.

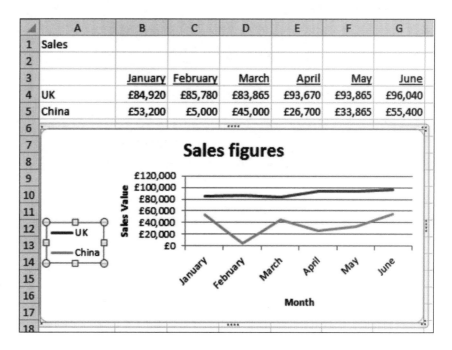

changing font size and style for a chart element

It is possible to change the font size and style for any of the titles or labels. To do this:

- Right click on the item
- select font and make the changes you require

changing the graph type for one data series

Once we have created our chart representing our data, it is possible to change how one of the sets of data is shown on the chart. For example, we may want to show the data from China as a bar chart, still keeping the UK sales as a line graph.

To do this:

- select **Design** from the **CHART TOOLS** menu
- select **Change Chart Type**
- select **Combo**

For the China data,

- select one of the **Column** chart types and OK

As shown below:

The chart should now look as shown in the image below:

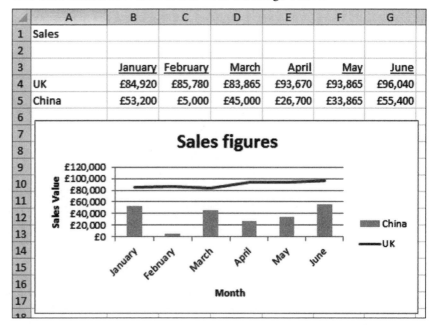

changing, adding or removIng a data series

Once we have created our chart representing our data, it is possible to add another set of data, remove one, or change what's included in a series.

To do this, with the chart selected:

■ use the **Select Data** option from the **Design** menu

Here we can see the two data series making up our chart – UK and China. If we wish to remove one:

■ click on the series name in the left hand box

■ click Remove

To **Change** the cells included in a series:

■ click on the series name in the left hand box

■ click **Edit**, make the required changes in the Edit Series box as shown below.

Edit Series	? X
Series name:	
=Data!$A$4	🔢 = UK
Series values:	
=Data!$B$4:$G$4	🔢 = £84,920, £85,7...
	OK Cancel

To **Add** another series,

■ click **Add** and then select the cells containing the data as required.

In Excel 2013® once you have created a chart, if it is selected, tools are displayed which enable you to easily modify your chart. These are shown to the right of the chart in the image below.

	A	B	C	D	E	F	G	H
1	Sales							
2								
3		January	February	March	April	May	June	
4	UK	£84,920	£85,780	£83,865	£93,670	£93,865	£96,040	
5	China	£53,200	£5,000	£45,000	£26,700	£33,865	£55,400	

Chart Title

£120,000
£100,000
£80,000
£60,000

CHART ELEMENTS

☑ Axes
☐ Axis Titles
☑ Chart Title
☐ Data Labels
☐ Data Table
☐ Error Bars
☑ Gridlines
☑ Legend
☐ Trendline
☐ Up/Down Bars

The first tool – **CHART ELEMENTS** – the green plus symbol allows you to decide what you want to include on your chart, as can be seen in the image on the left.

Note: if you move the mouse over the text of one of the elements in this list, a small arrow appears. Clicking on this reveals options relating to the element, such as positioning. This is shown in the example at the top of the next page, for Chart Title:

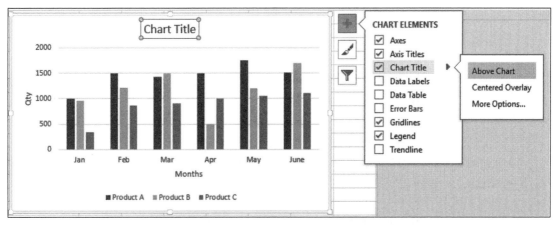

Or alternatively, if we moved the mouse over legend, and clicked the small arrow, we would see the options for the position of the legend, as can be seen in the image below:

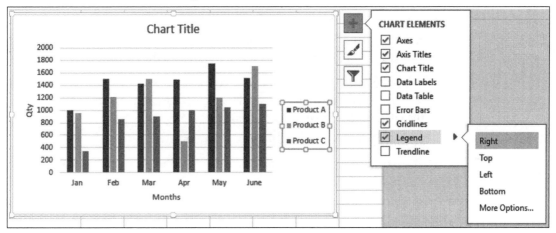

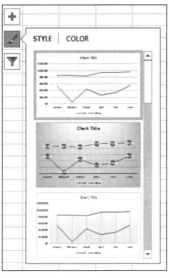

The second tool – **CHART STYLES** – the paint brush symbol, as shown on the left, lets you easily change the style of the chart and the colours used.

And finally – **CHART FILTERS** – the funnel symbol, as shown on the right, allows you to manipulate the data series, deciding which series should be shown, and which cells make up each series.

moving or resizing

Once you have created a chart as described in the previous steps, you may wish to resize or move the chart to a different location either on the same or a different worksheet, for example to avoid it covering some of the data.

To resize a chart:

- click on the chart to select it
- place the cursor over one of the corners of the chart frame, or the dots around the edges of the frame (you will see the cursor changes to a double headed arrow)
- click and drag to the required size

To move a chart:

- click on the chart to select it
- click and drag the chart to its new position

Moving charts, embedded charts and chart sheets

In Excel 2013® when a new chart is created it will be placed on the same worksheet as the data; this is known as an **embedded** chart.

Alternatively, the chart can be on a **chart sheet**, which contains nothing but the chart scaled up to occupy a full page. All the chart options still apply and the chart sheet can be printed as normal.

If you want to move the chart to a new sheet:

- right click within the space surrounding the chart, but still within the chart frame
- select **Move chart** from the menu

The following screen is displayed:

Move Chart	? ✕
Choose where you want the chart to be placed:	
⬚ ○ New sheet:	Chart1
⬚ ◉ Object in:	Sheet1 ▾
	OK Cancel

To select an existing worksheet and place the chart on it

- select **Object in**
- select the worksheet to which the chart is to move from the drop down list

To create a new chart sheet and place the chart on it:

- select **New sheet**
- enter a name for the new sheet, or leave it as Chart1

An example of chart sheet is shown below:

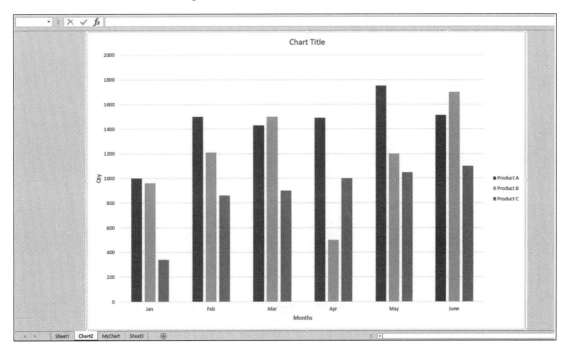

changing how a chart item is displayed

To change the properties of an item on the chart such as Chart Title or axis label, if you **right** click on the item you will get a menu allowing you to change how the item is displayed or formatted.

In addition, whenever you select an element on the chart, such as the chart title, a new pane of information and options opens on the right side of the screen allowing you set all the properties of the selected element.

An example is shown on the next page, for Chart Title:

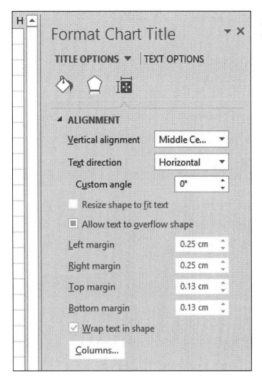

As you can see, there are many formatting options which can be changed.

more on pie charts

In the case of a **pie** chart, to make it more meaningful we would like each slice to show the value or percentage of the whole, as shown in the examples earlier in the chapter. To do this we would need to add data labels as follows:

To label a pie chart:

■ **right** click on the centre of the pie chart to select all slices, or on one of the slices if it is an exploded pie chart

■ select **add data labels**

The values represented by each sector are now displayed.

To change whether we see values or percentages or both:

■ **right** click on the centre of the pie chart to select all slices, or on one of the slices if it is an exploded pie chart

■ select **format data labels**

■ under **Label Options**, check or uncheck **Value** and **Percentage** as required

To create an exploded pie chart:

■ create a normal pie chart for your data

■ right click on the pie chart

■ select Format Data Series

The Format Data Series pane opens on the right as shown below:

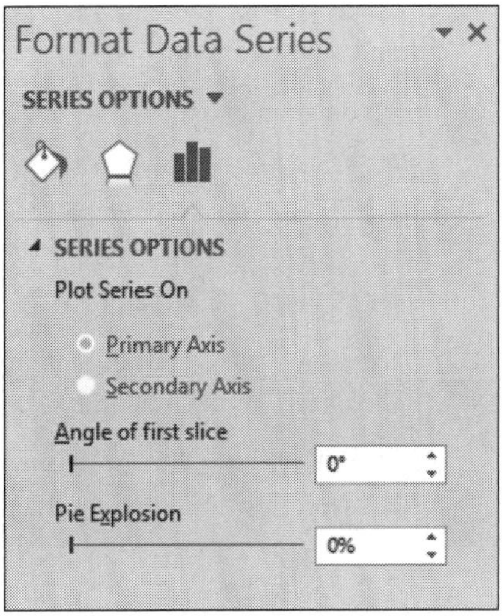

Format Data Series

SERIES OPTIONS ▾

◢ SERIES OPTIONS

Plot Series On

○ Primary Axis

○ Secondary Axis

Angle of first slice

0°

Pie Explosion

0%

■ in the pie explosion field, enter a value such as 20%

The pie chart will then appear exploded as illustrated below.

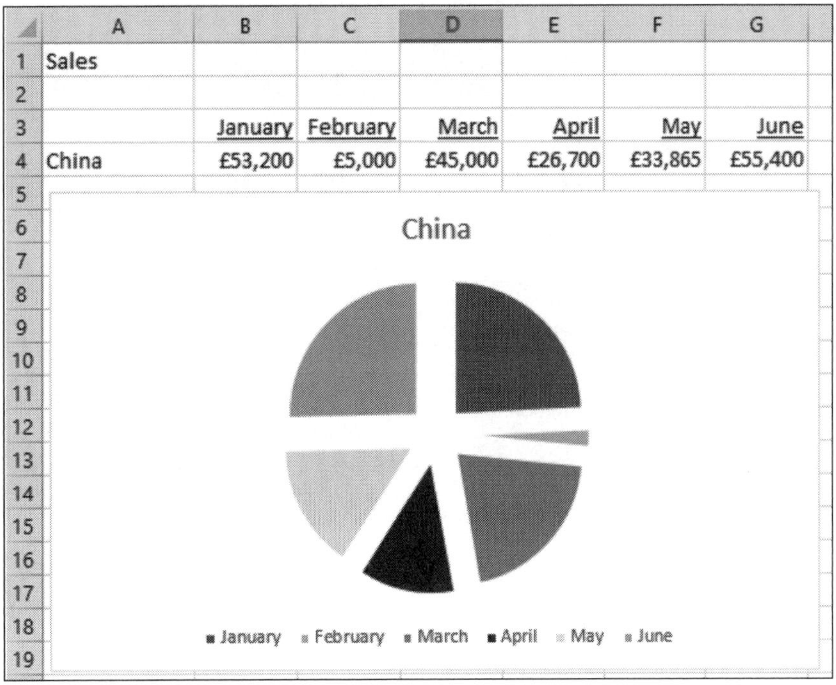

	A	B	C	D	E	F	G
1	Sales						
2							
3		January	February	March	April	May	June
4	China	£53,200	£5,000	£45,000	£26,700	£33,865	£55,400

China

■ January   ■ February   ■ March   ■ April   ■ May   ■ June

deleting a chart

Once you have created a chart it is possible that you may wish to delete it and start again, or just remove it from the sheet.

To delete a chart:

■ click on the chart to select it

■ press delete

printing a chart

Once you have created a chart it is possible that you may wish to print just the chart. To print a chart:

■ click on the chart to select it

■ select Print and adjust Page Setup as required

3D charts

Some charts types have the capability of being shown as 3D (3 dimensional). This is purely cosmetic but can enhance the legibility and visual impression of a chart.

For example a 3D pie chart is illustrated below:

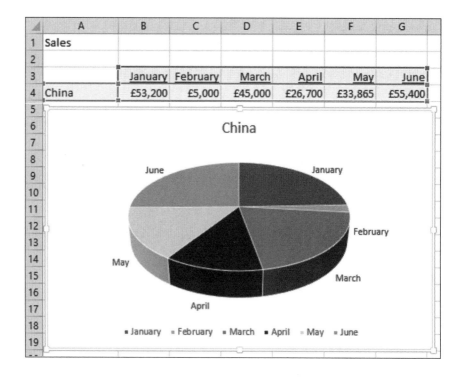

Column, Line and Bar charts can all be displayed as 3D To create a 3D chart:

- select the chart type
- select the 3D style from the choices if available

Or to change an existing chart to 3D

- select the chart
- select **Change Chart Type** from the Design menu select the 3D style from the choices if available

charts – learning about the software

As you will see from reading this chapter and also experimenting with the spreadsheet software, there are many things which can be changed within the chart layout itself, such as:

- the position of the legend
- displaying gridlines
- how the scales are to be shown
- how data points are to be shown on the lines

As you will see, not all these areas are covered in this text, but you are strongly recommended to experiment with your own data.

Spreadsheet software is an essentially practical 'hands on' subject. As previously mentioned, different software packages will step through the chart creation process in different ways, so it is important to familiarise yourself with the processes involved.

Chapter Summary

This concludes the text of this chapter, which has covered:

- types of charts
- creating charts
- modification of charts
- chart printing

You should now carry out some or all of the exercises on the next few pages in order to practise and reinforce your learning.

Activities

Exercise 1– creating bar and line charts

In this exercise we are going to produce a variety of bar charts, using some sales data.

Stage 1

In this stage we are going to create a simple bar chart from some product sales data.

1. Open a new workbook.

2. Enter the data shown in the table below.

Sales by Product	Jan	Feb	Mar	Apr	May	June
Product A	1000	1500	1430	1490	1750	1510
Product B	960	1210	1500	500	1200	1700
Product C	340	860	900	1000	1050	1100

3. Name your worksheet **Data**.

4. Save the workbook with the name **Ch7Exercise1**.

5. Select the cells A2 through to G5, this includes the column headings, row headings and data for the six months for each product.

6. Insert a vertical **bar (column) chart** to represent this data.

7. Move the chart and position it below the data. Resize it to the same width as the data.

8. If not already present, use chart **Design, Add Chart Element** to add titles for the Chart, Vertical Axis, and Horizontal axis to the chart layout.

    The Chart Title should be **above the chart**.

    For the Vertical Axis title, select type **Primary Vertical**.

    For the Horizontal Axis title, select type **Primary Horizontal**.

9. Change the Chart Title to **Sales January to June**.

10. Change the 'x' axis title to **Months**.

11. Change the 'y' axis, to read **Qty**.

12. Save your spreadsheet.

Your spreadsheet should now appear as shown at the top of the next page.

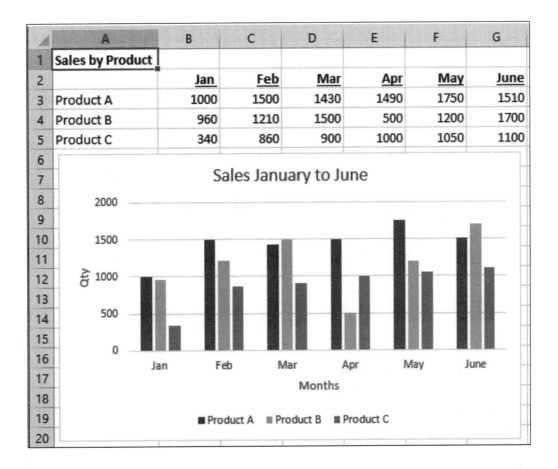

Stage 2

In this stage we are going to manipulate the chart we have created.

1. Add a new worksheet, name it **MyChart.**

2. Move the chart onto a new worksheet with name **MyChart**.

3. Change the size of the chart so that it covers approximately 13 rows, and 7 columns, starting in cell B2.

4. Change the **Chart Title** to **Product Sales Jan to Jun.**

5. Make the chart title bold italic, by selecting the text and using normal font options.

6. Change the **chart title position** from above to **Centred overlay**.

   Note to do this: use the Chart elements tool (the green plus sign), and clicking the right hand arrow which appears next to chart title, choose accordingly.

7. Change the **chart type** to **Column 3D**.

8. Chose the left most style from the **chart styles** – style 1.

9. Save your workbook.

Your workbook should look as shown on the next page:

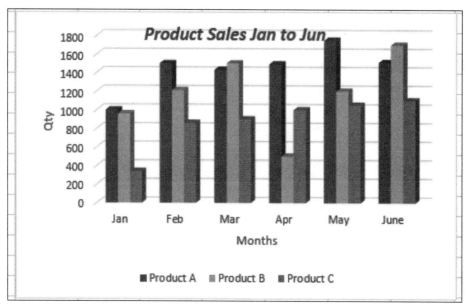

Stage 3

We are going to continue utilising the product sales data, and the chart created on worksheet MyChart.

1.   Change the **Chart type** to **Stacked Column**, not 3D.

2.   Change the position of the **Legend** to be on the **Right** of the chart.

3.   Add data labels to the chart, using the chart elements tool.

4.   Change the **x axis label** to **Months (2016)**.

5.   Change the **y axis label** to **Units**.

Your workbook should look as shown below:

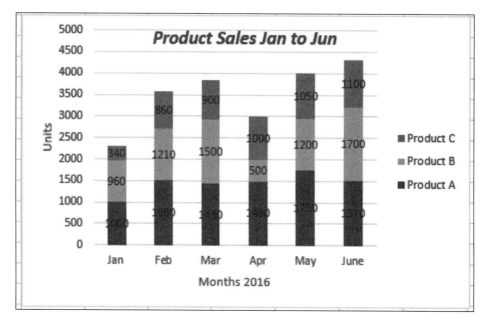

6.   Print just the chart.

7.   Save your workbook

Your print preview should look as shown below.

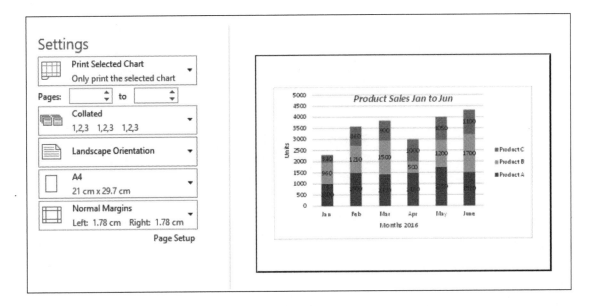

Exercise 2 – creating pie charts

In this exercise we are going to produce pie charts, using some sales data.

Stage 1

In this stage we are going to enter some regional sales data and use it to create a pie chart.

1.   Open a new workbook.

2.   Enter the Company sales data for each of the five regions shown in the table below:

Company ABC ltd	
Region	Sales
South	210,000
West	155,000
Central	412,000
North	327,000
East	523,000

3.   Name your worksheet **Sales**.

4.   Save the workbook with the name **Ch7Exercise2**.

5.   Create a pie chart to show the sales data by region.

6.   Resize and position the chart to the right of the data in your spreadsheet.

Your worksheet should look as shown below:

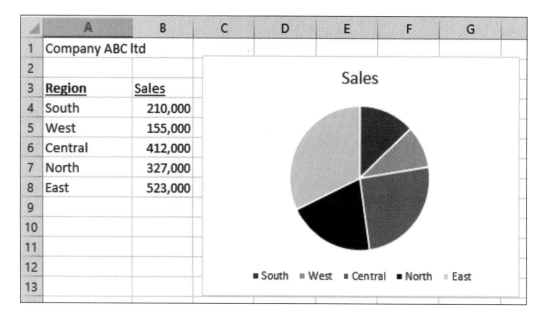

We are going to add value labels to the slices of the chart.

7.   Add **data labels** to the chart showing the value of sales in each region.

This can be seen in the image below:

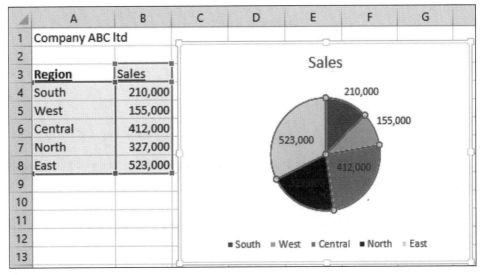

8. Format the data labels on the chart (using **label options**) to just show **percentages**.

Again this is shown in the image below:

	A	B	C	D	E	F	G
1	Company ABC ltd						
2							
3	Region	Sales					
4	South	210,000					
5	West	155,000					
6	Central	412,000					
7	North	327,000					
8	East	523,000					
9							
10							
11							
12							
13							

9. Save your workbook.

Stage 2

In this stage we are going to create an exploded pie chart.

1. Add a further row of sales data for the overseas region.

Region	Sales
Overseas	870,000

2. Edit the Data series for the pie chart to include this new row of data

3. Explode the pie chart to 15%.

4. Move the Series Legend so that it is to the right of the pie chart.

5. Format the data labels, to show both the value of sales, and the percentage each slice represents.

Your worksheet should look as shown below:

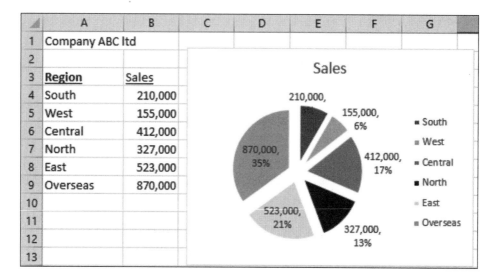

6. Change the Pie chart style to be 3D, and select one of the chart styles from the menu bar.

7. Save your workbook.

Your worksheet should look as shown below:

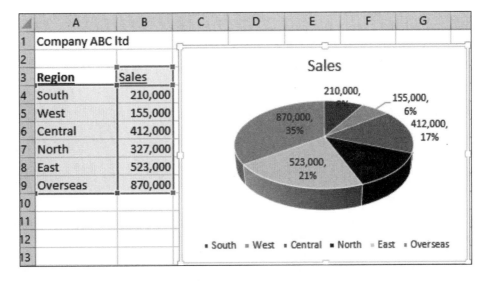

Exercise 3 – creating more charts

In this next exercise we are going to practise creating three types of chart:

- line
- scatter and trend line
- bubble

For some of the charts we will download the data, and for others we will enter a small amount of data.

To access and download the necessary workbooks, visit www.osbornebooks.co.uk ('Products and Resources').

Stage 1

1. Download the workbook **T7charts** from www.osbornebooks.co.uk ('Products and Resources').

2. Open the downloaded file, save the workbook with new name **T7Exercise3**.

The workbook should look as shown below:

	A	B	C	D	E	F	G
1	Company ABC Ltd						
2				£ (million)			
3		2010	2011	2012	2013	2014	2015
4	Turnover	2.1	2.3	2.9	2.6	3.2	3.5
5	Gross Profit	0.315	0.276	0.406	0.195	0.576	0.56
6	Cost of Sales	1.1	1.2	1.25	1.3	1.34	1.39

3. Select the worksheet **Turnover**.

Initially, we want to produce a line chart just for Turnover and Profit, so that we can compare the two sets of figures.

4. Select cells A3 through to G5.

5. Insert a chart of type **Line**.

6. Reposition and resize your chart to fit just under the data, in rows 7 to 18.

7. From Chart Styles, choose style 11 which will show data point values on the chart.

8. Add a **vertical axis title** set it to **£(MILLION)**.

9. Set the chart title to **COMPANY ABC LTD**.

10. Save your workbook.

Your workbook should look as shown below:

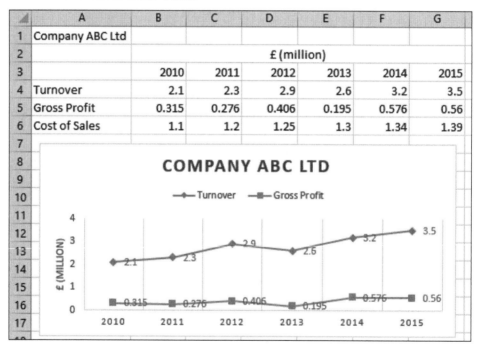

11. Add the data for **Cost of Sales** as another data series to our chart, again represented as a **line**.

12. Using **Change Chart Type**, change the chart type for **Gross Profit**, and **Cost of sales** to be **Clustered Column**, as shown below.

Choose the chart type and axis for your data series:		
Series Name	**Chart Type**	**Secondary Axis**
▮ Turnover	Line with Markers ⌄	☐
▮ Gross Profit	Clustered Column ⌄	☐
▮ Cost of Sales	Clustered Column ⌄	☐

13. Save your workbook.

Your worksheet should look as shown below:

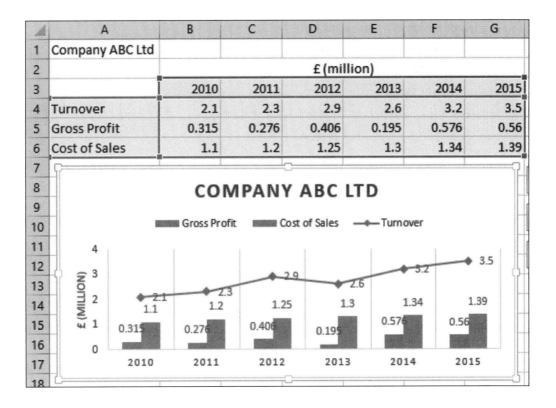

Stage 2

We are now going to use some financial data to create a scatter chart from a series of twelve values held in a previously created workbook. The data represents the values of two stock market indices which chart the value of the UK and US stock markets at different points in time. The stock market indices involved are the FTSE (UK stocks and shares) and the Dow (US stock and shares).

1.   Continuing with T7exercise3, select the worksheet **Scatter.**

The worksheet should appear as shown below. You should appreciate that there will be more values off to the right, which are not shown in this image.

	A	B	C	D	E	F	G	H	I
1	Financial data								
2									
3	FTSE	5,322	5,534	5,060	5,599	5,770	5,123	5,126	5,132
4	DOW	10,388	10,618	10,012	10,566	10,997	10,380	9,931	10,198

2.   Select all the data on the worksheet, cells A3 through to M4.

3.   Insert a **scatter chart** to represent this data.

4.   From Quick Layout, select Layout 1 which adds Axis titles to both axes.

5.   Edit the 'y' axis to **DOW.**

6.   Edit the 'x' axis to **FTSE.**

7.   Move the chart to a position below and to the left of the data.

8.   Change the chart title to **Financial Market.**

9.   Using **Chart Elements**, don't show the series legend.

Your workbook should look as follows:

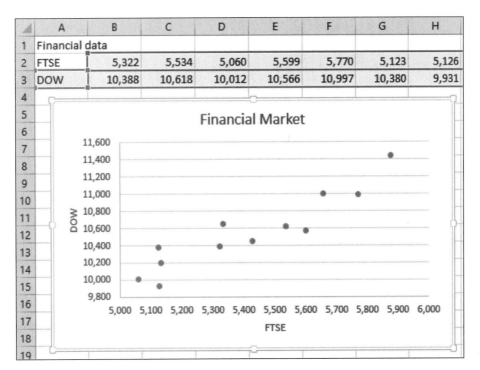

10. Using **Chart Elements**, add a **linear trendline** to the chart.

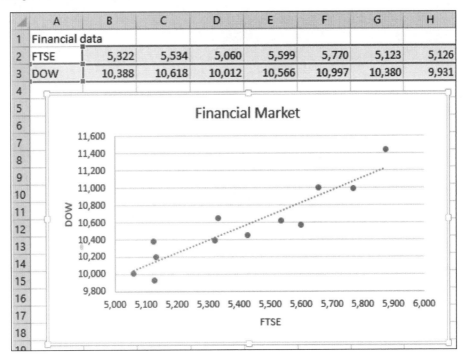

Stage 3

In the final stage, we are going to create a bubble chart.

1.   Continuing with T7exercise3, select the worksheet **Scatter**.

2.   Copy the data on worksheet Scatter to a new worksheet, name it Bubble.

3.   Add a new line of financial data in row 4 as shown below:

| NIKKEI | 16,110 | 16,357 | 14,865 | 18,123 | 20,952 | 16,090 | 15,231 | 17,255 | 15,911 | 16,522 | 19,221 | 19,422 |

4.   Create a **3D Bubble chart** of the 3 rows of financial data.

5.   Position the chart just below the data.

6.   Save your workbook.

It should look as shown below:

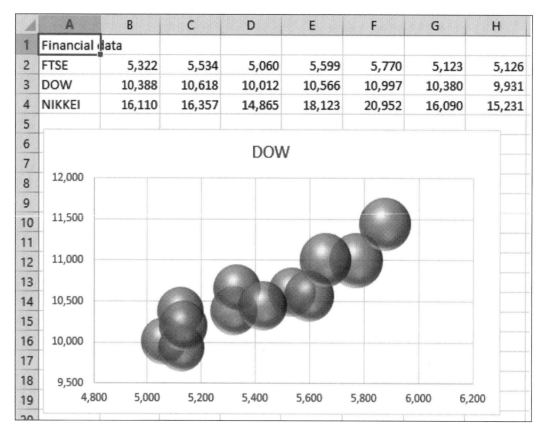

You have now completed the exercises for chapter 7.

8 Pivot tables and workbook management

this chapter covers...

This chapter covers some further spreadsheet techniques such as window management using Freeze Panes. It also explains the use of pivot tables and describes how they are created and formatted. By the time you have finished this chapter and carried out the exercises which follow, you should be able to produce spreadsheets which are very comprehensive, easy to read and containing pivot tables.

The concepts and techniques covered are:

■ *managing windows – using freeze panes*

■ *using the Paste Special function*

■ *working with multiple worksheets and workbooks*

■ *creating a simple pivot table*

■ *using subsets of data*

■ *formatting pivot tables*

■ *what-if scenarios*

■ *goal seeking*

■ *data tables*

■ *hyperlinks*

Note that the step-by-step instructions given in this chapter are based on the Microsoft® Excel model, but the concepts and techniques described generally relate to all spreadsheet packages.

WINDOW – FREEZE PANES

As we have seen in earlier chapters, we can scroll up, down and across our worksheet using the scroll bars positioned around the working area of the worksheet.

However, sometimes if we have a large amount of data, we want still to be able to see our row or column text headings so that we know what data we are looking at. The problem is illustrated in the next two screen images.

If we look at the image below, we can see the top portion of a large spreadsheet recording customer sales. The headings are clearly visible.

	A	B	C	D	E	F	G	H	I
1	**Name**	**Total**	**Month1**	**Month2**	**Month3**	**Month4**	**Month5**	**Month6**	**Month7**
2	*Farmhouse Foods*	£154	£0	£112	£0	£0	£0	£26	£0
3	*Engineering Services*	£554	£0	£0	£0	£0	£67	£0	£0
4	*Another Food Service*	£790	£0	£0	£0	£58	£116	£0	£0
5	*Top Quality Supplies*	£56	£0	£56	£0	£0	£0	£0	£0
6	*Halal Foods*	£36	£0	£0	£0	£0	£0	£0	£0
7	*Edwards Farm*	£195	£0	£0	£0	£0	£40	£0	£65
8	*Allen and co*	£1,412	£45	£68	£231	£0	£331	£37	£49
9	*Ahmed and son*	£340	£0	£0	£0	£0	£0	£0	£0
10	*Green & Sons Wholesalers*	£1,827	£700	£0	£104	£0	£0	£0	£0
11	*Higginbottom and son*	£389	£0	£0	£0	£0	£0	£0	£300
12	*W B Meats*	£135	£0	£45	£0	£0	£0	£0	£0

If we use the scroll bars to move around the data, we can end up in a situation where we cannot see the text at the top of the column, or at the start of the row. This is not very useful, as you can see in the image shown below.

	D	E	F	G	H	I	J	K	L	M
4	£0	£0	£58	£116	£0	£0	£174	£0	£0	£0
5	£56	£0	£0	£0	£0	£0	£0	£0	£0	£0
6	£0	£0	£0	£0	£0	£0	£0	£0	£0	£36
7	£0	£0	£0	£40	£0	£65	£0	£0	£0	£0
8	£68	£231	£0	£331	£37	£49	£0	£0	£100	£115
9	£0	£0	£0	£0	£0	£0	£0	£0	£0	£0
10	£0	£104	£0	£0	£0	£0	£0	£363	£0	£0
11	£0	£0	£0	£0	£0	£300	£0	£0	£0	£89
12	£45	£0	£0	£0	£0	£0	£0	£0	£0	£0
13	£0	£50	£0	£0	£0	£0	£25	£0	£0	£0
14	£166	£583	£225	£414	£365	£470	£490	£244	£423	£354
15	£40	£0	£0	£0	£0	£0	£0	£0	£0	£0

To get over this problem we can use a facility called **Freeze Panes**. This facility is found under the **VIEW** menu.

There are several choices within **Freeze Panes**, but the simplest is to select the first data cell (B2 in our example), then select **Freeze Panes** from the VIEW menu.

You are now able to scroll up and down with row and column headings staying in view, as can be seen in the image below, where we have scrolled both right and down. The slightly more solid lines at the bottom of row1 and to the right of column A indicate they are frozen and will not disappear out of view as you scroll around the worksheet.

	A	G	H	I	J	K	L	M	N
1	Name	Month5	Month6	Month7	Month8	Month9	Mont10	Month11	Month12
14	T F Curries	£414	£365	£470	£490	£244	£423	£354	£560
15	Fiber Optical Services	£0	£0	£0	£0	£0	£0	£0	£0
16	My Provisions	£0	£0	£0	£25	£0	£0	£0	£0
17	Alliance services	£0	£0	£0	£0	£0	£0	£0	£0
18	Aluminium casts	£360	£119	£72	£286	£0	£2,093	£0	£364
19	Impala	£0	£98	£0	£0	£0	£0	£0	£0
20	Tool Hire	£0	£0	£0	£0	£0	£0	£0	£0
21	Handyfreight	£0	£0	£0	£0	£0	£0	£0	£0
22	Steel Traders	£0	£0	£0	£0	£0	£0	£0	£0
23	Fruit Supplies	£0	£0	£0	£0	£65	£0	£279	£0

To turn off Freeze Panes:

From the **VIEW** menu,

- select **Freeze Panes**
- select **Unfreeze Panes**

It is also possible to freeze just the row headings, or just the column headings as follows:

From the **VIEW** menu,

- select **Freeze Panes**

Either

- select **Freeze Top Row**

Or

- select **Freeze First Column**

To turn off Freeze Panes:

From the **VIEW** menu,

- select **Freeze Panes**
- select **Unfreeze Panes**

PASTE SPECIAL

This is an extremely useful facility when we are copying data, whether it be a formula, just some text in a cell or group of cells or the way cells are formatted.

Paste Special allows us to decide exactly how we want to paste this copied information into its new location.

For example, if it is some text we are copying, formatted in Bold and Underlined, we may not want the copied text to be formatted in the same way. Or perhaps, we have a formula which we are copying, and we don't want to copy the formula, but the actual value it produces instead to paste in to the new location.

Looking at the image below, we have selected four cells of text, A6 to D6.

	A	B	C	D	E
1	Bank transactions				
2					
3	Opening balance	1500.00			
4	Closing balance	1289.05			**Down
5					
6	Date	Debit	Credit	Balance	
7	02/04/2016	95.34	0.00	1,404.66	

Paste Special dialog:

Paste
- ◉ All
- ○ Formulas
- ○ Values
- ○ Formats
- ○ Comments
- ○ Validation
- ○ All using Source theme
- ○ All except borders
- ○ Column widths
- ○ Formulas and number formats
- ○ Values and number formats
- ○ All merging conditional formats

Operation
- ◉ None
- ○ Add
- ○ Subtract
- ○ Multiply
- ○ Divide

☐ Skip blanks   ☐ Transpose

Paste Link   OK   Cancel

Then

- select **Copy**
- move to where you want to place the copy – in this case, cell A14
- select **Paste Special** from Paste on the HOME menu

The **Paste Special** options appear as shown on the left.

In this case we just want to copy the values, without formats, so we select Values, and OK. The results are shown in the screen image on the next page, with the copy of the unformatted text shown in cells A14:D14.

◢	A	B	C	D	E
1	Bank transactions				
2					
3	Opening balance	1500.00			
4	Closing balance	1289.05			**Down
5					
6	Date	Debit	Credit	Balance	
7	02/04/2016	95.34	0.00	1,404.66	
8	11/04/2016	0.00	25.50	1,430.16	
9	15/04/2016	0.00	34.78	1,464.94	
10	22/04/2016	67.90	0.00	1,397.04	
11	28/04/2016	107.99	0.00	1,289.05	
12	Totals	271.23	60.28		1,289.05
13					
14	Date	Debit	Credit	Balance	

By choosing the **Values** button you will paste the values resulting from formulas (rather than the formulas themselves) without formatting. If we look at row 12, which contains some formulas. The formula in E12 can be seen in the formula bar below.

E12	▼	⋮	✕ ✓ ƒx	=B3-B12+C12

◢	A	B	C	D	E
1	Bank transactions				
2					
3	Opening balance	1500.00			
4	Closing balance	1289.05			**Down
5					
6	Date	Debit	Credit	Balance	
7	02/04/2016	95.34	0.00	1,404.66	
8	11/04/2016	0.00	25.50	1,430.16	
9	15/04/2016	0.00	34.78	1,464.94	
10	22/04/2016	67.90	0.00	1,397.04	
11	28/04/2016	107.99	0.00	1,289.05	
12	Totals	271.23	60.28		1,289.05

If we chose to copy cells A12 to E12, use **Paste special**, and **Paste values** into cells A14 to E14, you can see in the image on the top of the next page that the value in E14 is correct, but no longer contains a formula.

E14		▼	⋮	✕ ✓ *fx*	1289.05	

◢	A	B	C	D	E
1	**Bank transactions**				
2					
3	Opening balance	1500.00			
4	Closing balance	1289.05			**Down
5					
6	**Date**	**Debit**	**Credit**	**Balance**	
7	02/04/2016	95.34	0.00	1,404.66	
8	11/04/2016	0.00	25.50	1,430.16	
9	15/04/2016	0.00	34.78	1,464.94	
10	22/04/2016	67.90	0.00	1,397.04	
11	28/04/2016	107.99	0.00	1,289.05	
12	**Totals**	271.23	60.28		1,289.05
13					
14	Totals	271.23	60.28		1289.05

Paste special offers many options when copying cells; one other which we are going to look at is **Paste Link**. This option pastes a direct link to the cell(s) being copied, so that if that cell changes so does the copy.

Using the same example, copying cells A12 to E12, if we use **Paste Special**, then **Paste Link**, E14 now contains a direct link to E12, ie the formula =E12

As can be seen below:

E14		▼	⋮	✕ ✓ *fx*	=E12	

◢	A	B	C	D	E
1	**Bank transactions**				
2					
3	Opening balance	1500.00			
4	Closing balance	1289.05			**Down
5					
6	**Date**	**Debit**	**Credit**	**Balance**	
7	02/04/2016	95.34	0.00	1,404.66	
8	11/04/2016	0.00	25.50	1,430.16	
9	15/04/2016	0.00	34.78	1,464.94	
10	22/04/2016	67.90	0.00	1,397.04	
11	28/04/2016	107.99	0.00	1,289.05	
12	**Totals**	271.23	60.28		1,289.05
13					
14	Totals	271.23	60.28	0.00	1289.05

To paste the actual formulas without formatting then the **Paste formulas** option should be chosen from the Paste special options.

Note: Once we have selected some cells to copy, moved to where we want to place the copy, we can use right mouse click to access the paste special options as illustrated below.

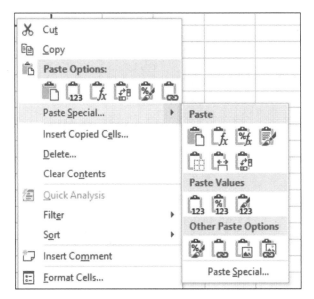

WORKING WITH MULTIPLE WORKSHEETS

When creating a formula, it is possible to use or reference data **on another worksheet** within the same workbook by including the worksheet name within the formula.

If we look at the images below, we can see a simple workbook with two worksheets, one named July, the other named Charges.

The July worksheet shows the opening and closing balances for a month:

	A	B	C	D	E	F
1	Transactions					
2						
3	Opening balance	1,500.00				
4	Closing balance	1,289.05				
5	Extra charges					
6	New balance					
7						

July | Charges ⊕

The Charges worksheet (shown below) is very simple, containing charges figures which need to be incorporated in the monthly balance.

	A	B	C	D	E	F
1						
2	Charges	May	June	July	Aug	Sept
3	Value		125	24	17	120	90
4						
5						
6						
7						

July | **Charges** | ⊕

In this case we want cell **B5** on worksheet **July**, to contain the charges value for July, found in cell D3 on worksheet Charges. To do this:

- Move to cell B5 on worksheet July
- Enter = (to indicate a formula)
- Move to cell D3 on worksheet Charges
- Press **RETURN** to complete the formula

Looking at the image below we can see the formula created in cell B5 in the formula bar of worksheet July:

=Charges!**D3**

The formula contains a direct reference to the work sheet Charges, followed by an exclamation mark (!) to indicate that this is a worksheet name, and then the cell reference D3 in the worksheet Charges.

B5	▼	⋮	✕ ✓ *fx*	=Charges!D3		
	A	B	C	D	E	F
1	Transactions					
2						
3	Opening balance	1,500.00				
4	Closing balance	1,289.05				
5	Extra charges	17.00				
6	New balance					
7						

July | Charges | ⊕

Alternatively, we could use the **Paste special**, **Paste link** option in cell B5 to insert a direct link to cell D3 on worksheet **Charges**.

To do this:

- move to cell D3 on worksheet Charges
- select Copy

- move to cell B5 on worksheet July
- select Paste special
- select Paste link

The resultant formula in cell B5 is illustrated below.

B5			✕ ✓ *fx*	=Charges!$D$3		
	A	B	C	D	E	F
1	Transactions					
2						
3	Opening balance	1,500.00				
4	Closing balance	1,289.05				
5	Extra charges	17.00				
6	New balance					
7						

| ◀ ▶ | July | Charges | ⊕ | | ⋮ |

The only difference using this method, is that the formula contains an absolute cell reference.

copying a worksheet

It is very simple to make a copy of a worksheet:

- select the worksheet you want to copy
- right mouse click on the worksheet name tab
- select **Move** or **Copy**

This operation can be seen below in the screen image below.

	A			D	E	F
1	Transactions		Insert...			
2		▣	Delete			
3	Opening balanc		Rename			
4	Closing balance		Move or Copy...			
5	Extra charges	▣	View Code			
6	New balance	▣	Protect Sheet...			
7			Tab Color ▶			
8			Hide			
9			Unhide...			
10			Select All Sheets			

| ◀ ▶ | July | Charges | ⊕ | | ⋮ |

- choose the workbook to which you wish to move or copy the selected worksheet

(This can either be within the current workbook, or another open workbook)

■ choose where the copy sheet is to be placed in the workbook

■ select the **Create a copy** check box, so that it is ticked

■ press OK

The screen will appear as follows:

Move or Copy		?	X
Move selected sheets			
<u>T</u>o book:			
Chap 8 mult sheets.xlsx			▾
<u>B</u>efore sheet:			
July Charges (move to end)			
☑ Create a copy			
		OK	Cancel

In the example shown above, a copy of the worksheet will be placed at the end of the workbook, named July(2) as shown below.

◢	A	B	C	D	E	F
1	Transactions					
2						
3	Opening balance	1,500.00				
4	Closing balance	1,289.05				
5	Extra charges	17.00				
6	**New balance**					
7						

July | Charges | **July (2)** | ⊕

WORKING WITH MULTIPLE WORKBOOKS

We may regularly want to work with more than one workbook open. In Excel 2013® each workbook is opened in a separate window. To switch between open workbooks, just right mouse click on the Excel icon in the taskbar, and select the required workbook from the list.

It is also possible to move or copy a worksheet from one workbook to another workbook. The procedure is very similar to moving worksheets within a single workbook. To move or copy a worksheet from one workbook to another workbook:

- in the **To book** box, select the name of the workbook where the worksheet is to be moved or copied to (in the example which follows we select **new book** from the drop down list)
- choose in which workbook the copy worksheet is to be placed
- select the **Create a copy** check box, so that it is ticked, and press OK

The screen will appear as shown below. If a worksheet is copied or moved in this way, any formulas will stay exactly as they were in the original sheet.

using Copy and Paste to move data

Moving or copying a worksheet as described above is an easy way of moving data from one worksheet to another, whether in the same or in different workbooks.

It is also possible to use the normal Copy and Paste to copy all or part of the data from a worksheet in one open workbook to a worksheet in another open workbook. In the image on the next page, you can see the bank transaction data on worksheet July in our file which is named **BankTrans**. (The filename is not visible on the image.)

▲	A	B	C	D	E	F
1	Bank transactions					
2						
3	Opening balance	1500.00				
4	Closing balance	1289.05			**Down	
5						
6	Date	Debit	Credit	Balance		
7	02/04/2016	95.34	0.00	1,404.66		
8	11/04/2016	0.00	25.50	1,430.16		
9	15/04/2016	0.00	34.78	1,464.94		
10	22/04/2016	67.90	0.00	1,397.04		
11	28/04/2016	107.99	0.00	1,289.05		
12	Totals	271.23	60.28		1,289.05	

◄   ►   **July**   Charges   ⊕

Suppose we want to copy some of the transaction data to a worksheet in another workbook. To do this we select cells A6:C11, and **Copy and Paste** onto **Sheet1** in another workbook, as shown below.

C2   ▾   ⋮   ✗ ✓ *fx*   0

▲	A	B	C	D	E	F
1	Date	Debit	Credit			
2	02/04/2016	95.34	0.00			
3	11/04/2016	0.00	25.50			
4	15/04/2016	0.00	34.78			
5	22/04/2016	67.90	0.00			
6	28/04/2016	107.99	0.00			

◄   ►   **Sheet1**   ⊕

We can see that cell C2 holds the value 0.

Alternatively, if we use **Copy** and then **Paste Special**, **Paste Link**, it would look as shown on the next page, with each cell holding a direct link to the appropriate cell in workbook **BankTrans**. Notice how the workbook name is included in the formula, enclosed in square brackets, then the worksheet name followed by an exclamation mark, then the cell on that worksheet.

Looking at cell C2:

| C2 | ▾ | ⋮ | ✕ ✓ *fx* | =[BankTrans.xlsx]July!C7 |

◢	A	B	C	D	E	F
1	Date	Debit	Credit			
2	42462	95.34	0			
3	42471	0	25.5			
4	42475	0	34.78			
5	42482	67.9	0			
6	42488	107.99	0			
7						

◂ ▸   **Sheet1**   ⊕   ⋮ ◂

We can see that it takes its value from cell **C7**, on worksheet **July**, in workbook **BankTrans**.

Should any of the original values in the **BankTrans** workbook change, the values in this workbook will change to match.

Note: Since we have not copied the formats across from the original worksheet, the dates are shown as serial numbers. This is easily changed using the normal **Format** options.

PIVOT TABLES – AN INTRODUCTION

what is a pivot table?

A **pivot table** is a very powerful reporting tool found in spreadsheet packages. Pivot tables allow us to generate and extract meaningful information from a large table of information within a matter of minutes, by creating an interactive summary from a worksheet containing numerous rows of data. This summary is known as a **pivot table**.

advantages of a pivot table

Instead of having to analyse vast amounts of data, a pivot table can sort, count, subtotal and total your numeric information. It can allow you to look at the data in different ways very quickly and easily.

It is possible to expand and collapse levels of data and drill down to details from the summary data to look at areas in more detail.

Changing the format in which the data is summarised, by moving rows to columns or columns to rows (pivoting) allows you to see different summaries of the same source data.

examples of pivot tables

If we look at the image below, we can see a small part of some extended sales data relating to the sales generated by individual sales reps:

	A	B	C	D	E	F
1	**Sales**					
2						
3	**Month**	**Product**	**Value**	**Sales Rep**	**Country**	
4	Apr	Other	£34.90	IO	SP	
5	Apr	Footwear	£1,460.40	TP	UK	
6	Apr	Other	£56.25	IO	IND	
7	Apr	Jewellery	£56.00	IO	SP	
8	Aug	Other	£1,500.00	IY	FR	
9	Aug	Luggage	£67.75	SM	PKN	
10	Aug	Clothing	£99.95	TP	UK	
11	Aug	Other	£1,460.40	IY	FR	
12	Dec	Luggage	£56.25	IO	GER	
13	Dec	Jewellery	£34.00	MP	SP	
14	Dec	Other	£1,500.00	IO	SP	
15	Dec	Accessories	£124.60	MP	GER	
16	Feb	Jewellery	£1,500.00	TP	UK	
17	Feb	Footwear	£220.00	IY	FR	

In the example pivot table below we are showing for each sales rep, the value of each product type sold (eg Accessories, Clothing etc) created from the sales data, and summarised in a simple table.

	A	B	C	D	E	F	G	H
1								
2								
3	**Sum of Value**	**Column Labels** ▾						
4	**Row Labels** ▾	**Accessories**	**Clothing**	**Footwear**	**Jewellery**	**Luggage**	**Other**	**Grand Total**
5	IY	1585.3	44.75	374.5	125.75	220	4705.55	7055.85
6	IO	334.75	1180		182.75	552.5	1647.4	3897.4
7	MP	124.6		253	34	2800		3211.6
8	SM		443.85	224.55	240	192.35		1100.75
9	TP	213.75	99.95	1586.15	1500		124.6	3524.45
10	**Grand Total**	2258.4	1768.55	2438.2	2082.5	3764.85	6477.55	18790.05
11								

pivot tables and workbook management

If we then wanted to see the detail of the Accessories sales made by sales rep IY, we could select cell B5, and 'drill down' to show the detailed sales which make up this subtotal, as can be seen in the image on the next page.

⊿	A	B	C	D	E
1	Month ▾	Product ▾	Value ▾	Sales Rep ▾	Country ▾
2	Sep	Accessories	34	IY	GER
3	Sep	Accessories	1460.4	IY	FR
4	Oct	Accessories	34.9	IY	PKN
5	Nov	Accessories	56	IY	FR

You can see that a pivot table provides a very powerful analysis and reporting tool.

CREATING A PIVOT TABLE

The techniques for creating a pivot table will vary greatly between spreadsheet packages, and even between versions of the same package, but the principles remain the same. In the steps that follow we will be creating a pivot table in Microsoft® Excel version 2013.

We will work with the sales data used in the examples above.

Step 1 – Setting up the data

The data should be set out in columns going down the worksheet.

The columns of data should be adjacent, and start in the same row.

Each column of data should have a title (name) which relates to the data it contains. In our example we have the following titles:

■ Month

■ Product

■ Value

■ Sales Rep

■ Country

These titles are normal pieces of text and should be placed in the cell directly above the first data cell, for each column.

The titles are also known as **fields** (of data) within the pivot table environment and are used extensively in the creation of a pivot table.

Step 2 – Selecting the data

Select all your data, including the column titles.

Step 3 – Creating the pivot table

You have two choices when creating a pivot table, you can either chose to create a recommended pivot table based on your data set, or create a blank pivot table which you will set up yourself. We will cover both options.

Creating a pivot table from scratch

■ select **PivotTable** from the INSERT menu.

The following message box should appear:

Check that the range entered in the **Table/Range** box is correct and includes all your data cells.

Leave the **New Worksheet** button selected – this will automatically create the pivot table on a new worksheet within your current workbook.

Select OK to continue, a screen similar to the one below is displayed.

Step 4 – Laying out your table

You can see our list of column titles (fields) in the small box (**Fields List**) top right, and below are the rows and columns boxes where we define which fields are to be the rows, and which to be the columns.

In our example we are going to calculate the value of sales for each **country** by **product**. These are the two fields of data which we want to display.

We want to have:

▪ products in columns

▪ country in rows

Working within the PivotTable Fields pane shown on the right, we select the appropriate fields, one at a time from the fields list (top right), and drag to either the **ROWS**, **COLUMNS** or **VALUES** areas within the pane.

We will first select the **Country** field from the **Field List**, and drag to the **ROWS** area, if not already there and release.

The layout immediately changes to reflect this, as shown below.

You can see that each of the different **countries** from our sales data is displayed in column A, one row for each country, sorted alphabetically, and with a Grand Total at the bottom.

In the **Field List** box, the **Country** field is now ticked to indicate that we have selected it.

Now we select the **Product** field from the **Field List**, and drag it to the **COLUMNS** area and release. The screen then appears as shown on the next page.

You can see that the titles for the different products from within our data are displayed in Row 4, starting from Column B. There is one column for each product, sorted alphabetically, and with a Grand Total at the end. In the Field List box, the **Product** field is now ticked to indicate that we have selected it. As you can see, the layout structure is becoming clearer.

One further step is now required to include the sales value data so that we can analyse the sales.

To include this field, we select the **Value** field from the **Field List**, and drag it to the **∑ VALUES** area then release.

As our pivot table has now taken shape, we can close the PivotTable Fields pane on the right hand side of the screen. If you want the box visible again, just select **Field List** from **PIVOTTABLE TOOLS**, **ANALYZE** menu.

We have our first simple pivot table – the **value** of sales for each **country** by **product** as can be seen in the image on the next page.

	A	B	C	D	E	F	G	H
1								
2								
3	Sum of Value	Product						
4	Country	Accessories	Clothing	Footwear	Jewellery	Luggage	Other	Grand Total
5	CHN		44.75		120		191.15	355.9
6	FR	1516.4	1180	220	125.75		2960.4	6002.55
7	GER	271.1		407.5	187.75	332.5	56.25	1255.1
8	IND	125.75	99.95				56.25	281.95
9	JPN	67.75				220		287.75
10	PKN	34.9		99.95		67.75	1554	1756.6
11	SP	154.5	34.9	124.6	149	344.6	1534.9	2342.5
12	UK	88	408.95	1586.15	1500	2800	124.6	6507.7
13	Grand Total	2258.4	1768.55	2438.2	2082.5	3764.85	6477.55	18790.05

Creating a pivot table using recommended table

■ select **Recommended PivotTables** from the **INSERT** menu

■ chose the layout which suits your analysis

In our example, we are offered a pivot table summary by each of our column headings ie by Sales Rep, by Country, by Product and by Month, not by Value since it is what we are going to total.

We choose by **Country.**

When we select OK, a new worksheet is added containing the pivot table, as shown below.

Row Labels	Sum of Value
CHN	355.9
FR	6002.55
GER	1255.1
IND	281.95
JPN	287.75
PKN	1756.6
SP	2342.5
UK	6507.7
Grand Total	18790.05

You can now adjust this layout as described in the layout section above. To achieve the same pivot table as previously, we would tick **Product** in the field list, and drag it to the **COLUMNS** area, as can be seen below.

Sum of Value	Column Labels						
Row Labels	Accessories	Clothing	Footwear	Jewellery	Luggage	Other	Grand Total
CHN		44.75		120		191.15	355.9
FR	1516.4	1180	220	125.75		2960.4	6002.55
GER	271.1		407.5	187.75	332.5	56.25	1255.1
IND	125.75	99.95				56.25	281.95
JPN	67.75				220		287.75
PKN	34.9		99.95		67.75	1554	1756.6
SP	154.5	34.9	124.6	149	344.6	1534.9	2342.5
UK	88	408.95	1586.15	1500	2800	124.6	6507.7
Grand Total	2258.4	1768.55	2438.2	2082.5	3764.85	6477.55	18790.05

Achieving the same result as before, but with fewer steps.

DRILL DOWN – SHOW DETAIL

The term 'drill down' is frequently used when analysing data and is used to describe the ability to display the underlying data values which make up a total or subtotal.

In the sales pivot table created on the previous page, if we wanted to see which individual sales made up £1516.40, the value of **Accessories** sales in **FR**:

■ move to cell B6 which shows the total value for Accessories sales in FR.

Then *either*

■ **double click** on this cell

Or

■ **right mouse click**

■ select **Show Details**

The detail making up this total is displayed on a fresh worksheet, as can be seen in the image below. This shows that when we **drill down** into the data, we can see that there were two sales of £1,460.40 and £56.00 making up this value of £1,516.40.

Note when you do a **drill down** there is, by default, no automatic formatting of data. As you can see in the Value column below, for example, the money amounts do not have '£' signs or a fixed number of decimal places. These can be formatted subsequently as required.

column C before formatting

	A	B	C	D	E
1	Month ▼	Product ▼	Value ▼	Sales Rep ▼	Country ▼
2	Sep	Accessories	1460.4	IY	FR
3	Nov	Accessories	56	IY	FR

column C after formatting

	A	B	C	D	E
1	Month ▼	Product ▼	Value ▼	Sales Rep ▼	Country ▼
2	Sep	Accessories	£1,460.40	IY	FR
3	Nov	Accessories	£56.00	IY	FR

REMOVING OR CHANGING A PIVOT TABLE

changing fields

If you want to change which fields you are including in the pivot table, within the PivotTable Fields pane:

Either

■ deselect the field in the field list box

or

■ select the field from the ROWS, COLUMNS or VALUE areas and drag it back to the field list box.

The effect of removing the country field from the pivot table is shown below:

	A	B	C	D	E	F	G	H
1								
2								
3		Column Labels ▾						
4		Accessories	Clothing	Footwear	Jewellery	Luggage	Other	Grand Total
5	Sum of Value	2258.4	1768.55	2438.2	2082.5	3764.85	6477.55	18790.05

PivotTable Fields ▾ ✕

Choose fields to add to report: ⚙ ▾

☐ Month
☑ **Product**
☑ **Value**
☐ Sales Rep
☐ Country

Drag fields between areas below:

▼ FILTERS   ▥ COLUMNS
                   Product ▾

▥ ROWS   Σ VALUES
                   Sum of Value ▾

If we wanted Product sales by Sales rep, we would select Sales rep, drag it to COLUMNS, and drag Product to ROWS, we would get the screen illustrated on the next page:

	A	B	C	D	E	F	G
1							
2							
3	Sum of Value	Column Labels ▾					
4	Row Labels ▾	IY	IO	MP	SM	TP	Grand Total
5	Accessories	1585.3	334.75	124.6		213.75	2258.4
6	Clothing	44.75	1180		443.85	99.95	1768.55
7	Footwear	374.5		253	224.55	1586.15	2438.2
8	Jewellery	125.75	182.75	34	240	1500	2082.5
9	Luggage	220	552.5	2800	192.35		3764.85
10	Other	4705.55	1647.4			124.6	6477.55
11	Grand Total	7055.85	3897.4	3211.6	1100.75	3524.45	18790.05

PivotTable Fields   ▾ ✕

Choose fields to add to report: ⚙ ▾

- ☐ Month
- ☑ Product
- ☑ Value
- ☑ Sales Rep
- ☐ County

Drag fields between areas below:

▼ FILTERS   ▥ COLUMNS
                           Sales Rep   ▾

▤ ROWS   Σ VALUES
Product   ▾   Sum of Value   ▾

clearing a pivot table

If you have started or created a pivot table, and you want to clear what you have done and start again:

- ▪ select **PIVOTTABLE TOOLS**
- ▪ select **ANALYZE**
- ▪ select **Clear** from the **Actions** menu

Note: To access the **PIVOTTABLE MENU**, **ANALYZE** and **DESIGN** tabs, click within your pivot table.

FORMATTING PIVOT TABLES

There are a variety of ways in which you can change the format or appearance of your table.

cell display

To change the way individual data values are displayed within the table, you can use the standard cell formatting options described in Chapters 2 and 3. In the pivot table created in this chapter, our sales values are displayed as decimal numbers, rather than the £ (UK pound) currency. To change this:

- ▪ select all the numeric data cells, including the Grand Total row and column
- ▪ select **Format Cells**
- ▪ select **Currency**, with the pound (£) symbol, and 2 decimal places

table style

Within the pivot table Design Menu there are a variety of styles which can be used for the table layout, colouring, and shading, all of which change the appearance of the table.

It is also possible to change other factors affecting the layout, for example row headers, column headers, subtotals and grand totals. This is an area where it is recommended that you experiment within your spreadsheet package to find your preferred style.

subsets of data

The pivot table we have created includes all the countries and products found within our data set.

It is possible that we may not want to include all values of one or other field. Suppose we only wanted to include countries FR, GER, SP and UK in our pivot table to show European sales values. This is easily achieved as follows:

■ select the drop down symbol to the right of **Row Labels** (cell A4)

The list of selected row labels appears, as shown below:

	A	B	C	D	E	F	G	H
1								
2								
3	**Sum of Value**	**Column Labels** ▾						
4	**Row Labels** ▾	**Accessories**	**Clothing**	**Footwear**	**Jewellery**	**Luggage**	**Other**	**Grand Total**
A↓ Sort A to Z			44.75		120		191.15	355.9
			1180	220	125.75		2960.4	6002.55
Z↓ Sort Z to A				407.5	187.75	332.5	56.25	1255.1
More Sort Options...			99.95				56.25	281.95
						220		287.75
▼x Clear Filter From "Country"				99.95		67.75	1554	1756.6
Label Filters	▸		34.9	124.6	149	344.6	1534.9	2342.5
Value Filters	▸		08.95	1586.15	1500	2800	124.6	6507.7
			68.55	2438.2	2082.5	3764.85	6477.55	18790.05
Search	🔍							
☑ (Select All)								
☑ CHN								
☑ FR								
☑ GER								
☑ IND								
☑ JPN								
☑ PKN								
☑ SP								
☑ UK								
	OK	Cancel						

- deselect CHN, IND, JPN, PKN from the list (as shown below)
- select OK

Sum of Value	Column Labels						
Row Labels ▾	Accessories	Clothing	Footwear	Jewellery	Luggage	Other	Grand Total
		44.75		120		191.15	355.9
		1180	220	125.75		2960.4	6002.55
			407.5	187.75	332.5	56.25	1255.1
		99.95				56.25	281.95
					220		287.75
			99.95		67.75	1554	1756.6
		34.9	124.6	149	344.6	1534.9	2342.5
		08.95	1586.15	1500	2800	124.6	6507.7
		68.55	2438.2	2082.5	3764.85	6477.55	18790.05

Dropdown menu:

- Sort A to Z
- Sort Z to A
- More Sort Options...
- Clear Filter From "Country"
- Label Filters ▸
- Value Filters ▸

Search 🔍

- ▣ (Select All)
- ☐ CHN
- ☑ FR
- ☑ GER
- ☐ IND
- ☐ JPN
- ☐ PKN
- ☑ SP
- ☑ UK

[OK]   [Cancel]

The pivot table adjusts to reflect these choices, as shown in the image below. This technique is a quick and easy way of displaying a **subset** of the data.

Sum of Value	Column Labels						
Row Labels ▾	Accessories	Clothing	Footwear	Jewellery	Luggage	Other	Grand Total
FR	1516.4	1180	220	125.75		2960.4	6002.55
GER	271.1		407.5	187.75	332.5	56.25	1255.1
SP	154.5	34.9	124.6	149	344.6	1534.9	2342.5
UK	88	408.95	1586.15	1500	2800	124.6	6507.7
Grand Total	2030	1623.85	2338.25	1962.5	3477.1	4676.15	16107.85

pivot charts

From the **pivot table** which we have created, it is possible to produce an interactive chart, which allows you to view subsets of the data graphically.

To create a pivot chart for your table

- select the **pivot table**, by clicking on any cell within the pivot table
- select **Insert**
- select **PivotChart**
- select your chart type eg column

A chart will be created as shown in the image below:

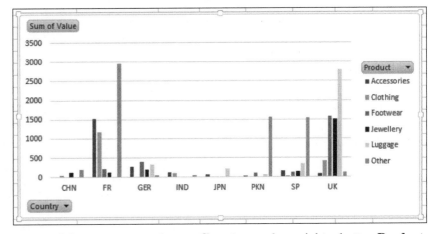

Bottom left you can see a button **Country**, and top right a button **Product**. Each of these buttons provides a drop down list so that you can refine the data that is included in the graph. In the example below we have chosen to show all Products, and only country UK.

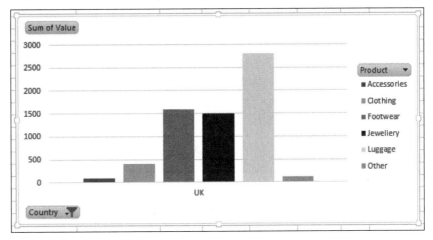

As you can see pivot tables and pivot charts offer a great deal of flexibility in your presentation.

WHAT-IF SCENARIOS

Spreadsheets are created to serve many purposes. One use is to have Excel analyse what the result would be if we applied different sets of values to one or more formulas. A simple example might be to see how different interest rates might change the loan repayments, and subsequently the profit, of a business. This could be achieved by having the interest rate built into a formula and manually changing it one value at a time, as required. However, Excel provides a powerful tool which allows us to offer up multiple scenarios and then automatically produce a report showing the various outcomes – these are known as **What-If scenarios**.

In the example below, we have a simple summary showing the calculated profit, based on a loan interest repayment rate of 15% and expected sales of €200,000. Cell B15 contains the formula necessary to calculate the profit. We want to see the effect on profit if we have higher or lower interest rates, or if sales don't meet our expectations.

	A	B
1	Example what if scenarios	
2		
3	Interest rate (%)	15
4	Loan	€ 100,000
5		
6	Sales	€ 200,000
7		
8	Loan repayments	€ 15,000
9	Salaries	€ 90,000
10	Insurance	€ 2,500
11	Rent	€ 19,080
12	Advertising	€ 20,000
13	Other	€ 19,950
14		
15	Profit	€ 33,470

To achieve this we will create our first scenario as follows:

- select What-If analysis from the Data menu
- select Scenario Manager
- select Add
- scenario name enter High interest
- changing cells enter or select B3 and B6 separated by commas (the cells containing the values for the interest rate and sales)
- click OK

As shown below:

Now we enter the **values** for these cells for this scenario:

■ enter 20 for B3, leave B6 unchanged, and click OK

We now select **Add** (another scenario):

■ **scenario name** enter Low interest

■ continue as before and enter 10 as the value for B3

Create two more scenarios:

Poor Sales using cell B6 and a value of €150,000.

High interest Poor sales using cells B3 and B6 with values of 20 and €150,000 respectively. The list of scenarios should appear as shown on the next page:

Now that we have defined the scenarios we wish to consider, we select **summary** to produce a report. This can take the form of a scenario summary or a PivotTable report.

We define the **Result** cell, which in this case will be B15 (the profit cell). We select **Scenario summary**.

The summary report is produced as shown below:

	Current Values:	High interest	Low interest	Poor sales	High interest Poor sales
Scenario Summary					
Changing Cells:					
$B$3	15	20	10	15	20
$B$6	€ 200,000	€ 200,000	€ 200,000	€ 150,000	€ 150,000
Result Cells:					
$B$15	€ 33,470	€ 28,470	€ 38,470	-€ 16,530	-€ 21,530

Notes: Current Values column represents values of changing cells at time Scenario Summary Report was created. Changing cells for each scenario are highlighted in gray.

It is showing us the values we can expect for profit for the different interest rates and forecast sales, showing that the what-if tool can be very useful for forecasting.

goalseek

Another tool within the **What-If analysis toolpak** is **Goal Seek**. This tool allows us to specify an outcome which we require, for example a profit of €40,000, and then a value (cell) which can be changed by the tool to achieve this outcome. So using our profit example above we want to know how big a loan we could take out, assuming an interest rate of 15% and sales of €200,000 to achieve a profit of €40,000.

To do this:

- select **What-If Analysis**
- select **Goal Seek**

And the Goal Seek option box is displayed as shown below:

◢	A	B	C	D	E	F
1	Example What If Scenarios					
2						
3	Interest Rate (%)	15				
4	Loan	€ 100,000				
5						
6	Sales	€ 200,000	Goal Seek			
7						
8	Loan Repayments	€ 15,000	Set cell:	$B$15		
9	Salaries	€ 90,000	To value:	40000		
10	Insurance	€ 2,500	By changing cell:	$B$4		
11	Rent	€ 19,080				
12	Advertising	€ 20,000	OK	Cancel		
13	Other	€ 19,950				
14						
15	Profit	€ 33,470				

The **Set cell** is B15, the cell containing the profit value, and the **To value** is €40,000 the profit we want to achieve. We allow the loan value cell B4 to change, in order to achieve this profit. (See image at the top of the next page.)

This shows that a solution has been found, a loan value of €56,467 would achieve a profit of €40,000. (See illustration on the next page.)

◢	A	B	C	D	E	F	G
1	Example what if scenarios						
2							
3	Interest rate (%)	15					
4	Loan	€ 56,467					
5							
6	Sales	€ 200,000					
7							
8	Loan repayments	€ 8,470					
9	Salaries	€ 90,000					
10	Insurance	€ 2,500					
11	Rent	€ 19,080					
12	Advertising	€ 20,000					
13	Other	€ 19,950					
14							
15	Profit	€ 40,000					

Goal Seek Status   ?   ✕

Goal Seeking with Cell B15 found a solution.

Step

Pause

Target value: 40000
Current value: € 40,000

OK   Cancel

If you don't want to change your spreadsheet to the values in the solution, click Cancel, otherwise click OK to accept the solution.

datatables

The final tool in the **What-If Analysis toolpak** is **Data Tables**, which provide us with the ability to change one or two variables in one or more of our formulas to a series of different (test) values. These test values are supplied as a series, in a row or column. Data tables provide an easy way of calculating multiple results in one operation and to then view and compare the results of all the different variations together in one place.

To illustrate the use of **Data Tables** we are going to look at a simple example shown in the image below.

◢	A	B	C
1	Example data tables		
2			
3	Sales	€ 200,000	
4	Annual growth in sales	2%	
5	Predicted sales	€ 204,000	
6			

We have our current Sales figures for the year of €200,000. We are predicting growth in sales of 2%. From this we insert a formula in cell B5 to calculate our Predicted sales. Now we will insert our series of growth values to be evaluated.

◢	A	B	C	D	E	F	G	H	I
1	Example data tables								
2									
3	Sales	€ 200,000							
4	Annual growth in sales	2.0%	1.2%	1.4%	1.6%	1.8%	2.2%	2.4%	2.6%
5	Predicted sales	€ 204,000							

To use Data Tables:

- select cells B4 through to J5 (this is to include our formula in cell B5 and our series of values)
- select **What-If Analysis**
- select **Data Tables**

◢	A	B	C	D	E	F	G	H	I	J
1	Example data tables									
2										
3	Sales	€ 200,000								
4	Annual growth in sales	2.0%	1.0%	1.2%	1.4%	1.6%	1.8%	2.2%	2.4%	2.6%
5	Predicted sales	€ 204,000								
6										
7										
8										
9										
10										
11										

Data Table   ?   ✕

Row input cell: $B$4

Column input cell:

OK   Cancel

The **Data Table** options are then displayed. We have put our series of values along a row, so we specify a **Row input cell** (and not a **Column Input** cell). The cell we specify is B4, the cell containing out current sales growth %. When we click OK, the table is completed and Predicted Sales figures are generated for each of the growth values, as can be seen in the image below.

◢	A	B	C	D	E	F	G	H	I	J
1	Example data tables									
2										
3	Sales	€ 200,000								
4	Annual growth in sales	2.0%	1.0%	1.2%	1.4%	1.6%	1.8%	2.2%	2.4%	2.6%
5	Predicted sales	€ 204,000	€ 202,000	€ 202,400	€ 202,800	€ 203,200	€ 203,600	€ 204,400	€ 204,800	€ 205,200

If you select one of the Predicted Sales cells, you see that the formula for the cell shows that it is part of a table based on cell B4, as shown below.

E5   ▾   ⋮   ✕ ✓ *fx*   {=TABLE(B4,)}

◢	A	B	C	D	E	F	G	H	I	J
1	Example data tables									
2										
3	Sales	€ 200,000								
4	Annual growth in sales	2.0%	1.0%	1.2%	1.4%	1.6%	1.8%	2.2%	2.4%	2.6%
5	Predicted sales	€ 204,000	€ 202,000	€ 202,400	€ 202,800	€ 203,200	€ 203,600	€ 204,400	€ 204,800	€ 205,200

As can be seen in the **Data Table** options, the series of values can be in a column instead of a row.

It is also possible to have two items that change, a series in a row and a series in a column. We will not be covering 2 dimensional Data Tables, and recommend that you experiment further.

Note: If the series is in a row, the formula to be calculated should be in the row below the series, and for columns, the formula should be in the column to the right of the series.

hyperlinks

Within a worksheet, it is possible to insert a hyperlink which will provide a quick route to either another file, a website or webpage or possibly an email address.

If we wanted to insert a link to the Osborne Books website:

■ select **Hyperlink** from the **Insert** menu

We would enter selections as follows:

This would result in a link being added to our worksheet in the current cell, as shown below:

Similarly we can add links to other files or documents.

An example of adding a link to an email address is shown below; notice that we can leave the subject blank:

An email link will be added as shown below.

Clicking on this link will open a new email addressed to Osborne Books.

To remove a hyperlink:

- Right mouse CLICK on the cell containing the link
- select **Remove Hyperlink**

Chapter Summary

The text of this chapter has covered:

- managing windows – using Freeze Panes
- using the Paste Special function
- working with multiple worksheets and workbooks
- the reasons for using a pivot table
- creating a simple pivot table
- using subsets of data
- formatting pivot tables
- what-if scenarios
- goal seeking
- data tables
- hyperlinks

You should now carry out some or all of the exercises on the next few pages in order to practise and reinforce your learning.

Activities

Exercise 1 – using Freeze Panes

In this first exercise we will use the window – Freeze Panes facility.

To obtain this spreadsheet visit www.osbornebooks.co.uk ('Products and Resources') and download filename **T8freeze**.

Stage 1

This stage uses the Freeze Panes and Unfreeze facilities to enable us to scroll around a sales spreadsheet with a large amount of data, and still be able to interpret the data.

1. Download the workbook **T8freeze**.

2. Open the downloaded file, save the workbook with new name **T8Exercise1**.

The top section of the workbook should look as shown below.

	A	B	C	D	E	F	G	H	I	J	K
1	Name	Total	Month1	Month2	Month3	Month4	Month5	Month6	Month7	Month8	Month9
2	Farmhouse Foods	£154	£0	£112	£0	£0	£0	£26	£0	£0	£16
3	Engineering Services	£554	£0	£0	£0	£0	£67	£0	£0	£0	£0
4	Another Food Service	£790	£0	£0	£0	£58	£116	£0	£0	£174	£0
5	Top Quality Supplies	£56	£0	£56	£0	£0	£0	£0	£0	£0	£0
6	Halal Foods	£36	£0	£0	£0	£0	£0	£0	£0	£0	£0
7	Edwards Farm	£195	£0	£0	£0	£0	£40	£0	£65	£0	£0
8	Allen and co	£1,412	£45	£68	£231	£0	£331	£37	£49	£0	£0
9	Ahmed and son	£340	£0	£0	£0	£0	£0	£0	£0	£0	£0
10	Green & Sons Wholesalers	£1,827	£700	£0	£104	£0	£0	£0	£0	£0	£363
11	Higginbottom and son	£389	£0	£0	£0	£0	£0	£0	£300	£0	£0
12	W B Meats	£135	£0	£45	£0	£0	£0	£0	£0	£0	£0
13	The Halal Centre	£205	£0	£0	£50	£0	£0	£0	£0	£25	£0

Customer Sales | Sheet2 | Sheet3

3. Select the appropriate cell, and then Freeze Panes, so that the column headings in Row 1 stay in view when you scroll down the worksheet, and the row headings in Column A stay in view when you scroll across.

4. Using the normal scrolling facilities scroll the view, so that cell I14 (T F Curries, Month7 value) becomes the top left-hand cell in the viewing area.

Your worksheet should look as shown at the top of the next page.

A	I	J	K	L	M	N	O	P	Q
1 Name	Month7	Month8	Month9	Month10	Month11	Month12	Month13	Month14	Month15 M
14 T F Curries	£470	£490	£244	£423	£354	£560	£309	£274	£376
15 Fiber Optical Services	£0	£0	£0	£0	£0	£0	£0	£0	£50
16 My Provisions	£0	£25	£0	£0	£0	£0	£0	£0	£0
17 Alliance services	£0	£0	£0	£0	£0	£0	£0	£0	£0
18 Aluminium casts	£72	£286	£0	£2,093	£0	£364	£1,750	£0	£72
19 Impala	£0	£0	£0	£0	£0	£0	£0	£45	£0
20 Tool Hire	£0	£0	£0	£0	£0	£0	£0	£20	£0
21 Handyfreight	£0	£0	£0	£0	£0	£0	£327	£0	£0
22 Steel Traders	£0	£0	£0	£0	£0	£0	£0	£0	£0
23 Fruit Supplies	£0	£0	£65	£0	£279	£0	£0	£71	£70
24 Food Safe	£0	£55	£0	£0	£0	£0	£0	£1,205	£0
25 Environmental Services	£112	£0	£112	£0	£140	£0	£0	£0	£0

| | Customer Sales | Sheet2 | Sheet3 | ⊕ |

5. We now want to freeze panes so that we can visually compare the figures in Month1, and the figures in Month7.

    Unfreeze Panes, then select the appropriate cell, then **Freeze Panes**.

    Then scroll to the top of your spreadsheet and scroll the view until Month7 (column I) is next to Month1 (column C).

    Your worksheet should look as shown below.

A	B	C	I	J	K	L	M	N	O	F
1 Name	Total	Month1	Month7	Month8	Month9	Month10	Month11	Month12	Month13	Mon
2 Farmhouse Foods	£154	£0	£0	£0	£16	£0	£0	£0	£0	
3 Engineering Services	£554	£0	£0	£0	£0	£0	£0	£0	£0	
4 Another Food Service	£790	£0	£0	£174	£0	£0	£0	£0	£0	
5 Top Quality Supplies	£56	£0	£0	£0	£0	£0	£0	£0	£0	
6 Halal Foods	£36	£0	£0	£0	£0	£0	£36	£0	£0	
7 Edwards Farm	£195	£0	£65	£0	£0	£0	£0	£90	£0	
8 Allen and co	£1,412	£45	£49	£0	£0	£100	£115	£77	£0	
9 Ahmed and son	£340	£0	£0	£0	£0	£0	£0	£0	£0	
10 Green & Sons Wholesalers	£1,827	£700	£0	£0	£363	£0	£0	£0	£0	
11 Higginbottom and son	£389	£0	£300	£0	£0	£0	£89	£0	£0	
12 W B Meats	£135	£0	£0	£0	£0	£0	£0	£0	£0	
13 The Halal Centre	£205	£0	£0	£25	£0	£0	£0	£0	£0	

| | Customer Sales | Sheet2 | Sheet3 | ⊕ |

6. We now want to freeze panes so that we can visually compare the figures for Allen and co (row 8), and the figures for T F Curries (row 14). **Unfreeze Panes**, then select the appropriate cell, then **Freeze Panes**, then using the normal scrolling facilities, scroll the view until T F Curries is next to Allen and co.

Your worksheet should look as shown at the top of the next page.

	A	B	C	D	E	F	G	H	I	J	K
1	**Name**	**Total**	**Month1**	**Month2**	**Month3**	**Month4**	**Month5**	**Month6**	**Month7**	**Month8**	**Month9**
2	Farmhouse Foods	£154	£0	£112	£0	£0	£0	£26	£0	£0	£16
3	Engineering Services	£554	£0	£0	£0	£0	£67	£0	£0	£0	£0
4	Another Food Service	£790	£0	£0	£0	£58	£116	£0	£0	£174	£0
5	Top Quality Supplies	£56	£0	£56	£0	£0	£0	£0	£0	£0	£0
6	Halal Foods	£36	£0	£0	£0	£0	£0	£0	£0	£0	£0
7	Edwards Farm	£195	£0	£0	£0	£0	£40	£0	£65	£0	£0
8	Allen and co	£1,412	£45	£68	£231	£0	£331	£37	£49	£0	£0
14	T F Curries	£7,245	£458	£166	£583	£225	£414	£365	£470	£490	£244
15	Fiber Optical Services	£90	£0	£40	£0	£0	£0	£0	£0	£0	£0
16	My Provisions	£75	£0	£0	£0	£0	£0	£0	£0	£25	£0
17	Alliance services	£327	£0	£0	£0	£0	£0	£0	£0	£0	£0
18	Aluminium casts	£7,625	£72	£54	£1,856	£0	£360	£119	£72	£286	£0

Customer Sales   Sheet2   Sheet3   ⊕

7. Save the workbook with the same name **T8Exercise1**.

You have now completed the first exercise.

Exercise 2 – Paste Special, multiple worksheets and workbooks

In this exercise we will work with **Paste Special**, move data and formulas from **one worksheet to another** and **across multiple workbooks**, and also use the **Move or Copy Sheet** facility. We are again going to make use of an existing spreadsheet, containing data relating to a Profit and Loss report. To obtain this spreadsheet visit www.osbornebooks.co.uk ('Products and Resources') and download filename **T8Paste**.

Stage 1

This stage uses **Paste Special** and requires you to move data and formulas from one worksheet to another.

1. Download the workbook **T8paste**.

2. Open the downloaded file, save the workbook with new name **T8Exercise2**.

3. The workbook should look as shown on the next page. You can see that the formula for the Total for the Ford row (row 6), in cell B6 is, as we would expect:

=SUM(C6:H6)

B6	▼	⋮	✕	✓	*fx*		=SUM(C6:H6)				

◢	A	B	C	D	E	F	G	H	I	J
1	Car Sales									
2										
3			*Max*	60,000	*Min*	930	*Count*	42		
4										*Average*
5		Totals	*Jan*	*Feb*	*Mar*	*Apr*	*May*	*Jun*	*3 month*	*6 month*
6	Ford	190,000	25,090	25,000	60,000	25,010	30,900	24,000	24,670	31,667
7	Volkswagen	98,510	13,200	6,150	32,900	15,130	15,040	16,090	12,457	16,418
8	Hyundai	9,000	1,000	1,500	2,500	1,000	1,000	2,000	1,500	1,500
9	Skoda	15,400	1,200	2,800	4,000	3,500	2,130	1,770	2,690	2,567
10	Kia	13,360	930	1,050	5,430	1,500	2,110	2,340	1,630	2,227
11	Renault	94,820	7,000	32,090	25,600	9,230	9,100	11,800	17,707	15,803
12	Vauxhall	166,750	22,000	10,500	55,000	25,050	24,100	30,100	21,883	27,792

4. Change the name of worksheet Sheet1 to **Car sales**.

5. Check that you have a second worksheet in the workbook you have open; if not add a worksheet (as described in Chapter 1) and name it **Copy1**.

6. Select all the data on the Car sales worksheet, select Copy (using the menu, or **CTRL** and **C**).

7. Select worksheet **Copy1**, move to cell B2, select **Paste Special** (from the menu), select **All**. The data from **Car sales** will be pasted onto the worksheet **Copy1**.

8. On worksheet **Copy1**, make Column A four units wide.

9. On worksheet **Copy1**, move to cell C7. You should see the formula for the Total for the Ford row (now Row 7 on this sheet):

    =SUM(D7:I7)

    This will have been modified to reflect the new row and column position, as shown below.

10. Save your spreadsheet (keeping the same name – **T8Exercise2**).

C7	▼	⋮	✕	✓	*fx*		=SUM(D7:I7)				

◢	A	B	C	D	E	F	G	H	I	J	K
1											
2		Car sales									
3											
4			*Max*	60,000	*Min*	930	*Count*	42			
5										*Average*	
6			Totals	*Jan*	*Feb*	*Mar*	*Apr*	*May*	*Jun*	*3 month*	*6 month*
7		Ford	190,000	25,090	25,000	60,000	25,010	30,900	24,000	24,670	31,667
8		Volkswag	98,510	13,200	6,150	32,900	15,130	15,040	16,090	12,457	16,418
9		Hyundai	9,000	1,000	1,500	2,500	1,000	1,000	2,000	1,500	1,500
10		Skoda	15,400	1,200	2,800	4,000	3,500	2,130	1,770	2,690	2,567
11		Kia	13,360	930	1,050	5,430	1,500	2,110	2,340	1,630	2,227
12		Renault	94,820	7,000	32,090	25,600	9,230	9,100	11,800	17,707	15,803
13		Vauxhall	166,750	22,000	10,500	55,000	25,050	24,100	30,100	21,883	27,792

◀	▶		Car sales	Copy1	⊕

Stage 2

In this stage we are going to use **Paste Special**, **Values**. You should use the same workbook **T8Exercise2**.

1. Check that you have a third worksheet in the workbook, if not add a worksheet (as described in Chapter 1) and name it **Copy2**.

2. Select worksheet **Copy2**, format Column B to be **Bold** and **Italics**, format Column C to be **Currency pounds (£)** and with **2 decimal places**.

3. Select the data in Columns A and B on the Car sales worksheet, select **Copy** (using either the menu, or **CTRL** and **C**).

4. Select worksheet **Copy2**, move to cell B2, select **Paste Special**, select **Values**.

5. On worksheet **Copy2**, make Column A two units wide, widen Column C so that all the data is displayed, Delete rows 3 and 4.

6. On worksheet **Copy2**, move to cell C5. There is no longer a formula for the Total for the Ford row (now row 5 on this sheet), only the value that was produced by the original calculation. You can also see that the cell formatting has been changed to the format we put in place on worksheet **Copy2**, as shown in the image below.

7. Save your spreadsheet (keeping the same name – **T8Exercise2**).

Stage 3

In this stage we are going to use **Paste Special**, and **Formats** within the same workbook, T8Exercise2.

We will change the format of the data on **Copy2** by copying the format from the original Car Sales worksheet.

1. Select worksheet **Car Sales**, select cells **B6:B12** select **Copy**.

2. Select worksheet **Copy2**, move to cell C5, select **Paste Special**, select **Formats**.

   On worksheet **Copy2**, you can see that the cell formatting of the totals cells (C5:C11) has been changed back to the format from worksheet **Car Sales**: there are no pound symbols or decimal places showing pence. The screen will appear as shown below.

	A	B	C	D	E
1					
2		*Car sales*			
3					
4			Totals		
5		*Ford*	190,000		
6		*Volkswag*	98,510		
7		*Hyundai*	9,000		
8		*Skoda*	15,400		
9		*Kia*	13,360		
10		*Renault*	94,820		
11		*Vauxhall*	166,750		
12					

◄ ► | Car sales | Copy1 | **Copy2**

3. Select the data in cells B5 to B12 on the Car sales worksheet, select **Copy** (using either the menu, or **CTRL** and **C**).

4. Select worksheet **Copy2**, move to cell E4, select **Paste Special**, **Paste link**.

5. On worksheet **Copy2**, move to cell E5. There is now a direct link to the cell holding the Total for Ford on sheet Car sales as shown in the image on the next page.

| E5 | ▼ | ⋮ | ✕ | ✓ | *fx* | ='Car sales'!B6 |

◢	A	B	C	D	E	F
1						
2		*Car sales*				
3						
4			Totals		Totals	
5		*Ford*	190,000		190000	
6		*Volkswag*	98,510		98510	
7		*Hyundai*	9,000		9000	
8		*Skoda*	15,400		15400	
9		*Kia*	13,360		13360	
10		*Renault*	94,820		94820	
11		*Vauxhall*	166,750		166750	
12						

◄ ► | Car sales | Copy1 | **Copy2** | ⊕

6. On the Car sales worksheet, change the figure for Ford in March to 40,000 ie cell E6.

◢	A	B	C	D	E	F	G	H	I	J
1	Car sales									
2										
3			*Max*	55,000	*Min*	930	*Count*	42		
4									*Average*	
5			Totals	*Jan*	*Feb*	*Mar*	*Apr*	*May*	*Jun*	*3 month*	*6 month*
6	Ford		170,000	25,090	25,000	40,000	25,010	30,900	24,000	24,670	28,333
7	Volkswagen		98,510	13,200	6,150	32,900	15,130	15,040	16,090	12,457	16,418
8	Hyundai		9,000	1,000	1,500	2,500	1,000	1,000	2,000	1,500	1,500
9	Skoda		15,400	1,200	2,800	4,000	3,500	2,130	1,770	2,690	2,567
10	Kia		13,360	930	1,050	5,430	1,500	2,110	2,340	1,630	2,227
11	Renault		94,820	7,000	32,090	25,600	9,230	9,100	11,800	17,707	15,803
12	Vauxhall		166,750	22,000	10,500	55,000	25,050	24,100	30,100	21,883	27,792
13										

◄ ► | **Car sales** | Copy1 | Copy2 | ⊕ | ⋮

The total for Ford has changed to 170,000.

7. Select worksheet Copy1 (created by copy and paste).

Nothing has changed on this sheet.

		Totals	Jan	Feb	Mar	Apr	May	Jun	Average 3 month	6 month
1										
2	Car sales									
3										
4			Max	60,000	Min	930	Count	42		
5									Average	
6		Totals	Jan	Feb	Mar	Apr	May	Jun	3 month	6 month
7	Ford	190,000	25,090	25,000	60,000	25,010	30,900	24,000	24,670	31,667
8	Volkswag	98,510	13,200	6,150	32,900	15,130	15,040	16,090	12,457	16,418
9	Hyundai	9,000	1,000	1,500	2,500	1,000	1,000	2,000	1,500	1,500
10	Skoda	15,400	1,200	2,800	4,000	3,500	2,130	1,770	2,690	2,567
11	Kia	13,360	930	1,050	5,430	1,500	2,110	2,340	1,630	2,227
12	Renault	94,820	7,000	32,090	25,600	9,230	9,100	11,800	17,707	15,803
13	Vauxhall	166,750	22,000	10,500	55,000	25,050	24,100	30,100	21,883	27,792

Car sales | **Copy1** | Copy2 | ⊕

8.   Select worksheet Copy2.

You can see that the copied total in cell C5 hasn't changed, but the linked total in E5 has updated to show the new total.

| E5 | | ▼ : | ✕ ✓ *fx* | ='Car sales'!B6 |

	A	B	C	D	E	F	G
1							
2		Car sales					
3							
4			Totals		Totals		
5		Ford	190,000		170000		
6		Volkswag	98,510		98510		
7		Hyundai	9,000		9000		
8		Skoda	15,400		15400		
9		Kia	13,360		13360		
10		Renault	94,820		94820		
11		Vauxhall	166,750		166750		
12							
13							

Car sales | Copy1 | **Copy2** | ⊕

9.   Save your workbook as **T8Exercise2**.

Stage 4

In this stage, we are going to manually create some formulas which link to a specific worksheet.

We will then copy the formulas from one workbook to another, using **Copy and Paste** and **Paste Special**.

We will make use of the same workbook **T8Exercise2**, and also create a new workbook to which we will copy data.

1. Check that you have a fourth worksheet in the workbook, if not, add a worksheet (as described in Chapter 1) and name it **Copy3**.

2. Select the data in Rows 1, 2 and 3 on the **Car Sales** worksheet, select Copy (using either the menu, or **CTRL** and **C**)

3. Select worksheet **Copy3**, move to cell A1, select **Paste Special**, select All.

    You will see that the values for **Max**, **Min** and **Count** are now zero, since we did not copy all the values which they reference. Rather than copy these values, we are going to link directly to the cells which held the results on worksheet **Car Sales**.

4. On worksheet **Copy3**, move to cell D3, enter the = (to indicate a formula), move to worksheet **Car Sales**, select cell D3, press **ENTER**.

    You should now see the value for **Max** from Car Sales displayed, and the formula includes a direct reference to the Car Sales worksheet.

5. Repeat for **Min** and **Count**.

6. Save your workbook as **T8Exercise2**.

    The Copy3 worksheet should now look as shown in the image below.

D3	▼	⋮	✕ ✓ *fx*	='Car sales'!D3				
◢	**A**	**B**	**C**	**D**	**E**	**F**	**G**	**H**
1	Car sales							
2								
3			*Max*	55,000	*Min*	930	*Count*	42
4								
5								
6								

Car sales Copy1 Copy2 **Copy3** ⊕

7. Open a new workbook, save it with name **T8Excopy**, name the first worksheet **Sheet1** (if it is not already called that).

8. Select workbook **T8Exercise2**, worksheet **Copy3**, select all the data on the worksheet, select **Copy**.

9. Select workbook **T8Excopy**, worksheet **Sheet1**, select cell A1, select **Paste**. The data from **Copy3** will be pasted onto the worksheet **Sheet1**.

10. On worksheet **Sheet1**, select **Show Formulas**.

11.   By adjusting the column widths, you can see the formulas as shown in the image below.

| D3 | ▾ | : | ✕ | ✓ | *fx* | ='[T8exercise2.xlsx]Car sales'!D3 | | | | |

◢	A	B	C	D	E	F	G	H
1	Car sales							
2								
3			*Max*	='[T8exercise2.xlsx]Car sales'!D3	*Min*	='[T8exercise2.xlsx]Car sales'!F3	*Count*	='[T8exercise2.xlsx]Car sales'!H3

You can see that the formulas in the new workbook contain direct references to the workbook containing the original data. If we did not want to retain the link to the original worksheet, we would use **Paste Special** and **Values**.

You have now completed Exercise 2.

Exercise 3 – using pivot tables

In this exercise we are going to create a pivot table, from some data in a prepared file, which can be downloaded from the Osborne Books website, filename **T8pivot**. We are also going to practise using **Move** or **Copy Sheet**.

To obtain this spreadsheet visit www.osbornebooks.co.uk ('Products and Resources') and download filename T8pivot

Stage 1

1.   Download the workbook **T8pivot**.

2.   Open the downloaded file, save the workbook with new name **T8Exercise3**.

3.   The top few rows of the workbook should look as shown below.

◢	A	B	C	D	E	F	G
1							
2		*Products*	*Quantity*	*Month*	*Value*		
3		Product1	3,063	Jan	£3,115.90		
4		Product2	406	Jan	£614.50		
5		Product3	192	Jan	£1,646.50		
6		Product4	97	Jan	£600.00		
7		Product6	47	Jan	£106.90		
8		Product6	13	Jan	£160.00		
9		Product1	4,661	Jan	£8,801.70		
10		Product2	975	Feb	£416.10		
11		Product3	407	Feb	£260.80		
12		Product4	163	Feb	£1,147.50		
13		Product5	128	Feb	£1,100.00		

We are now going to create a pivot table to allow us to look at product sales quantities by month.

4.   Select all the data in the worksheet, including the column titles (Row 2).

5.   Select **PivotTable** tool from the **Insert** menu.

6.   In the Create PivotTable options choose **Select a table or range**. This should display the full range of the data on the worksheet ie **Sheet1!$B$2:$E$86**. (Edit if necessary so that this is the range selected.)

7.   In the **Create PivotTable** options, select **New Worksheet**, and then **OK**, as shown below.

Create PivotTable ? X

Choose the data that you want to analyze
- ⦿ Se_lect a table or range
  - Table/Range: Sheet1!$B$2:$E$86
- ○ Use an external data source
  - Choose Connection...
  - Connection name:

Choose where you want the PivotTable report to be placed
- ⦿ New Worksheet
- ○ Existing Worksheet
  - Location:

Choose whether you want to analyze multiple tables
- ☐ Add this data to the Data Model

OK   Cancel

8.   Select the **Products** Field and move it to the **ROWS** panel.

9.   Select the **Month** Field and move it to the **COLUMNS** panel.

10.   Select the **Quantity** Field and move it to the **VALUES** panel.

      As shown on the right:

PivotTable Fields ▾ ✕

Choose fields to add to report: ⚙ ▾

- ☑ **Products**
- ☑ **Quantity**
- ☑ **Month**
- ☐ Value

MORE TABLES...

Drag fields between areas below:

▼ FILTERS | ▥ COLUMNS
| Month ▾

≡ ROWS | Σ VALUES
Products ▾ | Sum of Quantity ▾

11. Save your workbook as **T8Exercise3**

The pivot table showing product sales quantities by month should then appear on a new worksheet, as shown in the image below (possibly with different shading or colours).

	A	B	C	D	E	F	G	H	I	J	K	L	M	N
1														
2														
3	Sum of Quantity	Column Labels ▼												
4	Row Labels ▼	Jan		Feb	Mar	Apr	May	Jun	Jul	Aug	Sep	Oct	Nov	Dec	Grand Total
5	Product1		7724	15		125	856	3703	1383	13		257	429	2993	17498
6	Product2		406	10558	41		1281	1584	1763	5014	71		333	186	21237
7	Product3		192	407	33539	1972		17	2202	3055	27197	54		350	68985
8	Product4		97	163	279	7076	9		746	1243	2472	13251	15		25351
9	Product5			145	237	200	3026	38		212	273	356	355	2	4844
10	Product6		60		584	784	341	478	-40		127		288	2757	2360	7739
11	Grand Total		8479	11288	34680	10157	5513	5820	6054	9537	30140	14206	3889	5891	145654

12. Using the pivot table, select **Product2**, Quantity for **Feb** (cell C6) and drill down to show the detail for this quantity on a fresh worksheet. (You can double click on the cell, or right mouse and Show Detail.)

This will show us the individual lines of detail which make up the total of 10558 for **Product2** in Feb.

Your worksheet should look as shown in the image below (possibly with different shading/colours).

	A	B	C	D
1	Products ▼	Quantity ▼	Month ▼	Value ▼
2	Product2	9583	Feb	14472.7
3	Product2	975	Feb	416.1

13. Save your workbook as **T8Exercise3**.

Stage 2

We are going to create a new workbook by copying the data sheet from **T8Exercise3**.

1. With the workbook **T7Exercise3**, select worksheet **Sheet1**, and from the menu, select **Move or Copy Worksheet**.

2. In the **Move or Copy** options, for **To book**, select **New book** from the drop down list of choices. Then select **Create a copy**, so that it is ticked.

3. You will then be presented with a new workbook containing just the sheet of data which we have copied across.

4. Save this new workbook with name **T8Exercise32**.

5. Switch to the original workbook **T8Exercise3** and you will see that the **Sheet1** with all the data is still present in the workbook. If we had not selected **Create a Copy**, it would have moved to the new workbook, and disappeared from the old workbook.

6. Select the new workbook **T8Exercise32**.

7. Create a pivot table showing the Value of **Product by month**.

8. Save your spreadsheet (keeping the same name – **T8Exercise32**).

Your spreadsheet should now appear as follows, showing the **Value of each Product by month**:

Your spreadsheet should now appear as follows, showing the value of each product by month:

Sum of Value	Column Labels												
Row Labels	Jan	Feb	Mar	Apr	May	Jun	Jul	Aug	Sep	Oct	Nov	Dec	Grand Total
Product1	11917.6	41		2222	4100	11273.8	1110.5	191		1500	3884.8	4353.1	40593.8
Product2	614.5	14888.8	116		19110.7	11600	3256.3	2579.5	398		7200	2147	61910.8
Product3	1646.5	260.8	47628.6	2420		15.131	47285.8	5549.3	23361.5	490		1900	130557.631
Product4	600	1147.5	248.64	12086.8	45		4500	11962.9	3386.4	9917.2	562		44456.44
Product5		1126	391.1	306	5104.6	62		6200	3600.1	132.5	286.3	213	17421.6
Product6	266.9		5400	4800.1	1194.5	542.05	-293		1600	727.5	5089.4	617.9	19945.35
Grand Total	15045.5	17464.1	53784.34	21834.9	29554.8	23492.981	55859.6	26482.7	32346	12767.2	17022.5	9231	314885.621

9.   Name this worksheet **Pivottable**.

10.   Using the **Drill down** capability, display the detail making up the **Product4** value for **Oct**. The details should appear as follows:

	A	B	C	D
1	Products	Quantity	Month	Value
2	Product4	27	Oct	600
3	Product4	13224	Oct	9317.2

11.   Select worksheet **Pivottable**.

12.   Insert a **Pivotchart**, type **Clustered column** and position it just below the table.

13.   Using the selection drop downs for Products, display only the data for Product 4 on the chart. Your chart should look similar to the chart below:

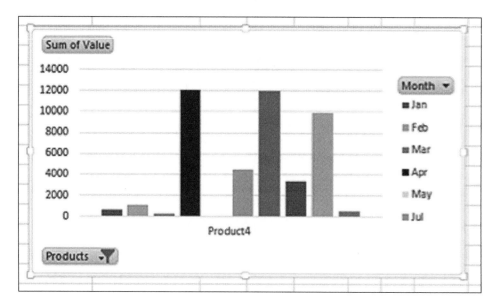

14.   Save your spreadsheet (keeping the same name – **T8Exercise32**).

Exercise 4 – What-If Analysis

In this exercise we are going to practise using the three tools within **What-If Analysis**, looking at the outcome of changing values, using **Goal Seek** to find out how to get a specific result, and creating a simple **Data Table**.

Stage 1

1.   Download the spreadsheet **T8WhatIf**.

2.   Open the downloaded file, save the workbook with the new name **T8Exercise4**.

3.   The workbook should look as shown below.

◢	A	B	C	D	E	F	G	H	I
1	Forecast for year								
2		Quarter 1	Quarter 2	Quarter 3	Quarter 4	Total	Assumptions		
3	Sales	£500,000	£525,000	£551,250	£578,813	£2,155,063	5%	(Growth per qtr)	
4	Cost of Sales	£100,000	£105,000	£110,250	£115,763	£431,013	20%	(Perc of Sales)	
5	Gross Profit	£400,000	£420,000	£441,000	£463,050	£1,724,050			
6									
7	Expenses	£125,000	£131,250	£137,813	£144,703	£538,766	25%	(Perc of sales)	
8	Income	£275,000	£288,750	£303,188	£318,347	£1,185,284			

This spreadsheet shows a forecast for Sales and Income based on a number of assumptions, as follows:

- sales will increase by 5% per qtr (cell G3)

- cost of sales is 20% of sales value (cell G4)

- expenses are 25% of sales value (cell G7)

The cells for each quarter are populated with the necessary formulas to use these assumptions and calculate the quarterly values.

We want to consider two scenarios.

The first where we are optimistic and hope that sales will actually be higher and both the cost of sales and expenses lower than we have specified.

4. Create a scenario named **Optimistic** with changing cells G3,G4,G7

Add Scenario   ?   ✕

Scenario name:

Optimistic

Changing cells:

$G$3,$G$4,$G$7

Ctrl+click cells to select non-adjacent changing cells.

Comment:

Protection

☑ Prevent changes

☐ Hide

OK   Cancel

Set scenario values:

Sales growth is 10%,

Cost of sales is 19%

Expenses is 22%

(**Note**: you will need to enter these values as decimals ie 0.1, 0.19, and 0.22 as shown below.)

Scenario Values   ?   ✕

Enter values for each of the changing cells.

1:	$G$3	0.1
2:	$G$4	0.19
3:	$G$7	0.22

Add   OK   Cancel

The second scenario will be **Poor**, with lower sales and higher costs.

5. Create a scenario named **Poor**

Set the scenario values as follows:

Sales growth is 2%

Cost of sales is 25%

Expenses is 30%

(Again, enter these values as decimals ie 0.02, 0.25 and 0.3 in the scenario manager.)

6. From the Scenario Manager, produce a **summary** report using these two scenarios, specify F3, F4, F5, F7 and F8 as the results cells.

The report should look as shown below.

Scenario Summary			
	Current Values:	Optimistic	Poor
Changing Cells:			
$G$3	5%	10%	2%
$G$4	20%	19%	25%
$G$7	25%	22%	30%
Result Cells:			
$F$3	£2,155,063	£2,320,500	£2,060,804
$F$4	£431,013	£440,895	£515,201
$F$5	£1,724,050	£1,879,605	£1,545,603
$F$7	£538,766	£510,510	£618,241
$F$8	£1,185,284	£1,369,095	£927,362

The $F$8 row which is the total for the Income row, shows the effect on income of the two different scenarios.

7.   Save your workbook as **T8Exercise4**

Stage 2

We are now going to use the **Goal Seek** tool. We want to determine the percentage value we need for cost of sales (cell G4) to allow us to generate **a total income** of £1,300,000 (cell F8).

1.   Open the workbook **T8Exercise4**.

2.   Move to worksheet named **Forecast**.

	A	B	C	D	E	F	G	H	I
1	Forecast for year								
2		Quarter 1	Quarter 2	Quarter 3	Quarter 4	Total	Assumptions		
3	Sales	£500,000	£525,000	£551,250	£578,813	£2,155,063	5%	(Growth per qtr)	
4	Cost of Sales	£100,000	£105,000	£110,250	£115,763	£431,013	20%	(Perc of Sales)	
5	Gross Profit	£400,000	£420,000	£441,000	£463,050	£1,724,050			
6									
7	Expenses	£125,000	£131,250	£137,813	£144,703	£538,766	25%	(Perc of sales)	
8	Income	£275,000	£288,750	£303,188	£318,347	£1,185,284			

You can see the current values for cells G4 and F8.

Goal Seek   ?   ✕

Set cell: $F$8

To value: 1300000

By changing cell: $G$4|

OK   Cancel

3. Select the **Goal Seek** tool.

4. Enter the necessary cell reference for the **Set Cell**.

5. Enter the required value.

6. Specify the **changing** cell (as shown on the right).

The tool will calculate a solution and display as shown below.

	A	B	C	D	E	F	G	H	I
1	Forecast for year								
2		Quarter 1	Quarter 2	Quarter 3	Quarter 4	Total	Assumptions		
3	Sales	£500,000	£525,000	£551,250	£578,813	£2,155,063	5%	(Growth per qtr)	
4	Cost of Sales	£73,385	£77,054	£80,907	£84,952	£316,297	15%	(Perc of Sales)	
5	Gross Profit	£426,615	£447,946	£470,343	£493,861	£1,838,766			
6									
7	Expenses	£125,000	£131,250	£137,813	£144,703	£538,766	25%	(Perc of sales)	
8	Income	£301,615	£316,696	£332,531	£349,158	£1,300,000			
9									
10									
11									
12									
13									
14									
15									
16									

Goal Seek Status   ?   ✕

Goal Seeking with Cell F8 found a solution.

Target value: 1300000
Current value: £1,300,000

Step

Pause

OK   Cancel

This shows that if the cost of sales could be reduced to 15% of sales, the total income for the year would be £1,300,000.

Stage 3

We are going to create a Data Table to evaluate a series of different growth rates for sales, to determine the effect on total income.

1.   Open the workbook **T8Datatables**.

The workbook should look as shown below:

	A	B	C	D
1	Sales Forecast for Quarter 2			
2		Growth Rate	5%	
3	Sales	Quarter 1	Quarter 2	
4		£500,000	£525,000	
5	Alternative Growth rates	1.0%		
6		1.5%		
7		2.0%		
8		2.5%		
9		3.0%		
10		3.5%		
11		4.0%		
12		4.5%		
13		5.0%		
14		5.5%		
15		6.0%		
16		6.5%		
17		7.0%		
18		7.5%		
19		8.0%		
20		8.5%		
21		9.0%		
22		9.5%		
23		10.0%		

You can see a range of growth rates for sales in the second column. We are going to calculate the possible sales for Quarter 2 for each of the growth rates using a Data Table.

2.   Use **Data Tables** to populate the values for Quarter 2, selecting cells B4 to C23, and since the new values are arranged in a column, we specify a column cell and the current growth rate, C2.

▲	A	B	C	D	E	F
1	Sales Forecast for Quarter 2					
2		Growth Rate	5%			
3	Sales	Quarter 1	Quarter 2			
4		£500,000	£525,000			
5	Alternative Growth rates	1.0%				
6		1.5%				
7		2.0%				
8		2.5%				
9		3.0%				
10		3.5%				
11		4.0%				
12		4.5%				
13		5.0%				
14		5.5%				
15		6.0%				
16		6.5%				
17		7.0%				
18		7.5%				
19		8.0%				
20		8.5%				
21		9.0%				
22		9.5%				
23		10.0%				

Data Table　　　?　✕

Row input cell:

Column input cell: $C$2

OK　　Cancel

The output should appear as shown below:

▲	A	B	C	D
1	Sales Forecast for Quarter 2			
2		Growth Rate	5%	
3	Sales	Quarter 1	Quarter 2	
4		£500,000	£525,000	
5	Alternative Growth rates	1.0%	£505,000	
6		1.5%	£507,500	
7		2.0%	£510,000	
8		2.5%	£512,500	
9		3.0%	£515,000	
10		3.5%	£517,500	
11		4.0%	£520,000	
12		4.5%	£522,500	
13		5.0%	£525,000	
14		5.5%	£527,500	
15		6.0%	£530,000	
16		6.5%	£532,500	
17		7.0%	£535,000	
18		7.5%	£537,500	
19		8.0%	£540,000	
20		8.5%	£542,500	
21		9.0%	£545,000	
22		9.5%	£547,500	
23		10.0%	£550,000	

3. Select cell C10

The formula should be as shown in the formula bar below, showing that cell C10 is part of a table based on cell C2.

C10	▼	⋮	✕	✓	*fx*	{=TABLE(,C2)}

◢	A	B	C	D
1	Sales Forecast for Quarter 2			
2		Growth Rate	5%	
3	Sales	Quarter 1	Quarter 2	
4		£500,000	£525,000	
5	Alternative Growth rates	1.0%	£505,000	
6		1.5%	£507,500	
7		2.0%	£510,000	
8		2.5%	£512,500	
9		3.0%	£515,000	
10		3.5%	£517,500	
11		4.0%	£520,000	

That concludes the exercises for chapter 8.

Index

for your notes

for your notes